a pageant is just the beginning...

PAGEANT
*I*nterviewing
SUCCESS

The Collected Series

Dr. Stephanie Raye, PhD
Former Miss American Petite

Pageant Interviewing Success: The Collected Series

© 2017 Stephanie Raye / Mindful Living Companies, LLC

ISBN-10: 1-943193-11-8
ISBN-13: 978-1-943193-11-0
Bast Cat Enterprises
P.O. Box 27783
Tempe AZ 85285-7783
http://www.PageantToPhD.com
http://www.PageantToPhDBlog.com

Kindle: If you prefer e-books, the individual books from this collected series are also available on Kindle.

Photographs: All photographs are from my personal collection to which I hold rights and free use.

Trademarks: Throughout the book trademarked names are used. Including the Trademark symbol is a distraction for the reader, so instead of using it each time, consider this as notice that using trademarked names in this book is done so in an editorial fashion and to the benefit of the trademark owner with no intention of infringement on the trademark.

Logo design by Christy VanDeman. Cover design by Cathy Lloyd and Christy VanDeman.

Pageant to PhD is a trademark of Stephanie Raye and Mindful Living Companies, LLC.

Publisher's Cataloging-In-Publication Data
(Prepared by The Donohue Group, Inc.)
Names: Raye, Stephanie.
Title: Pageant interviewing success : the collected series / Dr. Stephanie Raye, PhD, former Miss American Petite.
Description: Second edition. | Tempe, AZ : Bast Cat Enterprises, [2017] | Includes index. | Summary: A collection of the Pageant interviewing success series of books published in Kindle format.
Identifiers: ISBN 978-1-943193-11-0 | ISBN 1-943193-11-8
Subjects: LCSH: Beauty contestants--Interviews. | Interviewing--Technique. | Pageants.
Classification: LCC HQ1219 .R39 2016 | DDC 646.7042--dc23

Dedicated To:

The first-time pageant contestant as well as the more experienced pageant contestant, family member, coach, director, or judge, I wrote this with you in mind so you, your loved one, your clients or your titleholder will shine.

The woman at the fashion show who recognized my potential. I've been trying to do the same for others ever since.

Gratitude:

Many thanks to all those in my circle—my family, my friends, my teachers, my students—for their support in this endeavor and in the so many other ways they enrich my life. May I be as much a gift to them as they are to me.

Praise for
Pageant Interviewing Success:
The Collected Series

"When you are asked a question by a pageant MC or a judge in an interview, your answer often holds the key to your winning the competition. This book will help you present your best self, with knowledge and confidence. As you will read, there are a lot of things that can contribute to your 'spontaneous' answers."

~Vonda Van Dyke, Miss America 1965

"Every pageant contestant, no matter how beautiful, can always improve her interview skills. Dr. Stephanie Raye will help you boost your brains and streamline your answers in *Pageant Interviewing Success: The Collected Series*. Her interviewing advice applies both on and off the stage. By the time you're done reading this book, you'll be able to shine like the queen you are!"

~Allison Stavrakis, Teen & Mrs. Minnesota International State Director & 1988 Mrs. Queen

"Dr. Stephanie's book is not just for beauty pageant contestants – it's for *anybody* looking to sharpen their interview skills. The book helped prepare me not only for pageants, but also for internships, jobs, and law school. I felt really lucky to have had this insightful advice. Thank you, Dr. Stephanie!"

~Jasmina Cerimagic, Former Miss Teen Arizona

More Praise for
Pageant Interviewing Success: The Collected Series

"I read this comprehensive series of books on interviewing skills just to improve my interview skills in general as I wasn't sure I wanted to participate in a pageant at the time. Now I've learned more than I expected about interviewing, and now I'm more seriously considering entering a pageant for my personal and professional development."

~Samantha Perry, National Merit Scholarship Finalist

"The book is fabulous! It is highly informative, well organized, and very detailed. It would have been nice to have when I was new to the pageant interview world. (I could have avoided so many mistakes!)"

~Audrey Powell, Finalist in Miss Idaho-America

Pageant Interviewing Success:
The Collected Series
Table of Contents

Why I Wrote This Series of Books for You

As a former state and national titleholder turned PhD-level professional, I realize how valuable a foundation my pageant experience was to my later personal and professional life. And I know a critical component of my success in the pageant world and after related to how I prepared for and approached the personal and on-stage interview.

There's no doubt that interviewing well relates to all areas of life, so I decided to take the time to capture and share insights with others—

especially pageant contestants—so they too can be the best versions of themselves when they are in an interview and other "question & answer" situations.

Indeed, it is unfortunate when a smart, talented, and beautiful contestant fails to prepare for the interview component well, as what makes a Queen stand apart from all the lovely Princesses the judges see is what comes out of her mouth in interview. A pageant contestant that performs well in interview reflects well not only on herself but the pageant system and pageants in general. When she doesn't perform well, she undermines herself and accidentally fuels the opinions of people who wrongly think pageant contestants aren't smart.

Whether you are currently a contestant or just considering if entering a pageant is right for you, whether you are parent, coach, judge, director, or supportive friend, there's good information here for all as this material, while using pageants as the focus, is applicable to anyone who wants to do well in an interview situation.

My wish for you is that you understand and believe that a pageant is just one step—a fun and potentially important step. And that no matter what you want to do—small or big—you can leverage how you prepare for pageants, and what you learn in the process, to help you achieve your goals. Thoughtful preparation and skill building in pageants is a great step to help you reach your dreams in any arena.

This content was initially released as a series of shorter Kindle books to help pageant contestants target the specific area in which they needed support. But now we've collected the whole series of books together in this paperback edition as it really is a comprehensive guide to well-rounded, thoughtful preparation for a better pageant experience that will also improve life skills. And we added a little content at the end so stay tuned for that wrap-up. In my closing remarks I'll help you understand the importance of everything you just read, share my own success story, and emphasize one last time the value of these transferable skills.

With that said… let's get started!

"The most difficult thing is the decision to act, the rest is merely tenacity. The fears are paper tigers. You can do anything you decide to do. You can act to change and control your life; and the procedure, the process is its own reward."
~Amelia Earhart

---

a pageant is just the beginning...

PAGEANT *Interviewing* SUCCESS

Build a Strong Foundation

Dr. Stephanie Raye, PhD

Book 1
Build a Strong Foundation
Table of Contents

Pageant Interviewing Success:
Build a Strong Foundation

It's (Mostly) About You,
But It's More Than Just Talking

You may be thinking, "I've talked my whole life, how hard can an interview be?" Or maybe you're thinking, "An interview is just someone asking questions. No big deal, I can answer questions."

Yes, you may have talked your whole life but an interview is not an ordinary conversation and the questions they ask you are not the kind of questions you've typically answered before. Even if you've tried to think through a few potential questions you might be asked, that doesn't mean you are prepared. That's a good start but there's more to acing the interview than that.

I take interviewing pretty seriously (or I wouldn't have spent so much time studying it for years and writing this book series) but remember it is also *fun*. Or it can be! So while we're going to get down to some nitty gritty stuff, remember that it is all in the service of your being able to have a really good, successful time once you are actually *in* the interview.

So let's start with a simple question:

Are You a Bungler, a Smuggler, or a Sleuth?

Let me share with you why I ask that question because whether you are a Bungler, a Smuggler, or a Sleuth really could predict your interview success. I first learned this framework in terms of how, for instance, sales or religious organizations influence people (one of my professors in college was an expert on the topic of influence).

As the years have gone by, I've seen that people can be Bunglers, Smugglers, and Sleuths in any area of their lives...and definitely in interview settings. If you think about it, an interview is sort of a setting for influence or persuasion…you are hoping that your personality, qualifications, and interview skills will "persuade" them to select you for the job or title!

Bungler

A Bungler drops the ball and misses opportunities to highlight her qualifications. A Bungler doesn't understand what the judges want either because of inexperience, ignorance, or laziness. If you are entering pageants, you probably are *not* lazy…so it may be a matter of just not knowing when and what to highlight from your life experience and goals.

For instance, you can know a lot about something—like talking, like your own life, like your community service, etc. But if you don't use that knowledge then you just bungled away that opportunity, leaving any power from that information you could have shared on the vine to wither.

You may have seen this happen as you watch on-stage interviews. Or you may have felt that in one of your own interviews that you missed an opening. We don't want that to happen too often. You have a lot to offer the world. What a shame if you bungle away opportunities to show that to the right people at the right time.

YOU MIGHT BE A BUNGLER IF….

Ask yourself….
Have you ever left an interview feeling like you:

- Did not really understand the question?
- Understood the question but didn't know enough about the topic?
- Knew enough but your thoughts didn't come together well?

• Thoughts came together well but your words didn't come out right?

Ask yourself….
If you ever felt like the interview went "okay" but you:

• Didn't make a strong, positive impression?
• Didn't really convey your enthusiasm or "fit" for the title?

Smuggler

A Smuggler selfishly and dishonestly imports things into a situation that aren't really true or don't really belong there. A smuggler can know what people—like the judges—want to hear so they say it but it isn't true. If it isn't *true*, it is a form of dishonesty. It's not the *real* person, it's not the real *you*.

The Smuggler may try to "force fit" something into an interview (or their paperwork) to try to persuade the judges to think she is the best contestant but, in reality, it's just smoke and mirrors—an illusion. Most judges are pretty savvy, so I recommend against "smuggling" untrue information or misleading perceptions about yourself into your materials or interview.

It is best for everyone in the long run—including the titleholder— that the right person is selected for the title. If someone is being a Smuggler then she isn't the right person. She probably won't win…but *if* she does, she might be okay as the Queen for a while but neither she nor the pageant organization may be happy with the choice.

The director and judges may be fooled at first but eventually something will show. (And imagine being the Queen who must always worry that her dishonesty might be revealed. No fun!) We don't want this to happen either. And, no matter what you might be tempted to do, you really do *not* need to be a smuggler to do well in pageants. Quality pageants and contests are about integrity and they want their titleholder or Queen to reflect that.

YOU MIGHT BE A SMUGGLER IF....

Ask yourself....
Have you ever left an interview feeling like you:

- Pretended to care when you didn't?
- Led them to believe you were someone you aren't?
- Led them to believe you did something you hadn't?
- Said things you thought they wanted to hear but weren't true?
- In any way lied (either in the interview or on your paperwork)?
- Used a lot of "filler" to stretch your answers because you think you are too good to care enough about your personal development or the pageant to prepare?

Sleuth

"A wise man will make more opportunities than he finds."
~Francis Bacon

A Sleuth—that's another word for "detective"—examines the situation for clues that tell her what is a good lead to follow. She uses her powers of observation to appreciate matters of timing and when to offer—or ask for—more information. She knows more than "how to talk" as she knows that communication involves more than saying words.

A Sleuth listens well and chooses her words with care. She listens for the question *behind* the question—understanding what the judges are really hoping to learn about her beyond the surface of the question. She knows she is to answer that surface question, of course, but that there is usually something more behind it she can answer at the same time.

For instance, she knows that a simple personal question about her hobbies isn't because they are really that interested in her water skiing or her collecting _____ (you pick the collection!) but what her reply says about her values and character. She knows a question about a controversial issue or current event isn't so much about whether she is "for" or "against" something as much as how well informed she is and how diplomatic she can be in her response. She knows that any question—even a simple or silly one—is really getting at whether she is a good fit to be the titleholder.

A sleuth watches for the different kinds of questions and takes time to prepare for each kind. Let's explore that a bit more…

Categories of Questions

Different kinds of questions allow the judges to ascertain not just facts about the contestant but also facts that she knows and her abilities, analytical skills, and values. While this may be over-simplifying it, there are basically five categories of questions that may come up in pageant interviews, depending on your pageant:

- Personal
- Pageant
- Simple or Silly
- Current Events
- Controversial

These question categories overlap, of course. For instance, something that is controversial may be happening as a current event. And a pageant question or an apparently simple question also says something about you as a person. But breaking them into these five categories is a great way to think about them, as how you prepare for and respond to each category can be a little different. Watch for examples of these kinds of question in the book series.

Sleuths Know Themselves

A Sleuth is strategic (she has a strategy) on what information she shares and when, to help her solve the mystery of winning the crown. Knowing what to share requires that she *know herself well*.

How well do you know yourself? A Sleuth will know what is important to her and why; and how topics relate to those beliefs and values. She will know what she's good at and what she enjoys (skill and pleasure don't always overlap). And she will know how her past has helped shape her and where she hopes to go in life. Think these matters through.

Being observant of what others need and what you offer is a good thing. Having a "game plan" is not sneaky like the Smuggler or just saying what you *think* the judges want to hear. A game plan means being prepared, like when a sports team assesses the competition and arranges their players accordingly to maximize their success.

Or think of a Sleuth as being an ethical "spy" or investigator who is watching out for details that matter. Doing so is wise and helpful as it creates a "win-win" situation; it helps the contestant see the pieces of the puzzle she offers and the judges are then better equipped to select the right person for the title—and let's hope that is you!

YOU MIGHT BE A SLEUTH IF....
Ask yourself...
Did you research ahead of time:

- The pageant, to know about it (and the system)?
- The judges (if possible)?
- What they are likely looking for in a Queen or titleholder?
- Your "platform" (if required) and/or your hobbies and passions?

Reflect ahead of time about:

- What you offered in your paperwork and what it says about you?
- What skills and goals you bring to the table?
- The area/title (city, county, state, etc.) you are (or will be) representing (including age or competitions division)?

During the interview:

- Listen with care to answer what the judges *asked.*
- Look for (and answer) the "question behind the question."
- Work in, where appropriate, information about yourself that will help the judges appreciate your preparedness to hold the title.
- Share your enthusiasm for life, people, and the title.
- Avoid bringing up unflattering information about yourself.
- Avoid being ungraciously negative about others.
- Practice diplomacy to help people feel comfortable in uncomfortable situations (or in discussing hard topics).

Whether you prefer the image of having a "game plan" or the image of being an "investigator" remember that games and mysteries are fun and exciting! So part of what a Sleuth does is have fun and communicate warmth while she's using her head.

She doesn't just inform the judges of personal facts or values in a dry, boring manner and she doesn't sparkle just by being cute or witty—she blends the two together to "edutain!" That's *edu*cate and enter*tain* put together. So a Sleuth educates the judges about her overall fit for the title in an approachable, entertaining way to help stand out from the other contestants.

At the Pageant and Beyond

You can do this! You can sculpt yourself into a Sleuth whether you are a teen contestant who is just getting started in thinking about these things, or as a Mrs. or Ms. or "Senior" contestant who has more life experience and has already been building these skills.

Regardless of your age or competition level, my hope is that my materials will support and inspire you to be the best you can be *and* be a Sleuth about pageants. They are designed to do just that. And not *just* in pageants but beyond, as you'll find this increased awareness and skill set will help you do better in all areas of your life, including family and work.

"You may be disappointed if you fail but you are doomed if you don't try."
~Beverly Sills

After all, remember that a pageant or achievement contest is largely an elaborate job interview to select who will hold the title. That's part of why I call my pageant work "Pageant to PhD" as what you learn in pageants can set you up well to pursue whatever goal you have (even if you don't want to be a doctor) if you are thoughtful about what you are learning and doing along the way.

Mindful attention to your participation in pageants will help pave the way to your future—they can be a step to your winning in life, even if you don't win or place in the pageant. Let's get started on improving your sleuthing skills!

Interviewing is More Than Meets the Eye

A good interview has several components. Let's give you something to think about for each one. For some of you this will be new information. For some of you this will be review but chances are good you'll still learn something new even if you are an experienced pageant contestant.

Even if you've heard some similar tips before *ask yourself* if you are really doing it well. As we all know, we can know to do some things in theory but that doesn't necessarily mean we actually do them well, if we do them at all.

You're Applying (Competing) for a Job

And the competition is usually stiff! Good interviewing starts with good preparation and good performance at the interview. Both take attention, intention, and practice. So typically only those who see the potential power of the interview—in the context of the pageant, but elsewhere as well—may take the time to consciously work on it as a skill.

Those who do will be the "better" competitors. They are the ones who at least want to leverage the experience for all it can be worth. They are the ones who remember that the titleholder will make many appearances, give speeches, and interact with the public and the press. All of that has a lot more to do with interviewing than anything else in the competition.

So put yourself in the judges' shoes and imagine what they are thinking about as they consider each candidate. Here are the three main things they are concerned about:

- Can she do the job well?
- Is she likable and diplomatic?
- Is it a risk to choose her?

When you are being a Sleuth and listening for the "question behind the question" some form of these three concerns are behind each question. The "risk" concern cuts across the categories and is broad in that it can capture not just what you say or how you say it but could take into consideration, for example, your experiences and even your fashion sense. (We'll get to fashion sense more when we discuss pageant interview wardrobe!)

Even If It's Just for Fun, Research the Pageant

Even if you are in beauty pageants or achievement/scholarship contests only for the fun of them, you will benefit from what we talk about here.

And if you are in a pageant to place or to win hoping it will forward your platform or career goals—or realize that no matter how you score the experience will help you in jobs after the pageant—then you really want to practice these methods and skills.

Whatever your goal—fun, prizes, experience, opportunities—you'll want to be a Sleuth and find out what you can about the pageant first. Just like any activity or job, some are a better fit for some people than for others. It's good to know the requirements, judging categories, and the "look" of the contest to see if it fits with what you are willing to do. Some will be a more natural fit for you, others you'll have to work at (so you may decide to focus on, or at least start with, a different pageant).

"The most common way people give up their power is by thinking they don't have any."
~Alice Walker

Find the Best Fit for You

There are all kinds of pageants. Beyond the different age divisions and marital status divisions known by a variety of different names like Teen, Miss, Ms., Mrs., Elite (some pageants use this word for those competing over the age of 50) or Senior, there are pageants that allow for beauty to come in different sizes (for instance, Petite and Plus). And there are pageants that honor different heritages like Asian, African-American, Native American, Latin, and the like. So there is probably a pageant that is a good fit for *you*.

While most pageants have some components in common, they can vary quite a bit. One pageant that illustrates the range of pageants out there—and proves you can find one that fits you—is Miss Navajo Nation (a pageant since 1952) where the contestants do a lot of interesting things which include demonstrating, for instance:

Traditional Talents
Navajo drumming, story telling, Navajo singing or dancing

Traditional Skills
Spinning wool, weaving a rug, making jewelry, pottery, or a basket, or grinding corn

Modern Talents
Drama, painting, public speaking, dancing, singing, playing an instrument

Modern Skills
(In earlier days this was along the lines of sewing, floral arrangement, and typing) but the 2008-2009 winner, Yolanda Charley, spoke on a science/community related project about methamphetamine use on the reservation.

Food Preparation Skills
They must demonstrate/compete in butchering a sheep and making fry bread.

Knowledge of the Navajo Language
(Their interview questions are asked in Navajo.)

Knowledge of the Navajo Culture
A 45-minute interview that covers 18 questions on their teachings (on their stories of origin, basket design, knowing the Navajo words for different parts of ceremonial dress, etc.)

This pageant helps honor their culture and keep it alive for their own people as they also educate others about it. The young women must appreciate their heritage as well as be able to situate their culture in modern context and address problems in their community. The winners are often invited to visit other countries, as many people across the world are interested in Native American people, history, and culture.

Many Miss Navajo contestants were working on their Bachelor degrees or had them already (even dual-majors!) and were aiming for law school. Some former Miss Navajos have gone on to get their PhD degrees too (for instance, Dolly Manson, Miss Navajo 1981-82 and Karletta Chief, Miss Navajo 2000-01).

So as "unique" as their pageant may sound, it's really quite fabulous. These contestants work hard for their crown because of what the experience and opportunity means to them personally and to their people (not for big prize packages). Miss Navajo is truly an ambassador for her nation.

Talent

So talk about needing talent! Few of us could do everything one of the Miss Navajo contestants can do.

Still, some girls or women feel they can't compete in pageants because they don't have a "talent" or don't have the time for (or interest in) community service and platform work that is required in some pageants with a long, rich history (like the Miss America Organization). But, as we've discussed, there are many pageants so you can find a respectable one that does not require "talent."

On the flip side, you may have a talent that doesn't translate well to the stage or you prefer not to perform your talent for whatever reason. *If* that's the case, consider working with a talent coach to open up some possibilities for yourself. Some choose to master one or two brief performances just so they can slay that fear and open up the door to a wider variety of pageants.

But there is nothing "wrong" with starting with a pageant that doesn't require a talent. And there is nothing "wrong" if you choose to *never* compete in a pageant with a formal talent category. You are still a wonderful and talented person!

I bring this up because sometimes you'll hear folks say a pageant or contestant is "better" than another because of the presence or absence of a talent category. A graceful Queen (or titleholder hopeful) does not make such snap judgments and doesn't assume that just because one doesn't compete in talent that the woman is less good or has no talent.

A Sleuth will compete where she knows she can do well and/or is willing to strengthen the areas in herself to do well with time and practice. There are many great pageants that distinguish themselves in different ways, just as the contestants do. Thank goodness one size doesn't fit all.

And, to get back to the main theme of the book series, talent can be defined in many ways... *interviewing* well is certainly a talent but that's not the general interpretation of "talent" (even if good interviewing skills can win you the crown in *any* pageant). And some pageants allow other talents to show.

"No one can make you feel inferior without your permission."
~Eleanor Roosevelt

For instance, the Galaxy International pageants don't have a "talent" category, per se, but they have more categories for the demonstration of talent in modeling.

So know you can still be talented even without a traditional talent. (Don't put yourself down!) And also know that in the pageant world when they use the word "talent" they are generally talking about the sing, dance, act, play an instrument type of talent. You *can* do other things for talent, so think creatively if you do want to pursue a talent pageant.

Ask Good Questions (But Read First!)

A few paragraphs back I mentioned finding a "respectable" pageant. Let's get back to that for a moment. What I mean there is that you want to find one that is well run. If you have problems just trying to get the application, getting basic questions answered, etc., then you might hit similar problems later as a titleholder for that pageant.

That doesn't mean you should avoid a young or brand new pageant, but keep your eyes open and use your head. If they respond to questions in a reasonable amount of time and are professional in their other dealings with you, then great! Give them a try.

On the other hand, if a pageant website is really out of date or missing important information, if a pageant goes a year or two without a titleholder, if the number of contestants drops significantly, or if the fees are very high but what you get in return for that isn't much (and I don't mean just the prizes), then you need to weigh all this in your decision.

No matter the age or reputation of the pageant, ask good questions to be sure you understand the costs, the clothing requirements, and prizes, etc. If you don't know the rules, how can you follow them? But once you do know them, *do* follow them. Your ability to get paperwork in on time, follow rules, etc. helps them see you'd likely be just as responsible if you become the titleholder.

GOOD QUESTIONS TO FIND ANSWERS TO WHEN RESEARCHING A PAGEANT:

- What are the wardrobe requirements?
- What are the entry fees?
- What do the fees cover?
- What other fees are there?
- Will I get my scores or feedback? If so, when?
- What is the prize package/support for the titleholder?

*Be sure you understand the time schedule and expected commitments.
*Be sure you know the judging categories, rules, and time limits.

While I encourage research and questions don't be a bother about it or have a demanding attitude when trying to research a pageant. Always be polite and professional, notice when it is a good time to approach someone (some times are busier than others).

But *do* expect professionalism too. If you have emailed and haven't heard back in a reasonable amount of time, assume the best...maybe their computer misdirected it to their junk mail box. So re-send it. If you don't hear back again, pick up the phone and call. (Assuming there is a number available, of course!) Tell them that there may be an email glitch and then ask your questions. If you get a voicemail, leave a polite message explaining you've tried to reach them and asking them to return your call. (Be sure to speak slowly and clearly when you leave your number.)

Just as your preparation for the pageant is a small taste of what it'll be like to be the titleholder, how the pageant deals with you as a contestant is a taste of how they'll treat you as the Queen.

Ask yourself:

- Are you representing yourself well in how you deal with them?
- Are they representing themselves well in how they deal with you?

What is a "reasonable amount of time"? It is great if folks can get back to emails in 2 business days (don't count weekends and holidays) but everybody gets busy or takes a personal or sick day now and then. Things happen. So at 4 business days—which could be more like a week if a weekend intervenes—I start to get a little worried. So try again, maybe they were out of town.

And remember that during pageant week (or weeks!), it is possible folks will be *way* too busy to get back to anyone until the new Queen is crowned. So be aware of when that time is—it is usually on the website—if you are researching a pageant and waiting for an answer.

And before you ask a lot of questions, see what you can learn *first* by reading the website, application, and pageant handbook, etc. with care. If someone took the time to *write* it down somewhere and you are deciding to do this you should be willing to take the time to *read* it. Doing so saves irritation on both sides, shows respect for people's work, time, etc.

Anyway, if you or someone you know has avoided entering a pageant because you assumed they are all alike, then please know that they are *not* all alike. Find one that is a good fit for you to start with and if you get the pageant bug and want to stretch yourself to build a talent (or whatever area), then perhaps you make that a goal for a future pageant. But, otherwise, you can have a great experience competing in one or more pageants that don't require talent.

There really are a great variety of pageants. Beyond the various age divisions (like Teen, Miss, Ms., Mrs., and Elite) in the pageants that most people may think of like Miss America, Miss USA, National American Miss, Mrs. International, and American Queen, the table on the next page shows just a *few* of the others out there.

"Work joyfully and peacefully, knowing that right thoughts and right efforts will inevitably bring about right results."
~James Allen

A BRIEF SELECTION OF DIVERSE PAGEANTS*
(in no particular order)

Miss Rodeo America
Miss Wheelchair America
Miss Black USA
Miss Plus America
Miss America Latina
Miss National Teen
Miss Belleza Latina
Miss Latina US
American Junior Miss
Miss Int'l American Beauty
Miss Gay America
Miss Earth United States
Miss Tattoo
Miss Corporate America
Miss Indian Nations
Ms. Fitness
Ms. Senior America
Miss Deaf America
Miss Asian America
America's Perfect Miss
Miss Petite North America
Ms. African American United

*Remember, many pageants have other divisions than just "Miss."
*If you live outside the U.S.A., you will likely find a good variety in your own country. Many countries have pageants that lead to international competitions (like Miss USA leads to competing in Miss Universe).

Interviewing Separates the Queen from the Princesses

Why prepare for interview? Because the competition is stiff—winning the crown might be tough! It can be a close call. No matter the contest, it can come down to just a couple points difference in who wins.

Interview is an easy place for that difference to arise. Just as in a job where all the candidates meet basic qualifications, it is the interview where the employer really "sees" the personality of the person and decides if they are right for the job.

So it is in a beauty pageant or talent competition—all the contestants are beautiful and/or talented so what will make you shine brighter than the rest in your interview—where you can show your great personality, your intelligence, and ability to represent the title well. What you say and how you say it can be the dealmaker or deal-breaker.

Preparation is Key

Preparing thoughtfully in advance will pay off! While I recommend you start preparing weeks or months in advance (as a little each day is easier for any of us to do), even a few days preparation is better than none. Especially if the other contestants didn't happen to prepare!

Whether it is near the pageant time or you have left yourself plenty of time to prepare, the preparation doesn't have to be hard, and it can even be fun! But you do want to take this fun seriously and have the personal courage to lovingly examine your beliefs, thoughts, and actions.... and how that all translates into what you say—and how you say it—in interviews.

In the next book in this collection, we will cover whether or not interviewing preparation has to cost money, whether to work with a coach, and several tips to help you succeed. But before we go there, let's talk about a piece of advice you have probably heard time and again—or you will hear it if you haven't yet– and that is to "be yourself."

Being Yourself

You hear people say all the time to "be yourself" and then you read books like this or work with coaches or directors that seem to say, "this is the only way to do it" or "this is the right way." That may seem contradictory—you may feel that you *can't* be yourself and win. It's not contradictory….

You can be yourself because there isn't necessarily one "right" or "wrong" answer to an interview question. Lots of responses can work for (or against) you. The key is you *can* be yourself and still be *choosy* about *what* you share, *when* you share it, and *how* you share it. Being yourself doesn't mean having a "let it all hang out" approach that could come off as unprepared, careless, unflattering, or disrespectful.

And being yourself doesn't mean having a "take it or leave it; this is me" attitude that is insensitive to what the job of titleholder and what the image of the pageant is. It's all in how you say it and the feeling with which you leave the listener.

Later in this series (see, for example, the "Answer the Question" section of *Book 8: Being in the Win Zone* or the "Different Interviews, Different Questions" section of *Book 9: Answering Personal Questions*), I'll offer an example of how different answers from very different perspectives can work out just as well. You might want to say "yes" or "no" or not take a stand. Each choice is valid; it is simply *how* you handle it that matters.

Even though we'll cover it much more later, let me give you a quick example here. In the Miss USA 2009 pageant, Miss North Carolina-USA, Kristin Dalton (who ultimately won the crown) was asked the controversial current event question:

Judge, Kelly Monaco

"Do you believe that taxpayers' money should be used to bailout struggling U.S. companies, why and/or why not?"

Miss Dalton paused for a moment then said:

Miss Dalton

"That's a tough one. Um, no, I don't think that U.S. taxpayers' money should be used to bail out companies. Taxpayers' money should go towards bettering our education and our school systems, and and welfare, and the healthcare systems and that's what our taxpayers' money should go to. Absolutely."

She may have had a few extra "ands" and some unnecessary repetition in there (she said the words "taxpayer's money" three times), etc., but it was, in general, a good answer because she answered the "yes" or "no" question directly with her opinion on better alternatives for spending. She paused to collect her thoughts a little bit (which is good, or she may have rambled on or had still *more* "ands"), she smiled, made good eye contact, and sounded confident…she did well!

The crowd was pleased but clearly so were the judges. It is *just* as likely that she could have said "yes" and still won.

Let's pretend that she did in fact want to say "yes" in this alternate response… and here we will also have her improving her answer by acknowledging there are two-sides to the story (which acknowledges that others may have a different view from her). Perhaps something like:

Judge, Kelly Monaco

"Do you believe that taxpayers' money should be used to bailout struggling U.S. companies, why and/or why not?"

Potential "yes" answer

"That's a tough one. In general, I'd say "no" and that taxes should go toward education, healthcare, and welfare. But we are living in unusual times and I know everyone wants the economy to improve.... so while I haven't been happy with some of the bailout news, I feel some comfort that teams of experts are doing their best and if they say the bailouts are necessary, then I'm inclined to give their approach a try."

Here the contestant could say, "yes" to something that *might* be unpopular but if she does it in a balanced way, she's not likely to alienate too many people. It is especially good not to alienate the judges!

BALANCE IS KEY

- Just as you balance on your high heels, balance what you include in your responses. This is especially important in response to controversial questions.
- Don't tip too far to one side without offering a different perspective. Including "balance" helps you build good content for many questions and show diplomacy in delivery.

So whether you are *for* or *against* something, your opinion is *your* opinion and the judges don't have to agree with it (and they are not supposed to judge you on differences of opinion). But, how you leave people *feeling* about you and your opinion does matter. So practice being diplomatic about how you offer your answers; how good you are at that *is* something on which they will judge you.

The key is that you can be true to yourself in terms of beliefs, values, goals and what you say and still realize that there can be better and worse ways of saying things. Depending on where you are starting this process (your age, experience, education, etc.), improving the skill of knowing the "better" way of saying things might take building:

Awareness
Noticing your thinking and speaking habits that you may not have paid attention to before

Learning
More about yourself, including what you believe and why, about your potential careers and other goals

Involvement
With the community (perhaps through education or volunteer work) to build your appreciation of and experience with the world

Knowledge
Of your locale, as well as local, state, and national current events, and controversial issues, etc.

Practice
Learn and model successful techniques you see others (winners!) use and find your own way through educational materials like these

Empathy
Put yourself in the shoes of the judges or the public to appreciate what impression you are making through what you say and how you say it

Vocabulary
So you can use more precise and professional language to get your message across. As a start, use the words in this book to test what you know (or think you know) and work new words into your daily vocabulary use

That may sound like a lot but it is all *fun* and *do-able* – you can do it on your own easily enough but you don't have to be in it by yourself. I, among others, am out there happy to help make it easy for you to polish each component so you *shine*. And just imagine how this will also prepare you well for *any* area of your life.

"Be careful what you water your dreams with. Water them with worry and fear and you will produce weeds that choke the life from your dream. Water them with optimism and solutions and you will cultivate success. Always be on the lookout for ways to turn a problem into an opportunity for success. Always be on the lookout for ways to nurture your dream."
~Lao Tzu

Our Game Plan

As you know, I want you to learn how to be a Sleuth, rather than a Bungler or a Smuggler—so watch for how all we cover will help you do that!

Part of that—and part of preparing—is knowing what to expect, at least in general terms as every interview setting and experience will be different. So we'll start before you actually get to the pageant—with some things you can do in advance—and work our way through your personal interview day. We'll also give attention to the on-stage interview experience.

I'll cover several topics in some depth. Other topics I'll introduce and give some tips on but we can't do everything in one book—so some topics may have more detailed coverage in their own book so they can get the focused attention they deserve.

Review

Let's review what we covered:

An interview is more than just talking
While the style may be conversational, this is a "conversation" with two goals: the judges are looking for the "best" contestant to do the job as titleholder, and the contestant is looking to demonstrate she is the right person for the job.

Research the pageant
Find the one that is the best fit for who you are now. Understand and follow the rules. Understand what they are looking for in a titleholder and use that knowledge like a Sleuth.

Smugglers, Bunglers, and Sleuths
These are the three types of pageant contestants and/or ways to approach the pageant and the interview. Aim to be a Sleuth!

Pageant skills are valuable later in life
The skills you thoughtfully build in your pageant experience will be useful in your later pursuits (work, community, family, civic, military service, etc.)

Preparation is key
Competition can be stiff so you'll want to prepare as if interview *is* your "talent" as good interviewing skills separate the Queens from the Princesses.

You **can** *be yourself and win the crown!*
That starts with researching yourself (as much as you research the pageant) and ends with being diplomatic and sensitive in your interview responses. This book and other materials will support you in that.

Exercise 1.1: Self-Assess If You Bungle, Smuggle, or Sleuth

You may be a mix of two or three right now. (Hopefully you don't smuggle!) Just ask yourself the questions laid out in the book we've just wrapped up. Be honest with yourself about how you've done in previous pageant interviews.

If you haven't participated in a pageant, think back to any other situations in school, at work, at home, or in the community. Do you tend to handle conversations and opportunities like a Bungler, a Smuggler, or a Sleuth?

Determine in your mind and heart that you will allow yourself to grow into being more like a Sleuth all the time! (If you are already a Sleuth, imagine the skills coming more easily all the time or take on new dimensions.)

Exercise 1.2: Research a Pageant

… Or two (or three!) If you are just considering entering one, visit the websites of several and ask for more information if you need it. Reflect on what's a good fit for you.

If you are already signed up for one, consider if there is other information you'd benefit from knowing (as a Sleuth!) and seek it out. Also consider exploring other pageants for future reference in case you find one that is an even better fit for your strengths or goals.

"You are never too old to set another goal or
dream a new dream."
~C.S. Lewis

Exercise 1.3: Build Vocabulary

If in reading the book you skipped over words you weren't sure about or assumed you knew what they meant, take a few minutes now to go back and learn them. Look them up. It doesn't take long. Then try to use a new, different, or more specific word (or two!) each day.

"Our language is funny – a fat chance and slim chance are the same thing."
~J. Gustav White

Here I am being crowned by the national Queen at my state pageant.

a pageant is just the beginning...

PAGEANT
Interviewing
SUCCESS

How to Prepare

Dr. Stephanie Raye, PhD
Former Miss American Petite

Book 2
How to Prepare
Table of Contents

Pageant Interviewing Success
How to Prepare

As I've emphasized, and it will become more evident as we continue, preparing for interview ahead of time is a wise move. You may agree but still be very busy, strapped for cash, or confused about how to approach preparation. This book will help.

Do You Need a Coach?

Everybody is different, so the answer to this depends on several things:

- What is your skill level as you begin to prepare? Someone with more experience may not need as much prep, or not need as much structured support. On the other hand, if you are already fairly skilled, it may take a keen eye to help you see where you still need to improve.
- What do you already know about yourself, your pageant, the world?
- What is your personality or study style – Are you a Planner? Procrastinator?
- How much time is there before the pageant?
- How much time do you have in your general schedule —how many things are you trying to juggle? How are you with time management?
- What are your goals? To get past some fear? Improve a little in one area? Several areas? To master the whole process?
- Do you learn better from interaction? Materials and personal practice?
- What is your built-in (unpaid) support system for interview and pageant preparation?

While working with a coach isn't necessarily a "must" for everyone, it is important to realize that doing so will usually give you feedback and insight you typically can't get from family and friends (unless they are trained as coaches or have good, relevant experience). So do consider it if you have the money, if pageants are "serious business" for you, and/or you are cramming.

Most coaches will be a big help no matter what your preparation style, but if you are a "procrastinator" or have other time constraints keeping you from preparing well "on your own" then working with someone should help you stay on track and get the most out of time spent.

"I will study and prepare and perhaps my chance will come."
~Abraham Lincoln

How Much Do You Need to Practice?

Taking those questions above into consideration offers you some guidance on how much to practice. Also consider your experience and comfort level with the categories of questions you may get, depending on your pageant and age/division.

That said, no matter how great we are, we all can benefit from preparation. Even the most prepared contestants need to keep their skills up. It's not like you "get in shape" once and never have to exercise or watch what you eat again…so it is with interviewing. You can be pretty good and still benefit from practice.

How Often

I know from years of working with all kinds of students and clients that some people can prepare well in a few minutes a day, others can do a little bigger block of time (say, 10 - 20 minutes) two or three times a week, while others will try to cram a lot just before the big day (or test or whatever).

Research and experience tell us that cramming isn't the most effective way to learn or retain material so I'd encourage you to do little bits each day or a few regular chunks per week. (Sign up for my Twitter Feed and I'll send you an interview question several times a week to help you remember to practice and build your skill in thinking on the spot.)

But if you won't or can't prepare in a more planned out way because, perhaps, you only recently signed up for a pageant that is not far off or just recently came to appreciate that preparing was important, then do what you can do. You'll still be *much* better off than if you did nothing. So cramming is better than nothing. Just know that if you are the sort to wait until the last minute, you may be wise to spend some time and money with an interview coach to optimize that little bit of time you left yourself.

Experience Level

If it is your first pageant, you will likely feel the need to prepare more. Ironically, it could take you doing one pageant before you recognize the need to prepare. But not you! If you're a first-timer reading this book you are already ahead of the game over a first-timer who hasn't learned this valuable lesson.

Some people will "cram" and wait until a month or so before their pageant to start preparing for interview. That can work if you will actually put some time to it. Otherwise, you can start a few months before and give yourself more time to develop. You may do the same amount of time overall but spreading it out in smaller bits can improve your retention. Still, as I said, cramming is better than doing nothing.

Whatever you do, you *do* want to practice answering questions out loud. What we think in our head often doesn't translate into words the way we think they will! So it is better to actually talk some of your answers out. Once you get used to hearing yourself talk, you can work on increasing your content with the Sleuthing this book suggests, as well as work on tightening up your responses (if you tend to ramble).

Below, you'll find a table of elements to include in your practice. There are quite a variety of tasks there so you'll find that you can actually practice for interview in different ways at different times. If you keep your "thinking cap" on about how what you are doing relates to your pageant interview performance, you'll find all of these components add up.

Does Preparation Have to Cost Money?

The short answer is *no*. It does not have to cost money. Or at least doesn't have to cost much (in the grand scheme of things).

Again, it depends on your situation. If you work with a coach, then it will likely cost you some money. But you can do a *lot* (and maybe all you need to do) on your own or with smaller investments in materials, etc. The table below walks through some of the ideas to help you prepare on any budget.

If you want to prepare solely on your own—without the assistance of a coach on the phone, in workshops, or in person, that's okay! You'll still be much better prepared than if you did nothing.

INTERVIEW PRACTICE SHOULD INCLUDE:

- Practicing answering questions out loud (at *least* 30 minutes a week, however, if you want to split it up, that's fine. 10 minutes 3 times a week works.)
- Practicing your walk into the interview room (in your interview shoes)
- Practicing your sitting, standing, and gesturing (at least some of the time you should practice in your actual interview wardrobe)
- Practicing your eye contact

*All of the above should occasionally be done in front of the mirror, in front of others, and/or on videotape.

*Keep track of your improvements in both your answer content (what you say) and answer delivery (how you say it). You *will* see improvement! (You'll notice this on your own but you can also tape yourself to compare, and/or ask others to work with you.)

PRACTICE SHOULD ALSO INCLUDE:

- Following the news and becoming a more informed citizen (I offer specific suggestions on how and when elsewhere in this book.)
- Listening to or reading motivational and inspirational material (Keep yourself positive! Too much news by itself can bring you down.)
- Building your vocabulary
- Polishing up vocal characteristics
- Practicing relaxation techniques, if you need them
- Exploring your values, beliefs, and skills in Essential Pageant Interview Playbook, my forthcoming book (which will help with both your interview and your application materials)

Finding the Middle Ground

Preparation doesn't have to cost money, but you may want to find a "middle ground" approach.

That is, working one-on-one with a coach may be outside your budget but consider buying other materials like this book to help you. Consider investing in books of interview questions, audio CDs, my forthcoming Essential Pageant Interview Playbook™, etc. *If* you faithfully use the materials you buy, then you are getting a lot of useful info there. If you buy them and forget them on a shelf, then you've wasted your money.

Also, remember that you may be able to share a coaching session or two with a friend who is also competing. Or perhaps you (or your family) have goods or services a coach may be willing to barter for. So if you are short on cash, and *really* want to work with a coach, don't give up without trying. Call a couple and talk with them. Perhaps you can work something out.

DOES INTERVIEW PREP HAVE TO COST MONEY?

It can be totally free if you can prepare on your own and do this:

- Follow the advice in this book—which you already own
- Work with good practice questions—which you can make up if you are smart about it (but *do* come up with a *wide* variety). There are good question books (even some focused on pageants) and you can find some by watching videos of pageants that you could perhaps borrow from friends or the library.
- Follow the news in some way at least a few days a week. I will provide tips on this later in the book.
- Practice in front of a mirror
- Practice with friends or family
- Videotape yourself (free if you already own or can borrow a camera) watching and listening for areas to improve, as discussed in this book.

Whether you decide to go it on your own 100%, work with a coach 100%, or find some middle ground, please do *something* with the mindful intention of improving your interview skills and comfort with that part of the pageant (personal and on-stage).

And I do recommend that you consider your overall investment in the pageant and think about the wisdom of putting as much (or at least some percentage of) money toward interview preparation as you would toward any other category of competition. Here are some ideas on how to think about that:

HOW MUCH TO SPEND ON INTERVIEW PREP

You might consider allotting a portion of your pageant budget to interview preparation based on one of these ideas...
Spend as much as you did for your:

- Pageant swimsuit or Fitness attire
- Evening gown
- Interview wardrobe
- Fashion wear
- Or as much as you did for any one (or more) other garment, outfit, or shoes for the pageant

If interview is worth, say, 30% in your pageant, then spend 30% of your pageant budget toward interview preparation.

Spend as much as you did for other professional services, like what you spent:

- On the photo shoot for your professional picture (include make-up, prints, clothes).
- On one (or more) hair salon visits for your hair cut, color, extensions, or whatever you do
- On hair, nails and/or make-up consultations (and product)
- On your gym membership or personal trainer

Add up your various application and entry fees for the pageant – spend that amount on interview preparation.

Spend as much as you are asking your sponsors to spend.

You get the idea…whether you are competing on a tight budget or a generous one, you can choose one of any number of ways to decide how much to allow for interview preparation.

Once you figure out what's right for *you* and your budget, then, depending on the amount you determine, you can decide whether to prepare "alone" by working primarily from materials and books like this one, investing in a video camera to tape yourself, or if to add in some time working with an interview coach over the phone or in person, etc.

Whether you are in a pageant for the fun of it—like it is a fun activity but you aren't "serious" about winning—or whether you are really after the crown, the key points of logic to see here are:

- If you spend ___ dollars on your gown (or whatever else) and look *fabulous* but what you say when you open your mouth doesn't help earn you the crown, then maybe it would have been smarter to spend a little less on the gown and spend some of that money on interview preparation.
- Interview preparation is the gift that keeps on giving. It can help you win the pageant and more. Skill-building is cumulative in that usually you just keep getting better and more comfortable handling any kind of question, knowing more about current events, yourself, controversial topics, etc. and this will help you in *other* areas of your life (in pageants and afterward).

Fashions come and go, but who you become through the healthy body and mind habits you build to do well in pageants—including your thinking and interviewing skills—will help you for the rest of your life.

So make your pageant experiences count. Have fun with them while they are happening and all the while take pride in knowing you are helping yourself not just do well in the pageant right now but in building your future too.

Know Your Application Materials! – Resume, Bio, Fact Sheet

We'll cover this more later in the book series but, for now, suffice it to say that whatever you do, you will want to know what's on your application materials whether they call it your bio, your resume, your fact sheet, or whatever. You can count on being asked *something* from that material at some point in the pageant. At least a couple of these questions are asked of everyone as a gentle way of (usually) opening the interview to get to know you a bit and give you a chance to show your ease and comfort with questions you should know the answers to.

"Every great dream begins with a dreamer. Always remember, you have within you the strength, the patience, and the passion to reach for the stars to change the world."
~Harriet Tubman

After all, these questions are about *you* and what you put on your form so these should be "easy" for you. If you do well with them the judges will see your confidence and competence and likely raise the bar to more thoughtful questions. (Or they may ask what seems like "silly" questions just to see how you handle them—remember to look for the question behind the question!)

Similarly, know your platform if you and/or your pageant has one. Let's talk more about that…

Platforms and Passions

For those new to the pageant world, a "platform" is something you care about enough to learn about it, volunteer for, and speak about it if you win the title. If your pageant doesn't require a platform (like Miss USA does not require a personal platform at this writing), still read this section as it will help in general (especially the part on passions).

You can think of the word platform in this context in a couple ways including that it is something you "stand for" and something you "build on" as you go forward. Some pageants require platforms and may have you turn in a platform essay as part of your paperwork.

I'm assuming in this book that you have already filled out your paperwork so you already have selected a platform or know you don't need one at this time. I have other materials that will help you appreciate the value of a platform and how to narrow down your choices on choosing one but saying much more now is outside the scope of this book.

"How we spend our days is, of course, how we spend our lives."
~Annie Dillard

For now, let's just say that platforms are very useful to *everybody* in so many ways—so much great community work is done via pageants! In the immediate setting of the interview they help the judges know you and what you care about, and it gives them a focus area from which to ask you questions. And the flip side is that it is useful to you because you have something more to talk about than beauty, school, family, or hobbies.

So *know* about your platform. Look up and remember a few key figures in the field, know a couple stories (including any personal connections you can make) and a few statistics that help the judges (and the public) understand the scope of the problem or opportunity associated with your platform. Hopefully you've done and/or are doing some volunteer work around your platform.

If not, consider starting. And as things get busy, you may want to start now. Or if you have plenty of time to prepare, at least start soon. If you happen to have the luxury of having summers off from school or work, that'd be a good time to spend quality time on your platform. Even if you don't think "volunteering" fits in your schedule or is in your comfort zone, remember there are many ways to help organizations so there probably is something that would work for you. Just check it out as a start. You can find many sites that help you locate volunteer activities, like http://www.volunteermatch.org.

There are also sites that offer opportunities for more specific locations like, using Phoenix Arizona as an example, http://www.handsonphoenix.org. Similarly, many states or communities have sites like http://www.cir.org that help people find needed services, and those services often need volunteers. Search around a little and you will find a wealth of opportunities in your area.

Pageants Can Have Their Own Platforms

Some pageants have their own platform—they want the work they are doing to draw attention to a cause and educate the public. For instance, American Queen has DASH, which stands for Domestic Abuse Stops Here. If you enter their pageants obviously a *Sleuth* would know the basic facts (and preferably a bit more) about this as it matters so much to the pageant that they chose it as *their* platform.

So if you want to be a titleholder for them, you should care about it too. Not that you have to focus your volunteer efforts there if you are already committed to another cause, but you are a smart woman, you can learn about more than one cause to be able to answer some questions on it.

Passions

If you don't "need" a platform for your pageant, and don't happen to have some worthwhile cause you are involved in anyway, then at least identify your *passions* and know about them.

I'm assuming if you wrote something down on your application or fact sheet that you care something about it. Be prepared for the judges to ask you about your hobbies, activities, and sports and know a few things about whatever your particular passions are.

For instance, if you say you've played piano your whole life but can't name a favorite pianist or composer, that doesn't reflect well on you. If you run track in school but can't name any national or international track stars then it doesn't seem like you are that thoughtful about your sport. If you are a photographer (or hope to be) and don't know who Annie Leibovitz, Herb Ritts, or Ansel Adams is, as just a few examples, it may be time to look more into some of the "big names" in your hobby or profession to know about a few current and historic people in the area.

You don't have to be an *expert* on your passions but you should know a few things so think it through a bit. And the more serious you are about your activities, the more you should know.

Similarly, the more important winning a platform-based pageant is to you, the more you should know so you feel very comfortable with your platform. You could be considered an expert-in-training at least, because if you win a state or national title you'll likely need to learn more, stay current, and speak on your topic at appearances and to the media.

Current Events and Controversial Topics

I mentioned above that you can help prepare yourself for free by following the news at least a few times a week. (We can't always— or may not want to—follow it every day). I say that because it will help you know what's going on for some of the potentially "tough" questions you might get. We'll handle how to answer later, but *first* you need to know about the events so you have something to work with for your answer.

True, not every pageant will ask you questions about current events or controversial topics. Many will, at least at the preliminary levels, try to limit themselves to what you put on your fact sheet or to your platform. Still, you aren't just about pageants, are you? You also want to know about the world to help find your way in and perhaps make your mark on it, yes?

Even if you really are more about pageants (that's okay!), you would still be wise to follow the news and have thought through how you think and feel about some issues, especially if they might relate (even tangentially) to your fact sheet or platform as they just might ask you about them.

And, remember, every pageant happens in a locale, so you should at least know some information and/or current events about that area. Here's an example…

When I was competing in Arizona my state was in the news all the time because our Governor had done something wrong and was being impeached. So I took the time to think through how I'd respond *if* a judge at the state level asked my opinion or, say, at the national pageant a judge had asked me:

Judge
"What do you think about the scandal going on in your state now?"

If someone asked me that, I should at least know that "the scandal" (or one of them) was the governor's impeachment. I could then *ask*, "Do you mean the Governor's impeachment?" or *assume* the judge meant that and say:

Stephanie

"If you mean that our Governor is being impeached, I have mixed emotions. I'm sad that an elected official has fallen into a bad light but I'm happy to see the people can exercise their voice again by working to have him removed from office. That's one of the great things about America...what's happening in my state is an example of the democratic process in action."

Even if I assumed wrong—if there was some other scandal the judge had in mind—I at least sound intelligent and gave a good answer. Most judges would accept that and move on rather than admit their question was incomplete or poorly worded and they meant some other sort of scandal.

Alternatively, a judge could correct any assumption and re-direct you with something like:

Judge

"Oh, that's interesting. I didn't even know your state had that happening! But, sorry, what I meant was about your star baseball player using steroids."

Then you'd reply with what you think on that topic or, if you had no idea that was happening (and have no opinion) you might show your graceful way of handling such things by making a light-hearted attempt at taking a pass on the question, saying (with a smile in your voice and on your face):

Contestant

"Well, now it's my turn to not know something was happening! As you can probably tell, I follow politics more than sports."

And then leave it at that and hope they move on.

If they don't move on, or if you want to try taking the question on rather than using the opening to maybe take a pass on it, then you can use one of the other techniques we'll cover later in the book series.

The key for this section of this book is that you know some of the happenings in your state so you are prepared to discuss them like you would with a friend or with new people you meet. You don't have to know everything, but know key things going on and how you feel about them.

A final word on this: Be careful with assumptions.

You'll have to weigh out whether it feels safe to assume—take something for granted—and if what you'd offer in response to an assumption is adequately impressive to move on. Otherwise, you may want to ask a quick question to be sure you are on the right topic as that reflects well on you too. (Seeking clarity is rarely a bad thing.)

For instance, one could ask the judge:

Contestant
"Do you mean the Governor's impeachment?"

He might say "yes" and then, if it were me, I'd go on with the answer I provided above about the impeachment.

Or he might say "No, I mean the steroid scandal" in which case I'd hope I knew something about it or could think it through reasonably well on the spur of the moment. Again, other tips later in this series will help you with "spur of the moment" or "thinking on your feet."

Follow a Variety of News Levels

It can be tempting to just watch the local news. You might think they mention enough about national events to help you on that level too. It may be fine for *local* events but even then the local news is often bits of information that are so short and often not really very newsy on anything of lasting import—it is brief, brief, brief. It's like looking only at the headlines of a newspaper and rarely reading any of the stories.

That can be fine if you are just starting to listen to news or if you are competing in a local or preliminary pageant that might try to limit their interview questions to your application materials. But if your goals are set higher, you may as well start building your news "muscle" sooner rather than later. Building your awareness and understanding can take time so start small and work up.

Start by watching some local news. In addition, see if you can find more in-depth local coverage in the newspapers, on the radio or on the Internet. If you watch television news perhaps choose a news show sponsored by, say, a university which you may find on the local PBS (Public Broadcasting Service) station. You might find those over the network airwaves (meaning you don't have to have cable or satellite to get it) but also check your cable or satellite listings for other more in-depth local news shows.

And don't limit yourself to local news. All levels are important. Local news may be more important for local pageants but it is wise to keep an eye on news at all levels as it helps you be aware of current events and controversial issues that just might come up. And pay attention to news especially as it relate to your platform and/or passions.

> "Guts are important. Your guts are what digest things. But it is your brains that tell you which things to swallow and which not to swallow."
>
> ~Austin Dacey

So try to watch (or otherwise follow) the national news as well. Just as *local* news has mainly local news with a couple national stories (and once in awhile international), the *national* news will have mainly national news but usually also includes some *international* bits. The higher you go in pageants, the more important international news could be. (That is, if you are in a national level pageant it is more likely awareness of national and international situations would come up than it would in a local or preliminary pageant.)

To get better national and international news, you'll want to occasionally give international sources a listen, read, or look. For instance, Public Radio International (PRI; http://www.pri.org) has a show called "The World" which many find to be a good source.

And if you want a different angle, check out the BBC (British Broadcasting Company) which has several news programs or channels that are on U.S. radio and satellite airwaves and you can learn a *lot* of cool stuff about the world (including the U.S.) from them. Why? In part because the British Empire once encompassed a very large part of the globe so even their "national" news is much more international than ours in the U.S.A.

Seek Balance–Or Go For Neutral Sources

Beyond that, in terms of what station to watch, listen to, or read, I recommend following as neutral a news source as you can find—or at least check in with one now and then on issues that tend to polarize people. What do I mean by "neutral?"

Most news shows have a certain leaning or angle for or against a certain policy, political party, or even president. If the celebrity talk show personality, newscaster, big bosses, or editors are *for* something the news stories may slant the story that way. If they are *against* something they may slant the other way. The slant could be obvious or subtle. I'm not saying they are dishonest but they select what they emphasize or report. They take advantage of their position to use information to gently (or not) forward their agenda.

For example, at the time of my writing this, experienced media professors and professionals, and others "in the know" about media sources, tend to consider the Fox news outlet as politically "conservative" (or right-wing) so they emphasize stories in that direction. If you always watch Fox you may start seeing things only that way (which is only *one* way). On the other hand, a program like Keith Oberman's is considered more "liberal" (or left-wing). If you always followed his interpretation of the facts, you'd build a different opinion.

So you'd be wise to watch some of *both* so you can start to appreciate how the media works in this country and that will really help you figure out more where you really stand on matters for *yourself* rather than just through some other person or television or radio station's bias.

Being well informed and educated means collecting information and then thinking for yourself...not just adopting a belief you are handed. It can take time to build the willingness, openness, and skill to do that but all any of us can do is start where we are and keep growing.

Listening to both sides (though there are usually more than two!) is useful in the pageant and work world as it helps you understand people *and* helps you not say overly one-sided things in your responses to questions. Remember that balance is a key. Follow both sides or, perhaps *better*, find and follow what is traditionally known as a balanced or neutral news source from the start. One that is less tangled up by corporate ownership or worries over who will advertise during their shows. (Those sorts of things can impact what is covered or what said and what isn't.) So looking for a more "public" or "independent" new source might help.

For instance, a good more neutral news source is the *Christian Science Monitor*. I know, because the word "Christian" is in the title it might make some think it is a conservative source while others will think the word "Science" in the title makes it liberal. Those would be over-generalizations but doesn't matter because neither case is true! (And no, you don't have to worry that it is promoting Christianity if you happen to not be Christian. It's not about religion even if it has that in the title.)

The *Christian Science Monitor* is one of the oldest, most well written news sources in the U.S.A. (also available online). It is an internationally award-winning news organization and is widely considered balanced in the information they report and the kinds of questions they ask for all kinds of stories. You can judge for yourself when you start building your experience with different news outlets.

If your time and energy is short for the news, make it count and consider using one or two good, neutral sources like the *Monitor* or find a program or two that you can learn from on what many consider as a traditionally neutral or balanced sources like National Public Radio (http://www.npr.org/) or public television via the Public Broadcasting System (http://www.pbs.org/). And here's a source for both sides: http://www.procon.org/. Some other news sources include:

> *The Huffington Post* (http://www.huffingtonpost.com)
> *The Wall Street Journal* (http://www.wsj.com)
> *The Examiner* (http://www.examiner.com)

WORK CURRENT EVENTS/NEWS INTO YOUR DAY

Following a balance of local, national, and international news is a good habit for a Queen.

Here are some ways to work news into your busy day or week, don't make yourself crazy trying to do all of them! Just flex to different modes as you need to and find what works for you:

- Have a national morning news show on while you get ready for your day.

- Listen to radio news while you commute. Consider National Public Radio (NPR) or other radio news station known to be more in-depth (not just sound bites) coverage and more neutral (they take care to offer both sides of the story, have both liberal and conservative guests on, etc.).

- Watch the evening news (or read the newspaper) while you, for instance, walk on the treadmill for exercise. (Or while using other *safe* aerobic equipment—not all equipment is designed for you to multi-task while using it!).

- Read the newspaper over breakfast, lunch, or dinner. (Only if you are eating alone! People come first!) Catch some headlines, read a few stories, daily, or at least weekly.

- Follow respected Internet news sites or politically neutral truly journalistic (not sensational) news blogs. Perhaps subscribe to a free "feed" to help remind yourself. A few minutes a day add up.

- *Remember*, I recommend following a neutral source that will try to get balanced sources. That said, if you prefer to follow a very "left-wing" writer or organization, then *also* follow a "right-wing" one so you learn about "extreme" perspectives on both sides of the story.

How Much News Is Enough?

If following the news is not your natural inclination (it is for some people), then do not make yourself silly or sick following *too* much news too soon. Work yourself up to it and ultimately you will find what works for you as pageant preparation. Some will watch a lot of news in the weeks or months right before the pageant. Others will follow it more lightly but all year long. You do need to do some though!

If you live with, work with, or have a pageant friend or coach who is following the news, they might be able to work with you regularly on current events and controversial questions based on *their* experience. That is, they can ask you questions about what's going on and see how you handle it. Along the way, they'd be alerting you to what *is* going on and you'd indirectly be developing your views. But...

Obviously, it is best if you are following the news yourself. Maybe listen to local news a couple mornings a week while you get ready or drive to work or school or carpool the kids around. Then watch national news a couple evenings a week while you prepare dinner or workout. And find international news once or twice week. Create a schedule that works for you and matches the kind of pageant you are in and your level of education.

"Besides the noble art of getting things done, there is the noble art of leaving things undone. The wisdom of life consists in the elimination of non-essentials."
~Lin Yutang

What If You Don't Like the News?

Regardless of your age, experience, or level of education, you simply may not like the news. And if you are feeling "dumb" (you're not!) or "overwhelmed" when you watch, read, or listen to it that can make you like it even less. Sometimes more "in depth" news stories or shows will cover topics we've never even heard of...or at least not thought about in the sort of detail they might offer. That's okay.

Don't worry, you'll find your personal comfort level and your "education" starts to increase quickly if you follow quality news. At first, it can be pretty confusing and sometimes you'll just have to let some stories or topics go. There's only so much we can learn at once, and only so fast.

So if a particular topic of story makes your brain hurt, you can turn it off or listen to music for a couple minutes and come back to the news station after a brief break. Or just allow yourself to listen and see if you can start to get a sense of a new word or two. It may be a challenge sometimes but it doesn't have to be "work." Allow it to be interesting and fun and it will be!

So "get" what you can, let other things go or jot down the topic or words to figure out another time but, overall, have faith that you will start to get the gist of things and start having a broader, richer understanding of the world. Maybe not all at once but it is all good, so be proud of any progress!

The key is to not just *hear* or *read* or *see* the news but to process it in your heart and mind. Think about how you feel and notice what ideas come to mind as you hear the stories. Look up more information as your interest is sparked. Get a sense for what seems simple, but might really be a more complex issue (and vice versa).

"It is no longer enough to be smart – all the technological tools in the world add meaning and value only if they enhance our core values, the deepest part of our heart. Acquiring knowledge is no guarantee of practical, useful application. Wisdom implies a mature integration of appropriate knowledge, a seasoned ability to filter the inessential from the essential."
~Doc Childre & Deborah Rozman

Practice Positive Thinking, Motivation, and Inspiration

Finally, for some the news can be upsetting or depressing. After all, it can often be bad news! Not always…a lot of news is just to let you know what's going on. And there are upbeat stories too. But if you tend to take on the negativity from the news then consider *not* watching or reading the news right before bed—you may prefer to have happier, more relaxing thoughts in your head before you go to sleep.

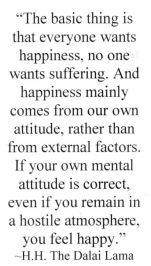

Also, whether or not you enjoy following the news, balance out that kind of preparation with positive, motivational preparation. Staying positive, believing in yourself and others, finding the bright side of situations and the like are important to your finding joy in your daily life. Reading inspiring books, listening to motivational recordings, or uplifting programs is a good antidote to the less happy things we personally experience or learn about on the news.

"The basic thing is that everyone wants happiness, no one wants suffering. And happiness mainly comes from our own attitude, rather than from external factors. If your own mental attitude is correct, even if you remain in a hostile atmosphere, you feel happy."
~H.H. The Dalai Lama

Staying positive will help a smile come more naturally to your face, it will help you assume the best of yourself and others, and it will help you relax—all are important to pageant success! Whether you start or finish your day with something to feed your spirit, do try to work it in there somewhere daily or at least weekly. It very well may help you sleep better and take life's ups and downs in stride.

For some uplifting spiritual inspiration, check out Sounds True, an independent multimedia publishing company. You can also find inspiring quotes on websites like http://www.brainyquote.com when you need a boost.

Review

Let's review what we covered:

- *Your goals, time frame, and ability to be a "self-starter" impact how you prepare.*

  Depending on your situation, personal learning style, and budget, you may prefer to work with a coach. There are several ways to determine how much might be a reasonable amount to spend on interview preparation.

- *You don't have to work with a coach to prepare— but* do *prepare.*

  There are plenty of free or less expensive ways to prepare without hiring a coach. But faithfully preparing *is* important as interview skills can 1) increase your chances of winning, 2) enhance other areas of your life, and 3) will last longer than a lovely gown.

- *Your experience level and goals affect how much time you should practice.*

  However, regardless of your experience level, there is always something to practice. Whether large or small, we all have major improvements or refinements we can make.

- *Practicing out loud (and preferably taping it) is important.*

  Practicing in your head will only get you so far. Hearing yourself saying the words and realizing if you ramble or are too terse can only happen in more "true to life" practice situations—the basic feature of which is to practice out loud.

- ***Good interview practice includes many components.***
  Beyond just knowing your application materials—including your platform and passions—you'll want to follow the news, practice in your interview wardrobe (including shoes), and practice positive thinking.

- ***News comes in all shapes and sizes.***
  Whether television, print, radio, or internet, look for news sources that are balanced and neutral or, at least, follow news sources from both sides of the political continuum to be more fully educated on the issues. This will help you develop your own opinions based on more complete information and help you give balanced interview responses.

Exercise 2.1: Self-Assess Your Interview Preparation Needs

Go over the questions in the "Do you need a coach" section as well as the boxes on what interviews should include. Based on your goals and your situation, get a sense of whether or not you'd like to work with a coach. If you think you might, start finding a coach in your area (realizing that many work remotely over the phone).

You may think an interview coach needs to be an expert in pageants but that may not be necessary depending on their training or experience, ability to appreciate the pageant situation (based on the information you provide them about what your pageant looks for), and their general skill level. As a start, you may be able to work with a high school or college speech teacher or someone experienced in communication. The main thing is that you get a good fit. And you can change coaches or work with more than one at a time as you may find one's style or knowledge base is a better educational tool for you.

Figure out your budget and goals. Ask yourself if you should adjust your budget to spend a little more on interview prep. That said, it is totally possible for you to prepare without spending much money at all if you do it wisely. Whether or not you work with a coach, be sure to take advantage of self-study materials (question books, audio CDs, etc.) and the other ideas presented in the book. Make yourself a practice schedule!

Exercise 2.2: Review (Or Plan) Your Application Materials

Take a few minutes to note the picture you present in those materials and imagine the kinds of questions you might be asked. Think through a little story or interesting fact about your platform and/or passion. Make sure you know some basic information (current and historical) about your hobbies and goals. Doing these things will help you be a prepared Sleuth!

Exercise 2.3: Explore News Sources

Check out some of the sources I offered in the book and find a few more of your own. Spend a few minutes here and there on each of the sites or listening to various shows. Make notes of what you like, what you find do-able. Start with a level that feels right for you but periodically allow yourself to "stretch" and "reach" for the next level. After you've tried a few things, start building a little "news schedule" for yourself but keep open to impromptu opportunities.

And start building your sense for if a source tends to be "slanted" rather than balanced. "Slanted" doesn't necessarily mean "bad" but it does mean you might be getting news that has been filtered a bit…so it'd be wise to also follow news that slants the other way to help you build your own thinking skills. A well-prepared pageant contestant (and person in any interview situation) doesn't just parrot what they hear on the news…they will have an appreciation for more than one way of looking at things and work on doing their own thinking.

Exercise 2.4: Explore Motivational and Inspirational Sources

For some, the idea of watching the news is off-putting. For others, the idea of actually practicing "thinking positive" or otherwise motivating one's self is off-putting or feels un-natural to them. But *both* the news and finding things that keep you feeling good about yourself and life are important to your success not just in pageants but in life. It doesn't have to be the same for everyone but find whatever it is for you! It may be an inspiring book, a certain kind of music (or particular song), it might be prayer or religion, or some particular comedy or talk show or motivational/inspirational speaker. Whatever it is, find what helps you smile and lifts your spirits. Make a little plan to bring that more regularly into your life so you keep yourself "up."

"Twenty years from now you will be more disappointed by the things that you didn't do than by the ones you did do. So throw off the bowlines. Sail away from the safe harbor. Catch the trade winds in your sails. Explore. Dream. Discover."
~Mark Twain

**Here I am shortly after winning
the Miss Arizona Petite 1988 title.**

a pageant is just the beginning...

PAGEANT
Interviewing
SUCCESS

❖

Personal
Characteristics

❖

Dr. Stephanie Raye, PhD
Former Miss American Petite

Book 3
Personal Characteristics
Table of Contents

Pageant Interviewing Success:
Personal Characteristics

The three main areas of a pageant interview performance are:

- Response content
- Response delivery
- And *you* (your personal characteristics)

This book focuses primarily on assisting you with your content—after reading this book, you will be better prepared to answer any sort of question in a more thoughtful way to show yourself in the best light, and help them make a good decision about whether you are the "best fit" to hold the title.

We will cover delivery to some extent when we talk about, for example, eye contact, body language, length of response, etc. And *you*—your personality, enthusiasm, likableness, fashion sense, beauty, quality of voice, and the like—cut across both content and delivery.

You come into a pageant with certain aspects of yourself and your behavior that you *cannot* change and other aspects you may *not want* to change. Still other aspects of you it may be very wise to change—whether or not you are aware of them just yet—to enhance your success in the pageant and in other arenas after the pageant.

So in this book we will touch on a few personal characteristics. As with the content and delivery aspects, there is additional support on enhancing personal characteristics if you need it through other materials, coaching, and classes.

Quality of Speaking Voice

Sound Like a Winner

You need to sound like a winner. Not like a whiner, not like a little girl, and not sexy, angry, bossy, or timid. You may not have thought there would be that much communicated in a voice but the simple sound of your voice can say a lot. Now it may not be accurate in what it says, but even if people do not jump to conclusions that stick, the first impression can still put them off. Perfection isn't necessary but…

…No one likes a voice that makes them cringe like fingernails scraping a chalkboard. And what rubs people the wrong way can vary…so having an overall pleasing voice is a good thing. It is less likely to bother anyone. This is so important so be sure to give it proper attention.

Going into too much depth on speed, tone, intonation, modulation, pitch, volume, regional accent, nasality, enunciation, diction (word choice), etc. are beyond the scope of this particular document.

But suffice it to say here that your speaking voice and vocal mannerisms are areas that we are so accustomed to, just like physical mannerisms, that we don't notice them. And our loved ones are so used to those same things about us they often do not notice either. If we do *hear* ourselves clearly we may not objectively appreciate the impact it has on people (just like with our visual characteristics and habits). A little focused observation and practice can make a big difference for us—in awareness and ability to improve.

For now, I'll mention just a few key points that add up to your sounding like a confident, capable person. We do not want to sound overbearing or shrill or too loud. Not too high-pitched. In contrast, neither do we want to sound too soft or have too low a volume like a little girl might sound. Not breathy. Not sultry. Not slurred or hard to understand.

Pitch

So what is "pitch"? In musical terms, it is basically what "key" your voice is in. For example, a deep male voice is low-pitched (it would be in a low key on a piano) and a high-pitched little girl voice would be in a higher key. Too high or too low a pitch in your voice quality can be problematic for listeners and give off the wrong impression.

Modulation

"Modulation" is about vocal variety—that is, as you talk does your voice naturally rise and fall around your natural center pitch point? Or do you talk in a monotone like a robot? A robot has no modulation—robotic speech is all flat and even. Interesting, pleasing voices have some natural lilt.

Enunciation

"Enunciation" is commonly confused with the term "diction." What most people mean when they say "diction" is really "enunciation" which is whether you form sounds and words clearly and distinctly as you pronounce the words. Put a different way, can the audience easily understand what you are saying?

Do your sounds and words run together or stand apart? If they run together, the speaking may sound slurred, sloppy, or "lazy." Ideally, each letter sound and word stands alone so the speech sounds more "clean" and precise. A Queen or titleholder should be easy to understand and be a fine example of spoken language and grammar.

Know that if you recently had braces or other dental and facial work your speech may change because how your tongue works with your teeth to produce sounds may alter. Regardless of what may be the cause, notice if you need to work on this.

Volume

Volume may seem like a "no-brainer" to mention as you probably know not to speak too loudly or too softly, right? You neither want them cringing because you are almost yelling at them nor do you want them struggling to hear you because your volume is too low. What may not be obvious, however, is that your volume may lower at the end of your sentences or at the end of your answers.

In other words, don't let your volume drift away to nothing as you finish a thought, sentence, or response. To sound confident and in control, end each sentence at about the same volume at which you started it. If you get nervous or ramble your way to lower and lower volume you come off as inexperienced and uncertain.

Stay on target, say what you need to say and then stop talking (smiling all the while)…don't dwindle your voice down to nothing. Especially if you tend to dwindle, you may want to aim on ending a response on a slightly "louder" volume to emphasize you are done.

As with any thing we discuss, be aware that you may not *think* you need to work on it. Again, it is hard to see and hear ourselves clearly at times. But audio record yourself (and/or get feedback from an objective party) and you'll get a sense of if you can improve in these areas.

Nasality, Regional Accents, Verbal Mannerisms

Practice eliminating nasal sounding voices or overly strong regional accents – one can usually reduce their impact with a little effort. Voices that sound very strongly of one area of the country may be just fine for local preliminary pageants—and possibly even at the state level. But the judges may favor a national contestant who sounds more region-neutral as the national titleholder will represent the whole country. There could be exceptions, of course, but region-neutral is more like a national anchorperson might sound—it usually isn't clear what part of the country they are from based on their speech.

And remember to get rid of unconscious verbal mannerisms which might include loud breathing or filler words. Ask yourself if you say any words or phrases like this without thinking about:

A FEW FILLER WORDS AND PHRASES

Er
Um
Like
You know
Really
I have to say
And so
And then
As if
Seriously
I mean
(Swear words)

Swear words?! I know a pageant queen hopeful would never do that but I mention it so you can start listening to people around you and on television and notice when folks use a variety of meaningless words to pad or fill out what they say. And the list I put above is *partial*...any word or phrase might find its way into mindless repetition in a given person's speech patterns.

If you try to fill silences with these filler words, perhaps as you are trying to figure out what else to say, that's not a good habit. If you say things like this habitually just as a part of talking (even if you aren't trying to think), and find that you say them more than once in a sentence or a response it could be distracting. Worse, it could make you seem less intelligent than you are.

Again, there is no one "right" speaking voice but there are several vocal components that you'll want to make sure are not "wrong." This is something you can adjust, so have the courage to self-assess on this (or get an outside opinion) and trust that you can optimize your voice for your success.

Speech Impediments

There are a lot of things we *can* do to improve our voices so we need to be honest with ourselves about what those are and work with the people who can help us do so. That said, there are other things we may not be able to fully change.

For instance, Miss International 2009, Jayna Altman was born severely premature which, among other complications, led her to have profound hearing loss. It was thought that she'd never speak. But not only did she learn to speak, she speaks very well. She is an articulate and well-spoken woman. (Note: many deaf people who can't or don't learn to speak the same way as those who hear are also articulate and well-spoken with sign language. Oral speech is only one form of communication.)

Jayna worked with professionals to improve her voice and while she may not speak as clearly as we are accustomed to, she's awesome. She didn't allow her circumstances, or anything else, to get in the way of her dreams. She is a great role model because of it. And, by the way, she's on record as saying she wants a PhD in Audiology— there we go, another "Pageant to PhD" winner!

So if you have a "speech impediment" you can still sound like a winner like Jayna who displayed the best voice she could and made it work. Her platform/mission was "Abilities First" with the motto "I CAN" (Inspiring Confidence in Abilities Now) and as one who has taught university level diversity classes (which includes work on the disabled or "differently abled") I truly appreciate her work on such an important issue.

Deafness can affect speech clarity as well. I remember back from my pageant days making friends with the Miss Deaf Arizona at the time. A great young woman and fabulous dancer! And you may recall that Heather Whitestone was crowned Miss America 1995, the first Miss

America with a known disability (deafness). It took her *six* years to correctly pronounce her name but she persisted. We can learn from and imitate her determination.

And Miss Siobhan Brindley-Lewis, was the first profoundly deaf contestant to compete in the finals for Miss Great Britain 2009 in the Miss Universe system. There are—or will be!—other examples inside and outside the pageant world. (Remember Marlee Matlin—the talented deaf actress.) The key to remember is…

Never underestimate what you can do in a specialized or non-specialized pageant if you put your mind to it. And even if you don't place or win you'll still be doing something important for yourself, at the same time you will shine for others too.

Know Thyself – Personality

Knowing your own personality when you enter an interview can help you succeed in it. It's no mystery that we all have different personalities. That's fine! We want you to be who you are.

That said, do you pay attention to what the strengths and challenges of your personality include? Do you pay attention to how you come off to others? Do you have the ability to flex with the situation? Do you have the ability (or are you willing to learn) how to "manage yourself" to tone yourself down or pump yourself up when need be?

I could write a whole series (check my website, I may have written more on this by now!) on key personality characteristics but for the purposes of this book, let's keep it simple and short. Let's talk about two key aspects that will help you succeed in interview.

How Do You Come Off to People?
Energy Level and Tone

As much as I encourage you to be positive and reasonably enthusiastic in your interview, I'm not suggesting you be fake or inauthentic. You do not have to be a cheerleader (as great as they are!) and be all bouncy all the time in your movements, attitude, and voice. I'm not suggesting that.

But if you are a really subdued, low-key sort of person, you may want to kick it up just a notch somewhere in your interview. Low-key can come off as calm and elegant (good things) or it can come off as bored and uninterested (not so good). If you are a somewhat "serious" professional sort, that's fine too, to an extent. But *too* serious and strictly "down to business" can come off as unfriendly or lacking a sense of humor.

Basically, too much of any extreme—too bouncy, too subdued, or too aloof—can be off-putting. Allow your personality to show some elasticity and adjust for the situation and the question. Pay attention to yourself in your practice sessions (practice out loud!) and audio and video record yourself from time to time to see yourself more objectively.

How Do You See the World?
Is the Cup Half Full or Half Empty?

The clichéd expression of "Do you see the cup as half empty? Or half full?" is a good thing to think about as you prepare for any interview. If you tend to see the cup as half empty you will more likely answer questions from a negative perspective. Without even realizing it, you may focus on the problem and forget to mention a solution.

For example, you may take a negatively worded question like "What do you see as a problem for youth today?" and run with the "problem" part of it so well that you forget to add something positive or to reframe the question entirely. Or you may take a neutral question like "What do you see as a challenge for youth today?" (challenges are not necessarily negative!) and go toward the negative side instead of including what's great with the youth today.

Without proper balance, a negative take on questions and answers can set a negative tone to the interview. That, in turn, can direct the judges away from choosing you. They may like you, think you are capable and intelligent but have some vague "negative" feeling about you that leads them to score you lower.

On the flip side if you *always* see the glass as half-full you may blow past a serious question or elect to skip the serious *part* of a question and come off as not living in the "real world" or as uninformed or not mature enough to address a "problem."

Balance is key but if you are going to be a bit off-balance then bending toward the positive side is a safer place to be. Which way do I lean? I don't see the cup as just half full or half empty. I see it both ways and say "Who cares; Are you going to drink that!?" Aim to see multiple sides to a situation (good, bad, and neutral) and deal with it (drink it). Try it!

Keep It Consistent and Real

Much of the rest of the pageant is about outer beauty, but the interview part is clearly to highlight inner beauty. And it helps the judges discover if the contestant carries herself as well in words and deeds as she does in her swimsuit/fitness attire and evening gown.

Stay humble without putting yourself down. No one is "better" than you are, just different. Everybody has strengths and weaknesses. Acknowledge what you have to offer but remember that every other person in the contest has something to offer too. So even if you're great, you aren't alone in it. Others will be great too.

Radiate confidence without coming off as arrogant or "too perfect." It is true that you may be better prepared than others—you may have it all together—but no one likes a "know it all" or a "show off" who thinks they are better than everyone else. Even if you don't think that, make sure you don't come off that way.

A Queen will inspire genuine admiration, she will not need to demand it or smuggle it in. She'll *be* admirable because of who she is, how she treats people, and her sensitive sleuthing. She'll be "all that" but she still needs to be approachable.

It's a fine line to walk. I remember when I was competing, I kept telling myself that all the other girls were beautiful and I was sure that they'd do a good job. But I knew I had prepared with great care and thoughtful specificity, and I knew I had the skills to do a good job for the year of Queenly duties. I felt like I was the right person for the job.

I was confident that if I demonstrated that in my interview, I'd win the crown. But if I didn't win, it would be because someone else was actually a better fit and I'd be happy for her. There is usually more than one lid for every pot (more than one contestant who'd do a good job). I knew I was good, but it was up to the judges and how well they felt I handled personal and on-stage interviews. I was confident without being cocky—that's the right balance to aim for and achieve.

Be Age-Appropriate

Youthfulness and beauty are generally valued in many areas of society—especially in the pageant world. And, yes, we want to have energy and (usually) look younger than we are. That said, be cautious that you don't act too much younger than you are or too much older than you are as it can backfire. Aging gracefully means accepting your age and making sure you're the best you can be *for that age*.

So aim to be age appropriate in your choice of clothes, talent, platform, and delivery of any words that comes out of your mouth.

An Example in Regard to a Child

"Age appropriate" (suitable for a particular age) in this context means, for instance, a very young contestant in a pre-teen or teen pageant should not be using words for which that they do not know the meaning. Think about it: It doesn't work out well if the judge asks them what it means and the contestant doesn't know!

Children can be practiced, sure! After all, we want them to be at-ease and prepared, but coming off as fake and robotic in repeating words they don't understand is not the goal. My recommendation: Teach them genuine vocabulary a little each day and they'll learn fast! Then as the pageant draws near, ask your little contestant what *she* wants to say and help her build on and shape that.

Similarly a contestant in a Miss, Ms., Mrs. or other mature pageant should avoid seeming too childish or immature. You can still be *fun*, just appropriate for your age. You can still be *smart*, just know what you are talking about.

And a person can be youthful and up-to-date without being child-like or too "hip" for their age group or title. In terms of your choice of words, in the pageant world slang is rarely—if *ever*—appropriate in *any* age group.

Just imagine if a contestant were asked the classic pageant question:

Judge
"Are you having a good time at the pageant?"

And she replied in some form of slang like:

"Yo, mad props on the pageant team. And the food has been off the hook. And isn't it sick how great the rooms are?"

Or something like:

"My roommate's the bomb. And I'm learning so much from watching the other girls… they really know how to pimp it."

Yikes! Responses like those may sound trendy, current, hip, or whatever. That may sound good to some people but slang like that is not appropriate. And many people won't even pick up the intended meaning of some slang so misunderstandings can occur. That would be like filling out your application paperwork in text message abbreviations! Let's expand on the importance of word choice…

Choice of Words – Diction and Vocabulary

I mentioned earlier that folks sometimes confuse "diction" with "enunciation"—it happens so often it almost has taken on that meaning! But diction really is what words you choose to express yourself. Very briefly here, diction choices fall along a few dimensions, for example, formality and precision.

On formality, do you choose slang, jargon, informal, common, or formal words? If you use too much slang or "jargon" people may not understand you. If it is too informal you may not seem professional enough. You wouldn't fill out your application in "Instant Messaging" or "Text Messaging" abbreviations, so you don't want your speech to be too informal either. Yet you don't want to be so formal in all choices that you sound like a snob.

On precision, do you choose vague or general words or are you specific and accurate? Too vague or general and you and the judges may *think* you are saying and thinking the same thing when you aren't—the words leave too much latitude for interpretation. Tending toward precise, accurate wording is better but not to the point where you torture yourself over finding the "perfect" word if it is going to delay the fluidity of your response.

A skillful communicator adjusts her speech to the audience and knows when to choose what words and tone—but to be able to do that you have to have several words available to you! That comes from reading, listening, looking things up, and in all ways building your vocabulary.

Yes, personality and beauty are important, but so is understanding the world around us and being able to talk to people of all walks of life.

A Queen needs to be able to use "big" words and "small" words depending on the situation to communicate well and help people feel comfortable around her. Since smaller words tend to come more easily to us (that's what the newspapers and television use most of the time), we often have to make an effort to build our familiarity and facility with new or different words that might better describe a situation, feeling, belief, or event.

I'm not suggesting you pretend to be someone you aren't. I *am* suggesting that you consider challenging yourself to keep growing toward a version of you that enjoys using an ever-widening variety of words. Why?

Because if *all* else was *equal* between two contestants—if in our imaginary scenario there were two identical twin beauties who had equal community service and talent and personality—the one who has better language skills would likely win. Why? Because she'd be able to communicate with people better and would overall better represent the title!

Consider how these two answers sound—they offer basically the same *content* in response to this classic personal question, but their choice of words communicate differently:

Judge
"Your bio says you just graduated so tell us a little about your time in school."

More casual language:

"School rocked. I went and got my 4-year degree and did really good. I never skipped class, not once. And I also did lots of things in school besides studying, like helping out the teachers and students with work, raising money for poor people and like the homeless. That was a ton to do so I had to take care of myself too so I was always at the gym because I didn't want to get fat or sick."

Less casual language:

"I enjoyed my education. I completed a Bachelor's degree with a B+ grade average and perfect attendance. But learning happens outside the classroom too so I also participated in extra-curricular activities. For instance, I served as an unofficial teaching assistant in leading study groups for my classmates and engaged in fundraising projects for three different charities. To manage all that, I had to stay healthy and energetic so you can bet I used my gym membership regularly!"

Which contestant makes a better impression on you? The judges? The public? The media? Probably the second one. Even if you are a teen, overly casual language should be avoided unless you are just hanging out with friends.

We could go over *many* examples of this and, with each one, we could increase the "level" of the words and the precision of the communication. But you get the idea. We don't need to overdo it, and neither do you. You don't have to sound like a genius and it is okay to show your personality with how you speak…just practice building your vocabulary and learn to adjust for the audience and situation.

"Eyes are more accurate witnesses than ears."
~Heraclitus, circa 480 B.C.

Body Talk –
What Is It Saying While You Talk?

Nervousness or Not?

Does what your body says agree with what your words say? Do you sound calm and in control but your body or face says, "I'm really nervous. I can't wait until this is over!" You're probably a happy, friendly person, so show it!

You need to look like you enjoy talking to people. After all, the titleholder will be talking to many people in many situations. Yes, interview situations will create a little nervousness that might not be there in some other situations. That's okay. But, as we all know, non-verbal communication says more than words—what your body language, physical mannerisms, posture, and facial expressions, etc., say can be "louder" and more meaningful than any words, so the judges will be listening to them.

And it may not be about nerves at all. You could actually be perfectly calm but have some odd habit that conveys a lack of self-awareness.

What Judges Want

The judges want to send someone out who presents a fairly-to-highly polished "has it together" image. That doesn't mean you have to be overly formal and you certainly don't need to be rigid and cold!

They want to see the sort of person we all like to be around—a friendly, intelligent person who is likeable, flexible, diplomatic, and has a positive impact on anyone they meet—a confident, trustworthy Queen who makes folks feel at ease. If you fidget and wiggle or shift your eyes, people may not feel like you are that confident or, worse, you may make them feel uncomfortable.

So have command of your body and expression. This doesn't mean you can't be spontaneous and natural. It just means get to know yourself and nix the mannerisms that send a contradictory message to what you intend. Let's review a few of those physical mannerisms now...

Do You Do Anything Like This?
Do You Have Distracting Habits?
Start paying attention. Notice if you:

- Fidget in your chair?
- Clasp or wring your hands?
- Pick at yourself?
- Swing a foot?
- Roll your ankle?
- Tap a finger?
- Twirl your hair?
- Roll your eyes?
- Wrinkle your nose?
- Wrinkle your forehead too much or at odd times?
- Sway or rock in your chair or when you stand?

In other words, do you do anything that is distracting to the judges or conveys that you are nervous? Nervous or not, do you have any annoying or unflattering physical habits? You may not be nervous at all and still have habits that don't help you shine.

What about your facial expressions? Ask yourself, do you routinely:

- Raise your eyebrows too often?
- Tighten your eyebrows so they pinch up your face?
- Over-exaggerate any expressions?
- Have overly large reactions?
- Frown or grin too big?
- Drop your mouth open too wide or too long?

- Fake pout too much, too long, or too big?
- Visibly tighten your jaw when you are tense or uncertain?
- Absent-mindedly bite or lick your lips?

If you do any of the above, I'd recommend stopping. But maybe you don't *realize* that you are doing it….

Consider Yourself Objectively

Expressions and habits that feel natural to you may not look natural—and you may have never noticed it because all the people in your life love you and, maybe, they don't see you objectively anymore.

They are used to your cute little habits! They may not realize that you do something that other folks might find distracting…or if they do, they may not tell you because to them it doesn't matter or they don't want to hurt your feelings. You can ask them to look at you objectively and give them permission to tell you anything they notice. But, whether you do that or not consider doing this…

Practice interviewing yourself in front of a mirror. Yes, you can start in front of your bathroom mirror looking at just your face but work your way up to sitting and standing in front of a full-length mirror to see what you do with the rest of your body. Do you hold yourself well? Wiggle around? Shift your weight?

After plenty of mirror practice, videotape yourself interviewing in front of a mock judges panel made up of your friends and family. It will help you see yourself more objectively. And it is good practice for "normalizing" the interview experience. The more you practice, the more familiar it will all be. So, again, practice both personal interview and on-stage interview at home and you'll be better off when the real interview time arrives.

You may already have a video camera. If you don't, perhaps you can borrow one from a friend or family member, or from work, school, church or some other group of which you are a part. If not, you can find them new or used in all price ranges. BestBuy is a good and reliable source for information, reviews, a range of choices, and good deals, which you can find at http://www.bestbuy.com.

"It is what they can show the audience when they are not talking that reveals the fine actor."
~Cedric Hardwicke

Review

Let's review what we covered:

- The quality of your speaking voice matters. We discussed vocal features and habits to avoid as you aim to sound like a winner.

- Know your personality characteristics and how people respond to your personality. Remember that your energy level and tone communicate a lot. And be realistic about whether you tend toward pessimism or over-optimism. Seek a balance but err on the side of positive.

- Being age-appropriate is a good idea no matter your age.

- The words you choose matter. We covered examples of casual and less-casual word choice, and we discussed the importance of avoiding slang.

- Interviews are about inner beauty but the judges can't help but notice your outer beauty too, especially up close in a personal interview or in the up-close camera shot of an on-stage interview.

Exercise 3.1: Self-Assess Your Voice

3.1.1 Review that section of the book and tape record yourself and *notice* if you do any of the things it is better to avoid. If you don't have a digital recorder or old-fashioned tape recorder, at least call and leave yourself a long voicemail message to see what you sound like.

3.1.2. Part 2 of this self-assessment exercise reaches beyond the "self" and involves getting the opinion of, or help from, others. Start with those close to you but remember they may not be objective. If you determine you have some room for improvement in this area, set about working on it. Set small goals and monitor your progress. Seek out the advice and support of professionals if that would help you.

Exercise 3.2: Self-Assess Your Personality

3.2.1 Start taking note of whether you tend to be "up" or "down" and how your comments and attitude affects other people. Keep a little journal or mark in something you carry around how often you catch yourself being positive or negative throughout the day. This takes *courage*, practice, and *awareness*. This is not an easy exercise but it is worth doing.

3.2.2. Similarly, if you have the courage to ask a few people who interact with you it may be helpful to you. You might try "I know this is an odd question but I'm looking for feedback so I know how I come off to people…in your opinion do I tend to come off like I have a positive attitude or a negative attitude?" See what they say. Just don't "defend" yourself if you don't *like* what they say. Simply say "thank you" or perhaps ask for an example if you don't understand what they said but whatever they say, take it in stride. Don't think negatively (or positively) about yourself from something like this—just see it as a potential source of insight for you.

Exercise 3.3: Pay Attention to Your Speech (And Watch Two Movies!)

3.3.1 Review that section of the book and start noticing if you tend to use slang too often. Or if you are too casual in your choice of words when you could be a little bit more formal or precise.

3.3.2. Watch the "old" movie called "My Fair Lady" (you can find it at some video stores, libraries, or on internet movie rental services). It's a fun movie and you'll see the importance of speech. There's a little of that sort of theme in the movie "Pretty Woman" as well but don't stop with watching "Pretty Woman." (Some of you may enjoy reading the play "Pygmalion" as well.)

3.3.3. Challenge yourself to improve your speech so you are better able to do so when it really matters (like in an interview!).

3.3.4. Challenge yourself to go back through this book and look up any difficult vocabulary words you skipped. Try to use a new word in your own speech each day.

Exercise 3.4: Self-Assess Your Physical Characteristics

Just as with your voice, your personality, and your speech, now it is time to look at your skin, hair, body, and physical movements. So this exercise is really 4 in 1.

Start with one thing at a time—wherever you feel most comfortable or most courageous—and take reasonable steps to improvement. One thing at a time, setting achievable goals (review Exercise 1.2 for how to set goals!) and you can really enhance the wonderful you that you already are!

3.4.1. Look at your skin and if it needs help then help it! Learn how to take care of your skin and use make-up.

3.4.2. Look at your hair and if it needs help or updated styling then set a goal for how you are going to make that happen.

3.4.3. Be honest about whether you are being good to your body. For some that may mean slimming down a bit in a *healthy* way (with good nutrition and exercise—just cut out the processed foods and your body will reward you for switching to a wholesome, balanced diet). For others, it may mean *gaining* a little weight or muscle mass by, again, sensible nutrition and exercise.

Whatever you need to do, focus on "right-sizing" for your body type and health rather than for some external ideal in a magazine or television show. You don't have to do this alone. If social support will help you reach your goals while you treat your body better, then join a group or form a "buddy" partnership, or see your doctor. Whatever, take care of *you*. (Actually, it is generally good advice for any of us to see your doctor before undertaking a weight loss plan or beginning an exercise plan.)

3.4.4. Finally, practice in front of a mirror and/or videotape yourself and watch for nervous habits or physical mannerisms or slumped posture, etc. Once you see it, start consciously stopping yourself from doing those things and substitute in a better choice for what to do with your hands, etc.

**Here I am in my swimsuit at
my state competition.**

a pageant is just the beginning...

PAGEANT
Interviewing
SUCCESS

Question Types

Dr. Stephanie Raye, PhD

Book 4
Question Types
Table of Contents

Pageant Interviewing Success: Question Types

Prepare as If Interview Is Your Talent

Preparation makes a difference! You'd never go out to do your talent without practicing. So you shouldn't do your interview without practicing either. You need to work with practice questions, practice sitting and standing, and practice *out loud*. No, practicing only by saying things in your head or writing down answers alone isn't enough, you need to speak it to hear yourself. Tape it or get feedback from others to see how you are doing.

If you haven't been winning, placing, or just haven't been feeling good in general about how you did, it could be because something is "off" in how you interview. So let's make sure all switches are turned on. That starts with good preparation. You're taking a good step by reading this book. It will definitely get you on a stronger path and give you suggestions for additional learning.

That Doesn't Mean You'll Sound "Rehearsed"

But let's be clear...preparation for interview does not mean to turn yourself into a robot. I'm *not* suggesting you memorize or prepare in such a way as to sound "canned" or "*fake*." But you want to practice handling a variety of question types because it will make it far easier to do so when the time actually comes.

If you compete more than once, it isn't uncommon to get the same sort of questions more than once. Why? Because you will have turned in a pageant application (resume, bio, form, etc.) that the judges will likely work from for part of their questions for you. Thus, remember, you want that paperwork to be helpful to showing you as a strong candidate so make sure it is thoughtfully prepared and flawless.

But even if they don't ask you the *same* questions you practiced, you'll find that you are more skilled at handling questions that previously seemed "hard" as you will be building your basic knowledge of current events and controversial topics. You are less likely to stumble over your words or look like a deer in the headlights (poor deer!) when you are asked questions you previously thought were too "personal." Answers will come more easily to you as you'll be getting in better touch with your values and goals. Fewer and fewer things will catch you off guard and you'll grow into a fine diplomat for your pageant (and yourself!).

You'll find the pointers in this book will help you succeed but you'll probably want to read some of the other materials too. And really, especially if you are preparing largely on your own, you'll benefit from my forthcoming Essential Pageant Interview Playbook. Even if you work with an interview coach (and I know that is not something everyone has the opportunity to do) this will help you work through a wide variety of exercises to increase how brightly you'll shine.

Review Your Bio and Other Application Paperwork Answers

Remember, as we've touched on already, those application forms (including fact sheets, resumes, essays, etc.) are there for a reason. One of those reasons is for the judges to get to know you…to give them something to work with to personalize your interview and determine if you're the right contestant for the title. Yes, of course, they could ask you some questions that are not related to your bio (that's short for "biography") or application answers, but they probably *will* ask some from whatever you turned in.

I'm assuming in this book that your forms are already done. Remember, though, that you should think about your interview *before* and *while* you fill out those forms and put together your paperwork. So I recommend you review the additional materials I have on my website about the topic of pageant applications to maximize your success by thoughtfully strategizing what exactly you include there.

But as a bonus sneak-peek for you here, let me give you a few quick tips about preparing your materials (your fact sheet, application, other forms):

- *Include information you want to be asked about and that shows you are a good candidate for the job of titleholder.*

  If the pageant requires both a platform and many appearances, be sure you include something about appearances you've made or your experience and comfort with public speaking.

- *Don't be a one-note orchestra.*

  Show the different sides of yourself that show you are a well-rounded individual. Show dimension and be willing to appropriately "talk yourself up" in your application paperwork. (Don't boast or lie but do communicate some of your great skills and successes.)

- *Don't take a scattershot approach.*

  Try limiting to what are the 4 or 5 most important themes to communicate in your paperwork. While you want to be well rounded, you don't want to tell about so many things that you dilute the power of your strongest areas. Again, you want to guide the judges to asking about what you are best prepared to talk about so don't put just anything down because you did it once or you think it looks good. Think it through like a Sleuth!

- *Think about what you want the judges and the audience to know about you.*

  The Master of Ceremonies (the "MC" or emcee) will likely be reading tidbits of it as you promenade in your fitness wear, gown, etc. For instance, the emcee might tell the audience who the contestants admire most as they take their turn in gown category, and what they listed as hobbies as they parade in swimsuit. Does the information that the judges hear there communicate you'd be a good choice?

- *Make sure your paperwork is accurate and professionally presented.*

  Most everything is downloadable or you might be able to fill it out on the computer these days but *if* by chance you have a paper application, find a typewriter somewhere (or re-type or recreate the form) as it is better if these materials are not hand-written. Regardless of the format, be sure it is error-free. Have someone else who is good with words and detail proofread it for you. (It is harder to see our own mistakes.) Do not fill it out in a hurry or at the "last minute."

- *Always follow the rules.*

  Some pageants will give you considerable freedom (allowing various formats, photos, etc.), others will be very strict. If they give guidelines for margins or page length, etc. then follow them or risk that your materials that exceed their length limits may be discarded.

- *Keep a copy!*

  Keep copies of everything you turn in for every pageant or job. Keep especially good records if you are entering more than one pageant in a year. Keep it all in a notebook or specific file. Know what you turned in for a particular pageant. All of us are "works in progress" so what we do—and what we put on our forms and in our resumes—will change, so keep track so you know what you said, and be willing to grow.

But for now—since your paperwork may already be in for this pageant—suffice it to say that you do *not* want to have a blank look on your face, or worse, because you forgot what you wrote there.

If you filled your form out in a rush, thinking it wouldn't matter that much, or a lot of time passed since you completed it, take the time to review it before you head to the pageant (and again once you are there).

Spin-Off Questions

We will spend a whole book later in the book series for tips on how to respond to personal questions (*Book 9: Answering Personal Questions*) but we'll introduce a type of personal question here.

You'd be wise to prepare in advance or, at the very least, review your materials the night before, or the morning of, your interview. Better yet, in the weeks leading up to the pageant, think of questions that might spin off from the information you provided to them. Think through what you'd say if they ask about anything on your bio or other application paperwork. For example, think about your:

- "Major" or studies in school (past, present, or potential future)
- What career(s) you have had or are considering
- Goals you mention
- Hobbies or activities
- Interests
- Community service
- Family
- Most embarrassing moment
- Who you most admire
- Favorite food, color, music, or movie
- (Teens and Miss may be asked about parents and siblings, Ms. and Mrs. may be asked about spouses and children.)

No matter what it is, think through your life so you are prepared for questions like:

- "How did you start doing _____ ?"
- "What does doing _____ mean to you?"
- "What are your favorite and least favorite things about _____ ?"
- "Why are you studying _____?"

At the teen level these questions would likely be simpler and more straightforward but if you are at other levels (like Miss, Mrs., Ms.), they will likely want to see that you've thought things through more carefully. In regard to items about what you study, what you do, or what you want to do someday, be *sure* you are ready to demonstrate your knowledge and/or skill in the area. In other words, be prepared to show your stuff.

Let's look at a question you might prefer not to get. This could come up anywhere but the example I'll offer is from the Miss Universe 2010 competition.

Judge William Baldwin

"What is one big mistake that you've made in your life and what did you do to make it right?"

Miss Philippines

"Thank you so much, sir, for that wonderful question. Good evening ladies and gentlemen; good evening Las Vegas! You know what, sir, in my 22 years of existence I can say that there is nothing major major, I mean problem, that I have done in my life because I am very confident with my family with the love that they are giving to me. So thank you so much that I am here! Thank you, thank you so much!"

Miss Philippines 2010, Yendi Phillipps, seems like a sweet and sincere woman, genuinely excited to be at the pageant. Maybe that excitement got in her way a bit, though, because her answer isn't strong. She bungled away the potential of that question.

It is fine that she has never made a major mistake, of course, and if she had it may or may not be appropriate to mention. But a smart pageant contestant will be prepared with a more thoughtful response to questions exploring her embarrassments and mistakes.

Let's try a different response working with what she offered and extending it.

Sleuth

"Thank you and good evening! A big mistake? Well, I've been fortunate to have a loving family that has helped me make good decisions I can feel confident about. My choices may not always turn out as I hoped—they might *feel* like a mistake sometimes— but I know I've tried to avoid hurting myself or others. Now little mistakes are another story! I'm human so I make those all the time and I've learned the best way to make it right is to acknowledge what you did, apologize, help fix it if you can, and aim never to do it again."

This response conveys what the actual contestant said and so much more, in only a few words more. She still doesn't admit an actual mistake but a response along these lines shows maturity, humor, self-awareness, gratitude to her family, and a realistic plan for when she might make a mistake in the future. Which would you trust with the crown?

Demonstration Questions

What do I mean? Well, if you say you want to be an anchor woman, then don't be surprised if they ask you to—right there and then!— give a pretend "on air report" of the pageant. Being ready to show that you are serious about, and ready to be, on camera like that one day (or perhaps already have been) will show you can think on your feet. So *if* they ask you something like:

Judge

"You say you are studying broadcast journalism to be a television reporter, pretend we're the camera and give us a 30 second report on the pageant."

You should be able to pick up the lead as if someone just said "And over to you, (fill in your name here)."

Contestant

"I'm here at the Orpheum Theatre in Phoenix Arizona where tonight ____ accomplished women will compete for the title of Miss Arizona. The weather is hot but these contestants are keeping their cool to put their best foot forward. The winner will be spending the year _____. Back to you in the studio, John."

You can fill in the blanks. But keep it *brief* and to the point. Choose an angle and report on the beauty, brains, and activities of the delegates (a word some will use instead of "contestants") or by saying something about the location (resort, city, state, country) of the event.

Add relevant detail to show you are knowledgeable about your pageant where you can. For instance, if you were asked to do this for the 2009 Miss Arizona-USA pageant, you might have said 43 women were competing. (I believe that's how many they had!)

Whereas if you were answering the question for the 2009 Miss Arizona-America contest, you'd adjust the number to 21, as well as adjust the judging categories, duties, prizes, etc. accordingly. It would depend on what you covered in your "demo."

But for you to do that, you have to keep your eyes and ears open and know about your pageant, yourself, and your career goals. For instance, if you are in the Miss America contest and want to go into broadcast journalism, you'd be well advised to know who Phyllis George and Gretchen Carlson are! They are both former Miss Americas who work in that field. (Miss Phyllis George really opened doors for women, especially in sports broadcasting.)

As additional examples, if you say you want to be a singer it is at least *possible* that a judge will say:

Judge
"Give us a few bars of your favorite song."

Especially if it is a pageant that does *not* have a talent portion where you may be showing that skill, they just might want to see what you have to offer "on the spot." It shows if you can think on your feet, handle pressure, go with the flow, etc.

If you've said you want to work in a certain industry or in a certain sport, you should know a little something about that industry or sport. Who are the key people? Maybe the ones who started or advanced the area, or are the "household names" for people who know that field or sport.

Think through how anything on your paperwork can connect to showing you are a great choice for the title. A Sleuth will realize that answering the question might also be an opportunity to connect to the job skills or values of that particular title.

Know Your Stuff – Pageant Questions

Speaking of which, you should *know* information about the area of the title you represent and are seeking. That has to do with both the *pageant* you are in and the *locale* that you will represent (the name of the city, county, state, etc., that will be on your banner).

Know Your Area

I hinted at this in *Book 2: How to Prepare* when I offered the example of knowing what was happening in my state with the Governor being removed from office. That's an example of knowing something about my state—since I *represent* that state, I should know a couple things.

At a more local level, you might pay attention to what's going on with the mayor. And you'd want to know basic facts about your city, county, state, or other area.

If you represent Phoenix Arizona, for example, you should be able to mention—if you are asked or it seems relevant to bring up—a variety of facts about the city, county, or metropolitan area. It is not uncommon for people to make small talk (judges and others) perhaps saying:

Judge
"So Phoenix has really grown...how big is it now?"

You don't want to go:

Bungler
"Uh...I don't know but it's really, really big."

When a better answer would be:

Contestant
It's big! Last I checked the overall metropolitan area had grown to over 4 million.

Know basic facts about your area's industries and concerns. Know who the state Senators are, who the Governor is, and other notable people your area or state has produced.

Showing you know the basics about your *current* title (or the one you are seeking) will help them see you as able to handle knowing *more* about a bigger area as you progress from the preliminary pageants up the ladder to State, National, and/or International titles.

Know Your Title/Pageant

Beyond knowing about the area or locale on your title, it'd be good of you to know a bit about your pageant. For instance:

- Do you know the name of the current or previous year's titleholder?
- Do you know how long your title, or the pageant, has existed?
- Do you know the name of the director of your pageant at each of the levels (local, state, and national)?
- Do you know about the history of the pageant?

You don't have to be an expert in it (though it wouldn't hurt), but it is a sign of respect and being "on the ball" and up-to-date to know what you are signing up for, what sort of organization this is, where it has been and where it is heading. Why would you want to be a part of something you know nothing about? Or, even if you are okay with being a "free spirit" in that way, remember that from the judges' perspective it may seem that you are not serious about winning the title (the job).

So if you are entering a pageant "just" for fun, maybe you will think you don't need or want to prepare as well. Maybe you won't take the few minutes to learn the answers to such questions and will take your chances that they won't come in handy. That's okay if it is your choice. But if you are serious about winning, I want you to realize that knowing a little bit about your pageant could come in very handy and set you apart from the other contestants.

These sorts of things you can learn by researching the pageant ahead of time. Most of the information may be on their website; other tidbits you may decide you want to learn by asking questions of the people you meet—including the director.

Ideally, you'd pick up on a lot of this from paying attention and from having looked into the pageant carefully before deciding to apply. Remember, as we covered earlier in the series, researching the pageant a bit *before* you enter may help you find the best pageant for *you* (they are not all the same) and your talents.

But if you didn't learn some of these facts beforehand, consider the value in learning them now—or at least before your interview. Don't bungle away points on "simple" questions that can really *help you shine* if you put just a little bit of effort into getting some basic information ahead of time.

In fact, if you are a *Sleuth*, you may decide to work in a little of this sort of information where *appropriate*, which will help you stand out. The judges may *not* ask about it directly as there are so many other things they could ask you about. But if you have the information somewhere in your head, you just might find a window of opportunity to share a bit of it and stand out from the other contestants. Don't force-fit anything; just keep aware of when it is appropriate to include such information.

One thing to think about in advance of actually going to the pageant is what you will wear for your interview. We'll talk about that in the next book in the series. For now, let's review.

Review

Let's review what we covered:

- Prepare as if "interviewing" is your talent, just as you would if you were planning to sing or dance.
- Know your pageant application paperwork (by whatever name your pageant calls it) and think

through what sorts of questions the judges might ask based on that information.
- We introduced the terms "spin-off questions" and "demonstration questions."
- Know the area (city, state, etc.) you are representing.
- Know about your pageant.

Exercise 4.1: Look at Your Pageant Paperwork

Go get it right now (or decide on a time and place when you will) and look what you've written there. What sort of impression does your paperwork give? What does it say about you?

If you haven't filled it out yet, make a copy and practice filling it out in pencil.

Think about how the different information you might put down would influence the kind of questions the judges might come up with.

Whether it is your "real" (already turned in) paperwork or just a practice draft…

Pretend you are a pageant judge and come up with two or three questions for each bit of information you put on there. Are you comfortable answering the questions in a *Sleuth*-like way? Get help coming up with the questions if you are being too easy on yourself. Show your paperwork to a friend, teacher, relative, pageant coach, etc., and see what *they* come up with.

Exercise 4.2: Self-Assess Your Local Area Knowledge

Review that section of the book and if you can't answer the sorts of questions and topics I mention there, then take a few minutes and find the information. If you haven't read my upcoming "Essential Pageant Interview Playbook" then write the information down on cards or sticky notes and keep them in a folder or notebook and gently quiz yourself on the details every day or two. Don't make it hard on yourself and feel like you have to *study*. Just lightly review the information a little every day or so and before you know it you'll have it!

Exercise 4.3: Self-Assess Your Pageant Knowledge

Just as we did in the previous exercise…Review the section of the book where we talked about the usefulness of knowing some facts about your pageant. If you can't answer the sorts of questions and topics I mention there, then take a few minutes and find the information and gently teach and quiz yourself on it (see the previous exercise) until you have it.

"You hit home runs not by chance but by preparation."
~Roger Maris

a pageant is just the beginning...

PAGEANT
Interviewing
SUCCESS

Optimize Your Outfit

Dr. Stephanie Raye, PhD
Former Miss American Petite

Book 5
Optimize Your Outfit
Table of Contents

Pageant Interviewing Success:
Optimize Your Outfit

Is It "You"? Is It "Right" For Your Pageant?

As we introduced in the last book, remember that in the personal interview part of the pageant the judges won't just be hearing what you say and how you say it, they will also get to see your beauty more closely as well as consider the suitability of your wardrobe choices. They'll be interested in how well you come off in a more personalized setting and, among other things, they are looking to see how you would present yourself in pageant appearances and to the media were you chosen as Queen.

We've mentioned the wisdom in focusing on grooming and beauty in personal interview, but you'll also want to pay attention to your clothes as well as your posture for both sitting and standing. Someone who has been practicing the Sleuthing skills we have covered (and will cover more later in the book) will pay just as much attention to the clothes she chooses and the image she projects as she will her words.

Interview as Performance

Dress for the part. What I mean is, to some degree, your interview is like playing a role or performing. Think of it as something like an "audition" to get the role of Queen. So what would the actress wear in this scene? Clearly she'd choose something that is flattering to her figure, in a color that works well with her skin tone and hair. She'd choose something that reflects her personality, yes, but she'd also think about what the audience expects. In this case the audience is the panel of judges.

As this part of the pageant is more of a job interview than a beauty contest, you want to remember that is the role you are playing—job candidate for that particular title. Many pageants will require a suit, but not all...trends change and pageants vary. Some may have you wear jeans! Some will allow flexibility, others will be very specific.

As with other aspects of the pageant, just know the guidelines set by the particular pageant you are in and make good choices within that framework. If you don't know the guidelines, see if they are explained in the application, the handbook, or on the website. While you are on the website, see if there are pictures of the previous years' contestants in interview attire. *If* there are, perhaps you can get a sense for what will work from that *but* realize that the guidelines *may* have changed so it is always best to double-check. If you can't find what you need, or need to clarify an expectation, contact the director and ask.

Whatever the pageant framework, be sure you choose something that is consistent with the image you've portrayed in other parts of the pageant—like in your paperwork and pageant photo. You may want to show "variety" but keep it within reason so it doesn't seem like you are confused about your identity. For instance, if it is a small-ish pageant, changing your hair a lot may be okay. But if it is a *large* pageant, you want them to remember you so keeping a somewhat consistent hairstyle may help with that. A Sleuth will weigh out the pros and cons (as, yes, your hair does have to work with your gown, etc.) so you don't have to be rigid about this—just mindful about your choices.

That and the judges may see many, many contestants in a short span of time so don't make it hard for them to remember you. Small to moderate changes are common but if your look is radically different from the picture they have in hand it may not work to your benefit. (That said, don't stress if you've improved your hairstyle or overall look and you can't change your picture for your current pageant. Judges know that can happen.)

When choosing what to wear:

Start with the **PAGEANT'S CRITERIA**

Then, within that framework, choose clothes that:

- Fit the tone of the pageant (some are more conservative than others)
- Fit the time of day (no evening wear for day time interviews)
- Are not too sheer (we don't need to see your nipples)
- Are not too short (we don't need to see your panties when you sit, stand, cross or uncross your legs)
- Are tasteful (nothing too gaudy or too trendy)
- Are age-appropriate
- Flatter the color for your skin and hair
- Flatter the cut for your body type/figure
- Fit properly in general
- Fit and look right when you sit, stand, gesture
- Enhance and highlight *you* (don't over-shadow you)

It's true, some pageant systems, especially at the teen level, may accept something more "trendy" but, in general, aim for something more "classic" that stands well on its own with minimal accessories. You never want too many pieces of jewelry and scarves and so on.

Some garments have their own flourishes of styling in terms of, say, an embellished collar or hem—for instance, lace, embroidery, beading, decoratively designed edges, ruffles, etc. That's great but, again, not *too* much of anything. And if your garment does have built in extras it is all the more important you choose your earrings, etc. with more care so they don't clash but, rather, compliment you and your garment.

If you are wearing a simpler (few or no embellishments) outfit, then certainly you'll likely want to bring it alive a bit with a *well-chosen* accessory or two. But if any one accessory is "dramatic" you may want to limit the number of other accessories (or keep them very simple). You don't want the judges distracted with accessories that are competing against each other and, at the same time, compete with you.

That's the key: any pageant clothing—not just your interview dress or suit—should highlight you, not compete with or overshadow you. Yes, choose an outfit and accessories that allow *you* to shine rather than one that outshines you. So, in general, keep jewelry appropriate and to a minimum.

Keeping accessories "appropriate" includes noting if the jewelry or scarves work with everything else in the outfit. For instance, the shape of your collar and your hairstyle should inform the size and style of your earrings and necklace (if any). Nothing should bump or tangle or otherwise be "too much." In other words, a high collar with lots of decoration may call for different jewelry than a lower or simpler one. If you have a high collar you may decide to wear your hair up and how you wear your hair influence which earrings you choose. Try out different things and be sure it works; don't wait until you are at the pageant to sort it out.

Keeping jewelry "to a minimum" includes thinking through the overall picture. Do you really need a ring on every finger, bracelets and/or watch on both arms, earrings (or more than one set if you have multiple piercings), a necklace, a brooch, toe rings, etc.?

Okay, I've gone overboard in mentioning all those items but that's the point. Don't go overboard. If you are the sort to wear a bunch of different things, consider not doing so for most pageants. You don't want a watch on one wrist and stack of jangling bracelets on the other, a necklace, rings on several fingers (try to keep it to one or two), etc. Choose what will really highlight you and work with your clothing.

"Less is more."
~Robert Browning, Peter Behrens, Mies van der Rohe

Style—Be Yourself and Be Consistent

We've talked about choosing clothes that fit within pageant guidelines and keeping things simple and elegant. But you still want to be yourself and look your best too. So definitely choose something that is "you." Do not try to be someone you aren't or choose clothes that are too far away from who you are and/or how you present yourself. You've probably had times where you've seen someone in an outfit that just doesn't fit who they are. (Or felt like you chose something that wasn't "you.") So pay attention to that with your interview outfit too.

For example, if you tend to be a soft-spoken sort with a gentle voice and style, it may seem "inconsistent" to see you in dramatic, bold colors or patterns and sharp lines to the garment's shape. Conversely, if you have a more professional "driven" way about your mannerisms and how you talk, it might seem a surprise to see you in pastel colors and soft ruffles. We all have different sides of ourselves, sure, but know what your strengths are and combine that with good advice and what's a good look for the pageant, and put that side forward. Be yourself no matter what you are wearing but let your clothes enhance the total image.

Style—Color

And since I mentioned color, don't fool yourself that you look just as good in every color. Even if you "love" a color that doesn't mean it loves you! So realistically consider your skin tone and hair color when making your choices. Look at yourself in different colors and see which ones really make you look alive and radiant. Get out clothes or go to a fabric store with lots of solid colors and drape them over your shoulder to see how your neck and face look in them. Do you "wash out" or do your hair, eyes, and skin come alive?

Often "your colors" might be the ones you get the most compliments in when you wear them but compliments can't be your only measure. Why? Because a) you are beautiful so you may get compliments no matter what color you wear. And, b) the person may really be saying that they like the color but not be saying that *you* look good in that color.

Consider that "You look great today" or "You look good in that color" are both a different sort of compliment than "I love that dress" or "What a fabulous color." The first compliments are clearly about you—*you* look great. The latter two compliments may be about you but they also may not be as one can like a dress or a color without thinking you look great in them. And since we are taught to be polite it is good to find something to compliment but we may just compliment someone's choice without complimenting how *good* they look in it.

For more on choosing the right color, visit:
http://www.wikihow.com/Choose-Your-Best-Clothing-Colors

Style—Fitting Your Body

Only you can decide what clothes fit your personality. And in the relatively short time the judges see you in personal interview it may or may not be apparent to them if you could have made a better choice there. But the judges (and everyone else) can see very easily if you chose clothes that don't fit your body well.

There's plenty of advice for you to find on this topic elsewhere but just be aware that not everything looks good on every body. Someone who has more of a curvy hourglass figure may want to enhance some curves while playing down others. Someone who has more of a straight figure may look better in certain styles. Some may be wise to try to focus on their waist (or "create" one if they don't have one). Others may want to draw attention away from their hips. For instance, if you are a little "hippier," no problem! Just steer clear of styles and color patterns that add visual width (or actual width with fabric) to your hips.

Sometimes a contestant will fall in love with a dress (interview suit, gown, or swimsuit, fitness wear or whatever) that looks great on the hanger and fits her image of what she "should" look good in but it just doesn't look good on her. She might like it so well, or think she should choose it because last year's winner wore something similar, that she stubbornly refuses to see that it isn't the best choice for her body shape. In the end, she may get that beautiful dress but not look as beautiful as she could have if she'd listened to the mirror or kept an open-mind to trying something different that may not look as good on the hanger but looks great on her body.

Don't make that mistake. Most pageant contestants are in some version of fairly good shape but, even so, our bodies vary. At any age (pre-teen to senior) and in any pageant (Miss, Petite, or Plus) we still have different shapes to deal with. Some say folks tend toward four basic shapes—hourglass, rectangular, apple-shaped, or pear-shaped. But don't worry about the labels. Just find what styles work for *your* body to diminish your figure "flaws" and enhance your figure "assets."

Similarly, thinking about the shape of your face relates to what may be better hairstyles for you *and* could help you choose more flattering necklines and collars. Don't *over*-stress about all this…your natural "eye" for what you look good in is probably already well trained. But if you don't think it is (and there is usually room for improvement) or if you just think this stuff is fun, then look into it more and play with it!

"Very little is needed to make a happy life. It is all within yourself, in your way of thinking."
~Marcus Aurelius

Here are some resources to get you started:

For information on face shape, go to http://www.beauty-and-the-bath.com/Face-Shape.html.

You can try different hairstyles on your face with The Hair Styler (http://www.thehairstyler.com).

Practice in Your Interview Clothes

As I mentioned above, you'll want to figure out in advance how to do your hair and what accessories are the best choice. That is part of "practicing" in your interview outfit. But you also want to practice walking in it, standing in it, and sitting in it. And you want to practice in the undergarments you anticipate wearing with those clothes. If anything seen or unseen starts to feel funny when you "live" in the outfit in some realistic-use situations, consider choosing a different outfit. You don't want to be fidgeting with your clothes during the interview. Know what the format of the interview will be before you go, but be ready for changes!

So go through the motions—and probably do so in front of a mirror, if at all possible. Do you have to stand or sit "just so" for your clothes to hang right? What if you gesture—does your outfit bind anywhere? What if you momentarily lose your "pageant" posture—is there something about the outfit that will exaggerate that lapse?

If it is an interview where you sit, posture and gestures are still a concern. And also be sure that there are no embarrassing gaps at your chest or waist; check that there are no unflattering fabric bulges that occur when you sit. (Fabric will fold when you sit, yes, but some looks better than others depending on the cut, etc.) Double-check that you can sit and get out of a variety of chairs without being awkward or revealing your undergarments.

How to Sit

Speaking of sitting, be sure you sit up straight without looking rigid. You don't want to lean too far back or forward so if sitting with your fanny and back all the way to the back of the chair feels awkward or puts you in an unflattering position, then simply sit closer to the edge of the chair. For instance, if your chair is soft (causing you to "sink" into it a bit) or if you have shorter legs and find yourself in a "deep" chair, you'd want to sit forward a bit too.

You don't want to be slouched back or find it awkward to gesture. A little natural gesturing within the range of your body helps you stay and seem comfortable. What's "within the range of the body?" Think of gestures as non-verbal "accessories" so just like your jewelry or clothes, you don't want your gestures to be too dramatic or distracting. They should enhance or emphasize what you say. So whether you are sitting or standing, you'd generally keep your gestures to no higher than your neck, lower than your hips, or wider than the distance your elbows would be if you had your hands on your hips.

Back to the chair…you'll have to wait until you are there with the actual chair to figure it out but if you start building your awareness to different sorts of chairs and how you need to adjust to sit "properly" in them, you'll be fine. The key is to control yourself in relation to the chair. Don't let the chair negatively affect you. And most pageants are aware of this and want you to be comfortable and successful. So, if they can, they'll usually choose a chair that is suitable to work with. But once you win the crown, you never know what sort of chair you'll be offered out at appearances so learn to adjust.

How to sit? Just be sure to sit "like a lady." So no spread legs or crossing or lifting your leg high enough to put your ankle on the opposite knee! (The way you'll see men sit sometimes.) Typically, you'd keep your knees together and inclined to one side, which leads to you keeping your ankles together (usually crossed) under you toward the other side.

Sitting like that (crossing the ankles toward one side) tends to create a nicer line for your body, calves, and ankles than crossing your legs at the knee. When you cross one leg over the other at the knee you also risk swinging or otherwise wiggling the foot that's now in the air. That would be distracting, so especially if you are a wiggler, keep your feet on the ground.

While this is good general advice, every body is different. And every outfit is different. You'll likely want to sit something like suggested here but, still, practice sitting in front of a mirror (and/or take pictures) to see what you naturally do and what you may be smart to change. Look for what is flattering or not for your body type in that outfit.

Good posture is important all the time but especially during pageant time. Good posture will make a difference in how your clothes look, can take "weight" off of you, and is an important overall piece of how you present yourself. It always surprises and saddens me to see a beautiful girl or woman (or man, for that matter!) slump while standing, sitting, or walking. Surely it is just a matter of them not realizing what a difference it makes?! Start paying attention to your posture now, if you haven't yet already.

Even if you haven't yet built (or are already maintaining) good postural habits as a matter of daily routine, then know that you should at least pay attention to it when you are at the pageant. You'll definitely want to do so when you are on-stage and in an interview but basically all the time at the pageant and in any pageant-related appearances. A Queen holds herself well while sitting, standing, walking, and dancing, etc.

You'll find information on posture while sitting, walking (gait), and standing in many places. To learn more search the internet on "correct posture" or "good posture" alone or with words like "exercises" or "tips." I also found some good information and products to build good habits when I searched on "posture page."

Three other quick points:

- Keep in mind wrinkle-potential. Choose fabrics that won't wrinkle much, if at all—especially if it is an interview where you sit.
- Aim to be at your goal weight a month or so before the event so you have time to get your clothes fitted differently, if need be. Or maybe you'll need to choose a new outfit. (If you do, practice in it!) But let's hope your weight or shape isn't fluctuating *that*

much. As we've discussed, for our physical health and mental clarity, healthy eating habits (no crash dieting) are important.

If you need support on *healthy* ways to lose weight or need to "get right" in your thinking about how to choose food, visit sites like *Self Magazine* (http://www.self.com) and focus on fitness and healthy eating. It is important to eat well even if there is no weight to lose but if you are in need of "right-sizing" (as I like to call it!) then please do it wisely and with support. You can also find many healthy food providers for different eating plans. It is also wise to see your physician before starting any weight loss or fitness program.

- It is probably best to *not* carry a purse (or your phone, or iPod, or whatever) into the interview unless you are told to. Usually you'll leave that sort of thing in your room or in a designated area outside the interview room.

Shoes

Make sure your shoes are appropriate and in good shape (probably "new" or just for special events like pageants). What's appropriate?

Styles change so it is hard to say *exactly* what you should favor and avoid but what I'll share is generally true no matter what the current styles are. There's plenty you can do and choose from to have shoes that work well with your outfit but here are a few things to keep in mind:

Don't draw attention to your feet. Your shoes can be pretty—unique even—but they shouldn't be the center of attention. So stay away from overly bright colors (they tend to draw the eye) unless they really "work" with your outfit. Consider avoiding rhinestones (or at least too many of them) or too unusual a heel, etc. Of course there could be times this would work or be tasteful (again, let the pageant style give you a sense of things).

No matter how tall you are or how cool the shoe is (even if it is *the* shoe right now), I'd steer clear of anything that visually shortens your leg length. For instance, straps that wrap around your ankles can visually "cut" the leg line. Generally, we look to extend the leg line so why introduce a horizontal visual stop right there when you really don't have to?

Still, as styles change, you may one day find yourself considering such a shoe. That's fine…give it a try! Each person, and how the shoe looks on her, differs. Just really check to see if they work with the overall line of your body and with your outfit. Choose what flatters you! Not just the latest style, but what enhances you. Use a mirror and take a photo of yourself in the shoes as you sit and stand to see the truth for yourself.

Now, just to be clear, this is good advice for interview (and swimsuit, and usually gown) but in your *talent*, you may decide for safety or artistic integrity that you need to go with a shoe with an ankle strap. That's for you and your talent advisors to decide with good sense. But for personal interview, consider avoiding shoes that draw too much attention and do not contribute to extending your leg line.

Practice in Your Shoes Too

You may think "Oh, I won't be wearing my interview shoes very long or have to walk in them *that* far, so I'll only practice walking in my gown or swimsuit/fitness or fashion wear shoes."

But you *do* want to practice walking in your interview shoes as well. I've seen interview situations where you only need to take a few steps to the chair or lectern, and others where you walk quite a distance from the entrance to where the judges are sitting (like they are tucked in a corner of a bigger-than-necessary meeting room) and they can watch you the whole way.

So a Sleuth would practice walking on a variety of surfaces so she is prepared and less likely to be caught off guard. Practice on smoother surfaces like wood and tile (sometimes those grout lines can catch ya!). If it is available, practice on highly polished or finished surfaces…it depends on the particular floor and material but some marble lobbies, etc. can be quite slippery. Practice on carpet (sometimes your heel will sink into carpet in a way that catches you off guard). Practice on a staircase or at least a few steps.

That may sound like a lot but if you generally have your walk down (meaning you generally know how to walk in heels, with good pageant posture and stride) then it only need take paying attention to what surfaces are available to you where you live, work, shop, and bringing your shoes to try them out for several paces.

Also, it is generally a good idea *not* to wear your shoes *to* the places where you might practice on different surfaces. You don't want to scuff them up or wear them out walking on unfinished concrete, asphalt, etc. But *do* wear them around at home enough to "break them in" so you won't get blisters and/or know how far you can wear them before you *start* to get blisters.

If you are inexperienced in high-ish heels (or it's been awhile) or if you are otherwise awkward in all or part of your walking style, then you may want to practice more and in a variety of shoe styles to find what works best for you overall.

If that describes you, consider building up your tolerance to high heels. Start with a lower heel and walk around the house at that level until you are fairly comfortable and then go a bit higher, working your way up to the heel height you desire. This gives your body time to build balance and your calf muscles and feet to adjust. If time is short, however, skip to your actual heel height sooner and spend more time practicing in the actual shoes you intend to wear.

All that said, I'd recommend going for a "comfortable" heel height. That may be higher for some and lower for others. If the pageant dictates what the heel height should be for certain segments of the pageant, then so be it. Otherwise, choose for yourself the balance between what's high enough to be flattering and fashionable but not so high as to make you uncomfortable or unsafe. Many will emphasize that high heels aren't particularly "good" for us, so try to wear comfy shoes with good support as much as you can (like at home and in rehearsals, if possible) while staying familiar enough with your high heels that you are fine in them.

The idea with practice and familiarity is to have a little "muscle memory" for how your feet and ankles work in these shoes so no matter what sort of surface you are entering on, then it will be a complete "non-issue."

Again, take comfortable shoes for long days of practice, etc. It is unlikely that you'd need to be in your heels the *whole* time in *every* rehearsal. Yes, you should rehearse some in your performance shoes but if you are practicing for 6 hours a day for the opening number (like they might, say, at the Miss USA pageant), then use your head and protect your feet when you can.

Visit Insolia for some good shoe resources: http://www.insolia.com. Getting the right inserts can increase your comfort (so you can wear your shoes longer) and actually improve how the shoe looks on your foot.

Mirrors, Photographs and Video

As I've tried to emphasize above, there is no substitute for practicing in your clothes and shoes to be sure they fit well, look right in all positions, etc. A Sleuth doesn't assume something looks good because it feels good or because a quick glance in one position looked okay.

A full-length mirror can be a great aid in helping you figure that out. If your home doesn't have a mirrored closet door, or the like, get a relatively inexpensive light-weight full-length mirror and sit in front of it in different positions, etc.

But you should *also* photograph yourself in your clothes and shoes and see how they look. Sometimes the angle we can see in a mirror isn't the same as what we'd see if we were sitting as far away as the judges, etc. So work it out to take photos of yourself—or get friends or family to help—in the different outfits and shoes in the various positions you'll be in (sitting, standing, walking).

As we've talked about, when we are in the heat of the moment of shopping, seeing something we think is perfect because of the style or color, we may miss that the color actually isn't good for us. Or that the style isn't so flattering when you are standing still or sitting (some garments really look better when in flow, in movement). A photo will help you see these things and show if a pair of shoes makes your legs look shorter and the like.

So take pictures and see what you look like when you are coming from the more objective or analytical side of your brain rather than more subjective or emotional side that was excited to find such a great outfit. The judges will be in the "objective" mode so a photo will let you put yourself in their shoes.

If you don't have video equipment or a camera to take photos of yourself, or don't have one you can borrow from a friend, a school, a church, or the like, see if you can find a new or used one at a store like BestBuy or on Ebay, etc. You can also find voice recorders there and at office supply stores. Most cell phones can take pictures and record video and audio too.

Preventing Wardrobe Malfunctions

If you find that some of your clothes aren't working quite right, you might consider choosing something else. Or you may be able work with what you have if you are a creative problem solver. Think it through and experiment a bit to see if you can work it out before giving up something you love (unless it is just plain unflattering!).

For instance, if something is gapping a bit or shows too much of this or that you might consider getting the garment altered a bit. Or, you might try a different undergarment. For instance, it is amazing the difference that a different style of bra can make on how a garment fits, etc.

And depending on the situation, you might try some of the great products out there now for everything from how to hide your nipples to how to avoid panty lines to taping fabric to your body (or other fabric) to help with gaps or prevent bra straps from showing. Check these items out and practice with them at home. I recommend keeping a variety of choices and little things like this in your "pageant kit" so you are ready for almost anything.

Have a Plan B Outfit

Okay, so let's say you have the "perfect" interview wardrobe selected. Here's what you do next...do it again! Pick a *second* interview outfit that you love hopefully just as much.

I understand budget constraints may make this sound like a silly tip for some, but it's a good idea. Why? Something could happen to your first outfit (snags, stains, etc.) or, while it is hard to imagine, you may see that someone may be wearing something so similar that you decide to go to Plan B. So if you can afford it (and there are less expensive ways to do most anything) have a back-up outfit planned.

"It's better to look ahead and prepare than to look back and regret."
~Jackie Joyner Kersee

By the way, is it the "end of the world" if someone is wearing your gown or interview outfit? No. Certainly not in personal interview as there are fewer eyes on you and the judges aren't seeing two contestants at one time. But it still may feel funny. If you find you are wearing the same thing as someone else and don't have another outfit to wear (or time to change) then your goal is to look and feel *your* best in it.

If you can turn the panic into power and tell yourself "No one looks better in this than me...I *rock* in this" then you'll be so great they may not even notice your dress. Sometimes the best outfit is the one people forget because that means you selected so well that it didn't get in the way of them noticing your beauty (and *you* should shine more than your clothes). And if you look fabulous in that gown or interview suit, then don't worry...it could work to your advantage that someone else is in it and you turn out to look better in it than they do!

So obviously the flip side is if the other person looks *way* better in it, then change if you can. But still, it is *who you are*, your attitude, and words that matter more than the clothes (assuming you didn't choose something really bad). The truth is you are likely to both look nice in your clothes or you wouldn't have chosen them. So I'd rather have you in something you feel *great* in (even if someone else is wearing it) than go to your Plan B outfit if you don't like it as well. So choose good Plan B outfits.

Ditto that with shoes. It's good to have more than one pair of shoes that will work with both your Plan A and Plan B outfits. If you do get a blister or the like, then you'll have another shoe that "fits" your foot a bit differently so it won't rub in the same place.

Pack Early and Pack Smart

You may think this an odd topic to have in a book series that is primarily about pageant interviewing but, as you'll learn in the next book, you want everything to go as smoothly as possible at the pageant. If you pack poorly, you could be distracted at the pageant or not easily find all the pieces of your interview wardrobe when the time comes. You will be busy at the pageant, make things easy on yourself by being organized!

Especially if you don't travel very often, it can be easy to forget how long it can take to pack and how organized you need to be to be sure you have everything. So start packing at least as *two weeks* before you leave.

Why *two* weeks instead of one? Because, ideally, you'll spend the week before you leave for the event being as "normal" as possible, keeping a good routine, getting *plenty* of sleep (you may not get much at the pageant). So if you are packing the last week that will consume a lot of time and thought. Thus, if you pack at least two weeks before then you can just re-check things a couple times and let your more relaxed mind help you remember whatever you may have forgotten. You can sleep easily in your last week before the pageant.

Okay, you got me…*two* weeks may be extreme if you are going to a pageant event that just lasts a day and night. If that's the case, you can get probably get away with less lead time to pack. But don't fool yourself, even if it is a smaller pageant, you still need lots of stuff.

On the other hand, two weeks may not be enough. If you are going to a pageant that lasts two to four weeks (yes, for something the size and scope of Miss Universe, you could be gone for *four* weeks), then you'll need even more time to pack. The longer you'll be gone, the earlier you need to start packing. (I've taught in London for a couple summers and being gone eight weeks means I start packing very early—and I'm not competing in a pageant while I'm there. I'd start even earlier if I were doing that!)

Start with making a big list with space to keep adding more items to the list as you think about them. Think in categories to get the bigger picture and then fill in the details. Some of the categories would be clothes (as well as shoes and accessories) for each judging category, clothes for rehearsal, appearances, etc. And categories like make-up, hygiene, mending (including items like a sewing kit, pins, tape, a travel size clothes steamer, a little iron—even if the hotel provides it!), etc.

Then work from there. You might try the approach that many favor which is to get a hanger for each outfit. Try to find a sturdy hanger with a metal top that rotates (so you can easily adjust what direction the outfit faces), has shoulder indentations (to hold straps), and maybe clips (for skirts). Then start collecting everything you need for a given outfit and center it all on that hanger.

For instance, write the name of the outfit on a piece of printer paper and with a big marker and then poke it over the top of the hanger. Then, with the creative use of bags and re-sealable "Ziploc" style bags, collect all the pieces. If the outfit needs a belt, put it in a baggie and write the words "belt for ___" and hook it on the hanger. Do that with the jewelry and other accessories. Do that for the undergarments that work with that outfit, the shoes, etc. Get it all together in one place for *that* outfit. Consider listing those items on the piece of paper on the hanger too.

Then use a garment bag to put all that stuff in and protect the garment. You can go as simple and inexpensive as leftover dry cleaning bags (those clear plastic bags they put over clothes when you pick them up). Or you can find garment bags of different size, strength, and features—the kind that zip and have enough space where you can put the shoes in the bottom. Fancy gowns sometimes come with a nice garment bag (though some are boxed).

Do that for each outfit and keep a master list of items (beyond the individual papers on the hangers) that are used for more than one outfit so you always know where to look to find them. If the pageant is local, you might be able to take your stuff to your room or dressing area just like that—hanging each hanger where it needs to be without re-packing.

If the pageant is not local, you will likely have to put all that stuff in a suitcase (or three!). If that's the case, then you can keep some of the items together per outfit by packing the outfit baggies together.

Or you may pack certain items together but even if you split up the baggies for one particular outfit you can put it all back together with relative ease once you get to your destination because you'll have labeled the bags, have your list per outfit, and your master list to keep everything organized.

When the time comes to pack, make use of the wonderful tools and information out there on how to do it well. For instance, there are "packing cubes" now, and the like, that keep everything tidy, together, and safe—you may decide to pack certain kinds of items in a single cube or put everything you need for one outfit in a cube. You'll have to see what works for you.

Packing is like a puzzle. You want the pieces to go in well and your stuff to be as in as good a shape as possible when it comes out. A little effort in packing can save you effort once you get to your destination.

"Destiny is no matter of chance. It is a matter of choice. It is not a thing to be waited for, it is a thing to be achieved."
~William Jennings Bryan

"Each problem has hidden in it an opportunity so powerful that it literally dwarfs the problem. The greatest success stories were created by people who recognized a problem and turned it into an opportunity."
~Joseph Sugarman

Review

Let's briefly review some points:

- Consider what you choose to wear as if you are auditioning for a role in a play—What is right for this role? For this audience? For how you as a person will "play" the part?

- Choose interview attire that matches your personality and is consistent with the image of your pageant. Balance out your need to show your personality with what is fitting for this situation. Don't choose clothes that "compete" with you.

- Accessorize to enhance not overwhelm. You want them to notice how you shine, not how your jewelry shines.

- Choose wardrobe items that fit well in general and that are complimentary to your particular body shape and other physical characteristics.

- *Practice* sitting, standing, and walking in your interview outfit. And I mean in all the pieces from top to bottom, inside to out. Pay attention to if it works or doesn't work in terms of gaps, length, bulges, etc. Figure out how to make it work through how you hold yourself or through permanent or temporary fixes to the garment before the interview. If you can't make it work, choose something else.

- Posture matters in all aspects of the pageant—including the interview. Practice good posture in sitting, standing, and walking.

- Shoes are as important as the clothes but should generally not be a focal point—we want the judges looking at your face! So shoes should be well chosen to enhance the outfit in a non-interfering way.

- Practice in your shoes with your outfit. And practice in them some more on different surfaces or if you need to get used to the height of the heel. You want to feel confident and safe in your shoes on any surface so you look natural and comfortable in them.

- Practice in front of mirrors, take pictures, and/or use video to see how you really look in your outfit.

- Learn how to fix or prevent wardrobe "malfunctions."

- Pack early and pack wisely.

Exercise 5.1: Assess Your Interview Outfit

5.1.1 If you already have one selected, go get it out. If you don't, go get a couple of your "maybe" outfits out just for practice. Look at what you've got and think about the job for which you are applying and the role for which you're auditioning when you are in a pageant personal interview.

Does your choice fit the part of a titleholder? Does it say you have good taste? Does it say you know your own body, personality, and coloring well enough to choose something "just right" for you? Does it show good sense in the level of modesty or skin you show?

5.1.2. Put the clothes on, wearing the undergarments you think you'd wear on the real interview day. Put on your accessories. Quickly (for the purposes of this exercise) arrange your hair up or down as you think you'd wear it with that outfit. Put on the shoes you have in mind.

Now look in the mirror and ask yourself the questions from the first part of this exercise. Do you need to change anything to make it a better overall look?

Exercise 5.2: Practice in the Interview Outfit

Take the assessment from Exercise 5.1 a bit further now and actually walk and talk in the outfit. Sit in a variety of chairs as well. You can start without a mirror just to get a feel for things.

Then get out a mirror and/or enlist the help of a video camera to give you a better idea of how the garment moves as you move. Have a friend help with this if necessary and consider taking some "still" photos too. Try a couple different outfits or ensembles (adjusting the hair, accessories, shoes, etc. too!) and compare the photos. Start to get a sense for what is really complimentary to you and what is not.

Adjust what you have by changing the undergarments or accessories, if that will do the trick. Or you may want to explore if something can be altered by a seamstress or tailor. You can also try the fashion tape, etc. (See the section on preventing wardrobe malfunctions.) Or, you may want to consider shopping for something different if need be.

Exercise 5.3: Learn Your Colors and/or "Season"

Take the time to "color drape" yourself or get the help of a friend or professional. Then go back to your interview outfit choices and see if you want to make any changes.

You can start with what you have in the closet and genuinely set aside your feelings toward the style of the garment and just look at the color at this point. Do this in good light for learning purposes. This may be enough. If not…

If you don't have enough variety to get a good sense of your colors at home, then go to a store with a wide variety of clothing colors or even a fabric store where they have bolts and bolts of solid color fabric. Sometimes they have mirrors in these stores too to help customers choose the best colors for the clothes they are about to make for themselves. Whether they have a mirror or not, you may want to have a friend (or friendly clerk) help you get a sense of it.

Some fabrics are inexpensive enough you could buy a foot or two of the material in several colors and take them home to play with.

The above methods will work and are helpful if you are watching your budget. If you really "get into it" and want to pay for it, you can likely get more and better information from working with a professional who does color draping. Despite its usefulness color draping goes in and out of style in the eyes of the general public so that can impact how hard or easy it is to find someone. But media professionals and politicians still need advice on what colors suit them the best so you can find folks who do this.

You may find color drapers as part of image consulting companies or wardrobe consulting companies. Some hair and make-up salons or stylists will do it. Some in-home cosmetic sales representatives will also do it (like some MaryKay consultants have or BeautiControl Cosmetics folks have. They don't *all* do it, but ask.) And you may be able to be color-draped in finer department stores (some still have "personal shoppers") and some cosmetic counter sales people may be equipped to do this. Ask around in your area.

If you find someone who does it, they usually have all the fabric color samples already, of course, and may put a white drape on you as the background for all the others. They may also help you figure out what colors you can use as accents or "away from the face" so that you have more variety available to you. Some will analyze your whole wardrobe as part of the deal, including looking at your body shape and face shape (which can be important in choosing necklines and collars.) Some will send you home with a little set of swatches so that you can carry them with you when you shop. That way you'll remember not just your best colors but the intensity level of your colors too (some folks look better in "smokier" colors and others in "truer" colors). Not everybody is equipped to be so "full service" but see what you can find.

Remember, I gave you a link to some resources in this book. You can learn a little bit from web pages but not get into "specific" colors too much as the computer monitor can affect things. And I believe one of the links I have available sells color-draping kits…so if you really get into it you might be able to share the cost of a kit with some friends (and make a side business to help fund your pageant expenses along the way—if you want to share your insider color secrets!).

Exercise 5.4: Practice Walking in Your Interview Shoes

So let's say that you did the exercises above and have selected a pair of shoes (or two!) that would work with your outfit. They fit the pageant criteria, look nice on you (in regard to your leg line, thickness of ankles and whatever else you should consider for *your* body).

Now practice in those shoes some more. Even if you are experienced in high heels in general, you'll want to practice walking in your interview shoes on a variety of surfaces. And if, by chance, you don't walk in heels that often, then step your way up to whatever level you need to (within reason!) by practicing. A variety of surfaces and how to practice in heels is laid out in the book so go review that.

Remember that unless the pageant requires a certain heel height for some reason, you should choose what works best for you. Walking confidently in a heel that is a bit shorter is better than wobbling around unsteadily on a higher heel. More is not always better and your *posture* will do as much or more for helping you look "taller" than a heel will. Yes, heels are typically *de rigueur* in pageants but still use your head. You can train yourself to do better in them but, even when you do, you still don't have to go for the highest heel all the time.

Exercise 5.5: Choose Your Plan B Outfit

From all you've just done in the previous exercises, you should have your Plan A outfit figured out or have a stronger sense for what to shop for. Do the same with a Plan B outfit. Ideally, it would also be in one of your best colors and cuts (so it'd be like you have *two* Plan A outfits) but if time or money constraints preclude that, then do what you can with a good Plan B outfit. Sometimes a scarf or changing the color of a blouse under a suit jacket can fix something up nicely.

Exercise 5.6: Explore Packing Options

Review the part of the book on packing and start making lists, collecting supplies, and make a timeline of when you want to get more serious about it based on when your pageant is.

"I adore the challenge of creating truly modern clothes, where a woman's personality and sense of self are revealed. I want people to see the dress, but focus on the woman."

~Vera Wang

a pageant is just the beginning...

PAGEANT *Interviewing* SUCCESS

Conquering Fears at the Pageant

Dr. Stephanie Raye, PhD
Former Miss American Petite

Book 6
Conquering Fears at the Pageant
Table of Contents

Pageant Interviewing Success:
Conquering Fears at the Pageant

You've arrived at the pageant and the excitement begins. If it is a pageant that takes more than a day, you've probably been booked a room in certain accommodations and assigned a roommate. Chances are good she's really nice. If not, don't let her get to you. (I'll tell you how Wonder Woman can help with that shortly.)

Either way, you'll be busy with all manner of things so you'll hardly be in the room. And when you are, keep it positive and keep yourself aware that soon your personal interview will occur. It often is the first judging category as it takes a fair amount of time to get all the contestants through this off-stage event.

Be Nice to Your Roommate

While we are on the topic of roommates, let's talk about them briefly. How's this for brief: *be nice*. Act like a Queen and be polite and gracious. Don't hog all the space in the bathroom, closet, dresser, on the floor or wherever. And if she hogs things, be diplomatic about getting your share back. Be courteous about sharing the bathroom and electrical outlets and everything else. Work it out. Be creative. (For instance, you might take a safety-inspected plug extender or extension cord.)

Don't quibble or fight, act like you'd act if the Judges were standing there watching you. Seriously, aim to be easy to get along with as the titleholder will need to get along with lots of different people in many situations. If you know you have some things about yourself that make you a challenge to live with, work on them.

And while a Queenly pageant contestant would never snoop in her roommate's stuff, if you know you are paranoid about people snooping through your stuff, take little luggage locks (combination locks, not keys! You don't want to lose the key!). Whatever it is that worries you or makes you worrisome, just deal with it so you can reduce such stresses while you are at the pageant.

And never say anything about your roommate behind her back. If she does come up in conversation, keep it to the good things you like about her, etc. Don't talk badly about anyone at the pageant. If you are put on the spot to tell the truth about a negative situation or person, remember what you've learned about being a Sleuth and how to respond to questions in balanced, diplomatic ways. Remember the tagline of my materials is "A pageant is just the beginning" because you'll want to use your Sleuth and diplomat skills in *many* situations outside the actual pageant interview.

Oh, and before I forget: It is nice if you can bring a little something for your roommate from your area or state to be welcoming and supportive of her. It shouldn't cost much, if anything—it could be homemade. Even a card is a nice gesture, as would be a t-shirt from your area. Or it could be something pageant-related, as something that was helpful to you in pageants might also be appreciated by her.

This is not obligatory, of course, so if it doesn't feel comfortable to you, then don't do it. And certainly don't *expect* it or act offended if your roommate doesn't bring you a token get-acquainted gift. (If you give her a gift and she doesn't give you one just say something genuinely nice (don't be a fake) to put her at ease as you do not want to make her feel poorly—that's the exact opposite effect we want! But do consider it because it is good manners and, you never know, it could help a nervous or grumpy roommate settle down a bit.

"I've learned that people will forget what you said, people will forget what you did, but people will never forget how you made them feel."
~Maya Angelou

The Night Before Your Interview

Review Your Paperwork One More Time

While I know (hope!) you did so at home, it'd be a good idea to re-review your paperwork again while you are at the pageant. In all the excitement of getting ready to go, we can get flustered. Looking at what you have to this point may help you feel more centered and grounded.

Errors

As I mentioned before, hopefully you filled out your paperwork wisely and with care. I'm sure that was your intention! And hopefully what you turned in to the pageant is free from errors. But if it wasn't, then you might notice that now.

If you find any, don't over-worry about it at this late date but do resolve to have future documents proofread (as errors in paperwork do not reflect well on you). Take special note if there is any information that is now inaccurate or was just flat out wrong to start with (either because of carelessness or because you used to be a Smuggler!). Something that doesn't "feel" right might cause suspicion in the minds of the judges, or may catch their attention as particularly humorous.

Either situation may lead them to ask a question about it, in seriousness or in fun. If you notice it now at least it won't catch you off guard if one of the judges happens to bring it up.

Get Some (Good) Sleep

Depending on what level of pageant you are competing in, you may spend the night at a hotel the night before your interview (you could be there several days or weeks for some pageants). Whether you are at home or at the pageant, do your best to get good sleep the night before your interview. Relax. Take it easy. Sweet Dreams.

Ideally, you'd have been getting good sleep all along (or at least for a solid week before the pageant) as it is of basic importance to your health and beauty. But now you are *at* the pageant! As tempting as it will be to stay up late chatting with friends or your roommate, don't do it—or at least keep it to a minimum. Obviously, if the pageant has you up practicing the group performance, or whatever, then you'll do that. But if you have free time, use it wisely. Rest. Rest. Rest. Rest, it is good for your beauty and your brains.

Some of you will want to exercise too. That's good as exercise is also good for your beauty and brains *but* you'll be so busy during pageant week and you've exercised so much up to this point that rest may still be the better choice. If you need to exercise a bit to blow off some steam in order to sleep better, that's one thing. But no long workout sessions mistakenly thinking it will make a difference at this late point in preparation—rest will be more important now.

But wait! What about the roommate? Sure, go have a little fun getting to know her and some of the other great contestants but head for your bedroom before you "have to" (or when opportunities arise) so you can have a little time to yourself. Even if your roommate is there, take a little time to review your paperwork and visualize how the interview will go. Keep your thoughts positive.

You can find plenty of relaxation audio files online. I've found audio to be a great source of progressive visualization for general relaxation and empowerment.

There are also plenty of great sleep resources online. One that I recommend is HeartMath (http://www.store.heartmath.com).

Trust me, if you will be sharing a room with someone, you may want to bring earplugs and a sleep mask or the like. Even pretty girls can snore or talk in their sleep.

Double-Check Your Interview Outfit

Once you get to the pageant check your interview outfit(s). Make sure it is ready to go and that nothing got crinkled or stained since you checked it last or on your trip to the pageant. Make sure you know where your accessories are. You want everything to be easy to find so you have an easy morning the day of your interview. (You actually want this *each* day of the pageant, so get in the habit of checking things every night for the next day's pageant events.)

If you find something is missing or damaged, don't panic. One of the reasons you are checking the night before is so you have time to find what you lost or figure out a replacement. (And if you followed the suggestion in the previous book, you can relax a little as you have a Plan B outfit and back-up hosiery and other items.)

Prepare a Little Just Lightly—No Cramming

If there is an evening paper in the lobby of the hotel—and if you have time early enough in the evening—scan the headlines and read a couple articles. That said, I do not recommend staying up late "cramming" for the interview or watching late, late news as your sleep is more important than last minute cramming. Yes, review your application paperwork and consider reading a bit of the newspaper but, really, the bulk of your preparation should be done by now.

Right Before Your Interview

Watch the News and Read the Paper

The morning of your interview—or right before it, whatever time of day it is—as opposed to "just waiting" remember you can do positive things with your time:

- Visualize your success.
- Take a few, easy, deep breaths to help you relax.
- Gently "yawn" to relax your throat (just once or twice).

- Make a new friend while you wait.
- Leave a little time to watch television news in your room as you get ready that morning.
- Catch the headlines on a local or national paper.

Those last two points help you prepare just a little bit more by being fresh on news that could come up in the interview. Even if the judges don't bring up a topic from the day's news, you might do so when, for instance, it is relevant to something they ask or it relates to your platform, hobbies, major, career plans, or community service.

As we've discussed, a good rule of thumb is to be aware of current events in general—be watching the evening news for months before the pageant, at the very least—but reviewing the *most* current events that morning could make you stand out from the rest of the contestants.

Arriving at the Interview – Show Up Early

Depending on the schedule for your pageant, you may be in some sort of rehearsal or activity before you go to your interview (sometimes they break the girls up in to groups, with certain groups waiting for interview, others rehearsing, etc.). Other times, you may be in the situation of getting to go to interview first thing in the morning or right after breakfast.

Wherever you are before the interview, keep your energy calm but positive and manage your time well. Feeling rushed right before you walk into your personal interview is *not* a good idea. Why?

- Something could happen that makes it so you go earlier than expected.
- You could cut into your own interview time (and you need every minute!).
- You could miss your time altogether.
- You want to be calm, cool, and collected....not looking like you just rushed in.

Remember, in many ways this is a job interview (or at least a very important part of your pageant fun) so if you are late or too frazzled, it won't reflect well on you. Running late or giving them the impression that you were "rushed" will not help you get chosen for the title. And it is courteous to others to be on time. You don't want to frustrate or delay anyone else based on your tardiness.

So plan to arrive early. If you run late habitually, tell yourself that your interview time is 30 minutes earlier than whenever you've been told to show up. If you don't tend to run late, plan to arrive at least 15 minutes early. You may be working within some restraints depending on the pageant schedule so you could be busy elsewhere with the pageant but no matter *where* you are or what you are doing, politely leave in sufficient time to arrive *early* to your interview.

Getting there early relieves one big potential stressor and gives you time to relax and visualize your success. If you are nervous, you can turn your attention inward a bit—keeping a gentle smile on your face, of course!—or you can lightly chat with others who are waiting.

Be sensitive to what your mind and body need and be sensitive to others' needs. That is, don't force a conversation with another contestant to help relieve your nerves when it may be she wants to silently prepare. Just as you can politely avoid a lengthy interchange with someone if you need a few minutes to yourself before you are called in.

Attitude as You Wait – Keep It Calm and Positive

Focus on being calm and positive. And, as we are all human, it is possible that you may *look* calm and positive but *feel* more nervous than you look. Either way, allow me to suggest that you avoid showing any anxiety you might feel to the degree that you can (we all show it a little!).

What I mean here is avoid displaying clear indications of stress or anxiety. For instance, do not pace around. Choose instead to remain gently still and emotionally centered. Don't tap a foot or your fingers impatiently. If you happen to be sitting with your legs crossed, resist the tendency to swing your top foot around.

If you feel you need to "do" something to calm yourself, you can bring the newspaper to further review headlines and stories. As we've covered, that'll serve to both distract and prepare you a little more.

But, really, now is the time to not busy yourself but to center yourself. Unnecessary pacing or physical agitation may magnify your nerves and cause others to feel nervous around you. Yes, feelings can be contagious! If someone else is overly nervous or agitated, let it sweep right past you. Stay positive, upbeat, and keep a good sense of humor—let that be the emotion that gets spread around.

Invoke the Power of Wonder Woman

You've got the image and persona of a Sleuth in your mind to help you prepare well for the pageant and do great in the interview segments. But what about while you are at the pageant? What image or persona can help you keep your edge, your focus, and your positive energy up there? Well, the Sleuth will still be in play but let's up the ante and move from being an investigator to a super hero!

You might recall the super hero Wonder Woman. If you don't, it's high time you learn about her. In DC Comics or on television she was (still is!) a big hit. She's the perfect image for a potential pageant queen to think about to help calm herself down and pump herself up at the same time. Wonder Woman even has a tiara! And, as an aside, she was played on television by former pageant queen Lynda Carter. (By the way, she's another Arizona girl!)

> *Lynda Carter represented Arizona and was crowned Miss World USA in 1972. She made it to the semi-finals at the Miss World competition. Her mother was

Mexican making Lynda, to my knowledge, the first U.S. national pageant winner of Mexican descent. In 1985, Miss Laura Martinez-Herring was the first naturalized Mexican-American to win Miss USA.

So try this: Imagine yourself as Wonder Woman and make use of some of her skills and tools. Wonder Woman experiences great stress in her mission to improve the world and fight evil but she handles it like a pro. It is as if she has an indestructible force field that surrounds her as her golden bracelets can deflect anything. And, among other things, she has a cool invisible airplane at ready whenever she needs it.

Imagine yourself in that invisible plane or force field as you go about your business at the pageant. You are protected such that anything that isn't positive just bounces right off of you. And anything negative that does make it through the force field loses its power so it cannot harm you. If you are waiting for your interview, or anything else at the pageant, and there are unkind words, looks, or whatever coming from one or more contestants, it won't stick to your Wonder Woman self.

"When I dare to be powerful, to use my strength in the service of my vision, then it becomes less and less important whether I am afraid."
~Audre Lorde

Visualizing yourself as protected can be especially helpful to remember if, by chance, you are assigned to a room with someone who is, say, "snippy" and acts superior or maybe is, for instance, overly fearful or perhaps a "downer" in her words or attitude about herself, the pageant, you, other contestants, or the world in general.

Don't worry ahead about this, you *probably* will be with someone wonderful. (I was. Miss Arkansas was very sweet.) But *if* you happen to get one of the (hopefully ever more rare) pageant prima donnas just visualize your shield and laugh off her wicked ways.

You certainly don't want anyone impacting *your* performance—that'd be giving them some influence over you and Wonder Woman wouldn't let that happen.

Okay, so you are centering yourself and being friendly as you protect yourself with your Wonder Woman imagery. You're getting focused as you wait for your personal interview to begin. Nothing is going to get you off track but what about the contestants around you who might be nervous or agitated?

Good Sportsmanship (Or, Rather, Sportspersonship)

If you enter pageants with more of "me" or "winning *really* matters" focus, I suppose you can take secret comfort in someone else being more nervous than you are. You can't always tell who feels what but if it is really showing then, yes, you'll probably do a better job in interview than that person.

But, to me, pageants are more about "competing against yourself" than against anyone else. If you agree—if you enter pageants with a more "sportsman-like" spirit—you may want to say something to help that other contestant keep it all in perspective (not make too big a deal of anything). Tell the nervous contestant, and yourself, that being a bit nervous is totally normal. Even the most prepared people will have a little bit of nerves.

While it is true that your being calm (or at least looking it!) is a competitive advantage over others who are not, remember that it is more important to be the good person you are.

Being calm and positive is something we don't have to keep to ourselves. Being genuinely kind and gracious is a Queenly attribute we all need to practice daily. But if it is still all about the competition for you, remember that you never know who is watching or over-hearing, so "if you can't say something nice, don't say anything at all" might be reasonable to keep in mind.

The walls have ears—always be on your best behavior. Sincerity and authentic caring—being a "real" and genuinely nice person—is something that most of us appreciate in those around us. And for those of you who are still focused strictly on competition aspects, remember the fact that you are being nice just might earn you a Miss Congeniality prize.

But, really, just know there can be some mean, spiteful, selfish people in *any* group and you may encounter a few at the pageant as well (thankfully, *most* pageant girls are gracious and likeable). I recommend against being a mean girl. Be nice to others.
Remember…

…This book series is as much about how all this relates to *after* the pageant so what kind of interpersonal habits are you building *during* the pageant? Hopefully positive ones! Whether you may work or compete with these women again or not, don't build bad blood. Even if you don't think you will *ever* see someone again, being kind is just the right thing to do. (We all have bad days or moments…but if you do, keep them *rare* and try to apologize to whomever you were unkind.)

"There is no beautifier of complexion, or form, or behavior, like the wish to scatter joy and not pain around us. 'Tis good to give a stranger a meal, or a night's lodging. 'Tis better to be hospitable to his good meaning and thought, and give courage to a companion. We must be as courteous to a man as we are to a picture, which we are willing to give the advantage of a good light."
~Ralph Waldo Emerson

No More Worries

The time for worrying is done. Move into the mental space of enjoying the interview. All your work up to this point is so you can *relax* and be your warm, friendly self. Or your dynamic, powerful self. Or both. Whatever *your* personality is!

Spend the last few minutes while you wait to prime yourself one last time to pay attention to what they ask, flex with the situation, and be positive. If you do what I suggest here as we proceed through this book, you will be so prepared there will be nothing to worry about. Just focus on shining your true self in this great opportunity to meet some interesting new people who are definitely interested in *you*.

"Worry gives a small thing a big shadow."

~Swedish proverb

Nervousness and Confidence

Standard Nerves

Feeling nervous tends to decrease as your confidence increases. That said, even a confident, experienced contestant might feel nervous. It's only natural. If you don't feel a little nervous, you are fortunate (and unusual). Whatever you feel, don't make more of it than it is.

Sometimes when we focus on something too much or in the wrong way, we can make a big deal out of something that is pretty normal (making a mountain out of a mole hill). So if you have a few butterflies in your stomach, smile at them and what they are trying to tell you...which is that you are taking a calculated risk and putting yourself out there a bit to stretch and grow.

That natural nervousness is a reminder to be proud of what you are doing and to bring your "A" game (do your best). Again, take some deep breaths, focus on the opportunity to meet some interesting new people, and enjoy the process.

Super Nerves

We'll cover more on "stage-fright" later in the series that may also help you with your personal interview. But, for now, what if you feel more than the standard, "natural" amount of nervousness? What if you actually feel afraid or *really* worried? A person might feel that way for any number of reasons. A few reasons, and potential solutions, that come to mind include the possibility that you could:

- Have had a bad interview or public speaking sort of experience before and some left over fears from that are still hanging around
- Benefit from preparing more thoughtfully and/or farther in advance
- Benefit from regularly doing a guided visualization to relax and focus on your interview success
- Consider engaging in a few specific tasks to build your skill in this area (like volunteer work, speaking training, etc.)
- Consider engaging in a series of steps to help desensitize you to what stresses you about interview (or other aspects of the pageant)

Each of these things are outside the scope of this book but the advice in this book overall will go a long way to reducing "nerves" and building confidence. There's other support for you out there, too, if you need more. Ask if you need help finding it.

"Without faith a man can do nothing; with it all things are possible."
~Sir William Osler

While we could all benefit from the techniques and strategies to reduce stress and relax, you may especially want to consider taking a few simple steps to help yourself out if you are one who feels more than a little "natural" anxiety before, during, or after your interview.

Review

Let's review some key points:

- Be nice to your roommate. It's the right thing to do and you want things to be peaceful and easy in the room. That will help you both.
- Check your interview outfit once you get to the pageant and again the night before. Be sure everything is okay and easy to find. Re-review your pageant paperwork briefly one more time.
- Get plenty of sleep (as much as you comfortably can) the week before and certainly the *night* before the interview.
- Show up early for your interview and keep a calm, positive, "sportsmanlike" attitude. Invoke the power of Wonder Woman if you need to protect yourself from other stressful or negative people.
- Focus on your interview being a great opportunity to meet some nice people—you are ready! No need to be too nervous.

Exercise 6.1: Think About Your Potential Roommate

If you are in a pageant where you will spend a few nights with a roommate, think about what may make a nice but not too expensive gift for a roommate. What is unique to your area? What is supportive? Even a card wishing them success in the pageant is sufficient. Think through what you can do to make it easier for you to share limited space with her. Perhaps a safe extension cord? Perhaps a sleep mask for your eyes to block out light? Perhaps earplugs? Think it through. If *you* snore or are otherwise noisy, maybe bring some earplugs for your roommate!

Exercise 6.2: Practice Being Wonder Woman

Review the section on this so you know that I don't mean try to do more stuff than you already do. I don't mean being Wonder Woman like that. I mean in terms of protecting yourself and keeping yourself strong, calm, and energized. Set a timer and spend five minutes practicing your Wonder Woman imagery now (and regularly) so it comes to mind easily when you need it.

"How important it is for us to
recognize and celebrate our heroes
and she-roes!"
~Maya Angelou

Here I am in my evening gown at my national pageant.

a pageant is just the beginning...

PAGEANT
Interviewing
SUCCESS

Making a Strong
First Impression

Dr. Stephanie Raye, PhD
Former Miss American Petite

Book 7
Making a Strong First Impression
Table of Contents

Pageant Interviewing Success
Making a Strong First Impression

Smile – First Impressions Matter (So Do Second Impressions!)

Technically, the first impression the judges will get of you is from your application paperwork. So that would be your resume, your bio, your application, your fact sheet, or whatever materials your specific pageant requires. We've already talked about how those should be thoughtfully and accurately completed.

But the first "in person" impression is typically when you walk in for your personal interview. First impressions can matter so much that in some pageants it is actually something the judges keep in mind while scoring you! What's the best way to make a positive first impression? *Smile!* Pair that with eye contact (arguably the second best way to make a good first impression) and you'll be in good shape.

When you smile you help yourself and you help others. Smiling is the single most important non-verbal communication or facial "gesture" you can master. Worldwide, a smile shows warmth and kindness and good humor. (Okay, not those creepy evil smiles, but you won't do one of those!) Whether it is common sense or scientific research (yes, they've researched smiles), we know that a smile conveys friendliness, approachability, and likeability. All good things.

Yet this one simple thing—smiling—is often forgotten or under-estimated. Many times I'll watch a pageant interview (or any interview) and think "*Smile!* This isn't a funeral." They may not be frowning or looking sad but they've stopped paying attention to their facial expression. We may not realize it but sometimes when our faces are just in their natural "no expression" look, it doesn't look neutral like we might think it does. Our "no expression" may be unflattering to us. A slack face or a face you aren't paying attention to can give the wrong impression and on a "looks" level can appear a little sad, angry, heavier, or older.

Don't worry, it's not like you have to plaster a *fake* smile on all the time as that won't look natural (you do want to be genuine). The hope is that you will *want* to smile more often than not, and that you know how to move through different versions of your smile (and other positive facial expressions) that keep you happy and looking positive. So even if it isn't your great big "smile-for-the-camera" smile, do smile somehow *all* the time.

Remember, smiling isn't just to make other people feel good or increase the chances they'll like you. *You* will feel better if you smile. University researchers have run studies where people are induced to force a smile—to fake it—and their mood improves. Making yourself smile can make you happier. But you'll be happy to be at the pageant so you won't be faking it…you'll just be *reminding* yourself to keep your face smiling or looking happy.

Practice Smiling

Smiling naturally takes practice. First, start noticing when you neglect or forget to smile and then do it—smile! And it does take practice, not just to notice the absence of a smile but to hold one for long periods of time. Try it, you'll see!

If you are a student, practice smiling as you walk to classes. If you work, try it to and from and around the work site. If you are not working or in school, then try it around the house, in dealing with neighbors or shop owners, the mail carrier, and in your volunteer work. Regardless of what you do, experiment and practice. Have fun with it.

Notice how people respond to you when you smile at them. Or when you are just walking along smiling like you just thought of something funny or that makes you happy. Yes, a few people may be surprised or think you are strange but most people will smile back. Smiling can be contagious!

Practice your general "pleasant face" too...holding your face in a positive expression short of a real smile. Your face and demeanor looks happy, your eyes lively, without really smiling. Why not try it right now?

Holding a natural-looking smile for a long time (on stage for instance) takes little muscles you may not have known were there. So, like any other muscles, your smile muscles may need a little training to get them in shape.

Aim to smile way more than you think you need to when you are at a pageant. While it doesn't have to be a *big smile* 100% of the time you want to know your expression is at least positive. Your lips should at least be uplifted in a gentle smile even when it's time to relax the "show" smile for a bit. (Even on stage sometimes you'll want to give your face a rest and to look like a human being rather than a robot!).

When Not to Smile

And there are certainly times that it is appropriate to *not* smile. When the topic turns serious, a big smile may seem out of place. When we are listening intently, a full-scale smile may be too much. So practice your expressions, learn how to use your face like you do your words. Can you look like you're listening with a gentle, no-teeth smile? No need to frown and knit your brow to show that you are paying attention. Your expression can still be pleasant.

And, remember, our faces tend to look "down" when we have no expression at all. We may not *feel* unhappy or angry but we might look that way. Even when a smile isn't appropriate, don't let your facial muscles go totally slack. Practice holding your face in a gentle expression of attention.

Why We Might Not Smile

So if smiling is such a great feeling and so important to do, why don't we do it more? There could be many reasons. Like maybe you smiled a lot as a kid (children sometimes smile more freely than adults) but then a grumpy adult or two said harshly "What are you smiling at!?" like it was a bad thing.

Some folks can be so sensitive sometimes that they take everything personally even if a kid is smiling "just because." You've probably seen this happen even as an adult: someone in a bad mood might think they are being laughed at or something when they aren't. Or they hold to that expression that "misery loves company" so if they don't have a reason to be happy they don't want you to be either.

Too bad! Don't let other people pull down your mood. Even if you weren't discouraged from smiling growing up, few of us still smile as much as we could on a daily basis—let alone as much as you need to for a pageant. Again, there could be many reasons, but here are a few that come to mind. You may:

- Not be in the habit of smiling
- Find smiling does not come naturally to you
- Forget to smile because of nervousness
- Think it is important to look "serious"
- Want to hide discolored or crooked teeth
- Want to hide braces
- Not realize how important a smile is!

Simple mindful awareness (noticing) can erase several of these reasons. Practice can take care of a few too. And hopefully this little section on smiling has erased concerns that you must look negative to be taken seriously. Indeed, if you cultivate a look of "interested attention" you may be surprised at how many people (teachers, friends, co-workers, you name it!) will start to think you are a better listener (even if your mind still wanders).

But what about if you think there is something "wrong" with your smile?

Find the Beauty in Your Smile, Or Fix It

Hiding your smile is not recommended. No matter what your smile looks like, a smiling face is a good thing. And *beautiful* and famous people have had less than perfect smiles. Do you remember the super-model Lauren Hutton? (If not, ask your parents or grand-parents or "Google" her.) Some consider her the *first* model to reach super-model status—even with a noticeable space between her two front teeth.

Lauren Hutton made it work for her because she *embraced* her "flaw" as part of her natural beauty. If she had tried to, for example, lower her head, cover her mouth with her hand when she spoke, or keep her mouth closed all the time to hide her teeth, she'd *never* smile and she'd never have had the great success that she did.

So if you have a smile that has a little space between your teeth it doesn't have to be a problem. And some folks don't like their smile because it "shows a lot of gum." Well, that same smile may not bother someone else at all. Whatever the case, just love the smile that comes naturally for you. A space between the teeth can be a "beauty mark" like Cindy Crawford's mole that she kept when some may have counseled her to have it removed. (Cindy is another super model for you to "Google" if you haven't heard of her. She's still around but her heyday may have been earlier than some of my readers will remember.)

All that said, *if* you can't find a way to love your smile and use it freely to show your wonderful personality then you may want to do something about it. It can take practice and courage to train ourselves to smile if for years we've hidden our smile because we thought our teeth were too crooked or discolored. True, sometimes if you have a less than perfect smile, you'll notice people look at your teeth and some may not be nice about how they "react." *If* that happened to you too often growing up then you may find you don't smile much at all.

If you are reading this book, chances are good that you have "nice" teeth already. Or at least "nice enough." You may have been blessed with good genes from your parents so have pretty good teeth naturally. Or you may have had parents that could afford to get you braces and such as you grew up. If in doubt about your smile, remember how fortunate you are as some people are born with facial deformities. This might even be an opportunity for you to check out organizations like Smile Train (http://www.smiletrain.org) and Operation Smile (http://www.operationsmile.org).

But there are a lot of different people that might be reading this book so we want to be of help to them too. If you inherited less attractive teeth or your family didn't have the money to help you take care of or straighten your teeth, that's okay. And remember in some cultures what people's teeth look like just isn't as important as it is in mainstream U.S.A. society where we tend to "overdo" things sometimes or strive for "perfection" when there are plenty of lovely people in the world with slightly irregular teeth. (I say this from the knowledge of having experience traveling and living in other countries.)

Wherever you are from and whatever your background, start with practicing smiling no matter what your teeth look like and start considering if or how you'd want to improve your teeth.

You'll want to consider that because you may only be able to get so far in certain pageant systems *if* your teeth are severely discolored or severely misaligned. I say "severely" because a little misalignment or off-colorness probably won't get in the way in most cases. It's all a matter of degree, your goals, your pageant, and your own degree of sparkle and confidence. You can be so fabulous that no one will notice little flaws in your smile or, if they do, they'll "forgive" them. But if your teeth are severely discolored or misaligned and *if* you are serious about winning a pageant (versus entering primarily for fun or the good life and work experience they provide) you may want to consider some teeth whitening, orthodontics (teeth-straightening), or other cosmetic-dentistry.

Speaking of whitening, teeth do not have to be super-duper white "glow-in-the-dark" teeth. In fact, over-white teeth can look too fake. You've seen those teeth—the ones where you feel like you need your sunglasses to look at them! If you are "into" that, fine. But it isn't necessarily a "must." Know and trust yourself but also Sleuth it out as you become more experienced and determine if the "whiteness" of your teeth is really a deal-breaker for your success.

In the meantime, realize that there are many shades of white and you do *not* have to whiten your teeth in order to do well in a pageant. (Some people choose not to whiten their teeth because there is a downside to most anything—and they might be sensitive to the ingredients, etc.) Chances are the color of teeth you were born with works well your skin tone, assuming you took care of your teeth. Staining from certain foods and drugs, etc., can mess them up a bit. But even then changing toothpaste can do a lot of good without using teeth whitening kits or the like.

"A smile costs nothing but creates much good. It enriches those who receive it without impoverishing those who give it away. It happens in a flash, but the memory of it can last forever. No one is so rich that he can get along without it. No one is too poor to feel rich when receiving it. It creates happiness in the home, fosters good will in business, and is the countersign of friends. It is rest to the weary, daylight to the discouraged, sunshine to the sad, and nature's best antidote for trouble. Yet it cannot be bought, begged, borrowed, or stolen, for it is something of no earthly good to anybody until it is given away willingly."
~ Dale Carnegie

In the end, I do not suggest "fixing" a smile to mean yours isn't good enough or that you need to hide it ever. A genuine smile can melt hearts even if it is a totally *toothless* smile. But, realistically, we must acknowledge that top pageant winners are more likely to have teeth that don't attract attention one way or another. The smile is more important than the teeth. Teeth are there to serve the smile (and to chew food, of course) not to be the focus of attention.

If you cannot love your smile and use it freely, then get it fixed. Maybe ask family members to contribute as you save up your own pennies. You might ask them to help with your teeth in lieu of other sundry gifts you might get this year for your birthday, holiday, or gift-giving occasions.

If you are married, you might ask your husband for invisible braces for your anniversary rather than another something he might give you that may just be "extra." (Even if the gift is nice, it could be something you don't really want or need or something that will collect dust somewhere. If you'd really like something different— ask.)

At any age or marital status, consider volunteering or trading some product or services you have access to for dental services. Maybe you could do some work in the office or go speak to a few of their favorite schools or charities. You might even consider asking if a qualified dentist might donate all or part of the services (perhaps at a discount) to be prominently featured as one of your sponsors. (Need more insights about sponsors, how to approach them, and how to maximize that opportunity? Please see my website for support on that—it is outside the scope of this book but well worth learning more about!)

If you decide to do whitening at home, you can find tooth-whitening kits in most grocery stores these days but there are pros and cons to different approaches and you may find it better to work through a dentist in the end. And, of course, there are less expensive (and more chemical-free) tooth-whitening "remedies" our ancestors used to use. You might try some of those first. There are many resources and products for teeth whitening, teeth and gum care, and teeth straightening out there!

Make and Keep Eye Contact

Cultural Differences

Unless you are competing in a culture-specific pageant where custom would dictate otherwise, plan on making quality eye contact with the judges throughout the interview.

No one culture is better than another but we are assuming in this book that we are dealing with "mainstream" or "general" U.S. American culture where good eye contact communicates confidence and respect. In general, in the U.S.A. avoiding eye contact in a pageant can convey that you are uncomfortable with the judges and/or uncertain about yourself.

I say "in general" because the U.S.A. is made up of people from many cultures. Many of our citizens have been naturalized and others were born in the U.S.A. but may retain some customs of their ancestral culture. Either way, if you are competing in a different culture or a culturally specific pageant where the expectations are different, learn what those expectations are and practice them. Remember, a good Sleuth will do her homework! Or if you are from a family where eye contact has a different meaning, you may have to work extra on this for mainstream pageants. It's okay, you can do it!

Conversely, any Queen—from any pageant in any country—could find herself in a different cultural setting than her usual one. That can be part of the job! Think of the Queen of England and how many places she's gone to represent her country…and how many foreign cultural representatives she's entertained. She has to be *sensitive* to the situation and the people.

As Pageant Queens we may not have the high stakes involved that an actual Queen of a country does (and we certainly don't have the staff to help us navigate the cultural differences!). But every Queen should be able to adjust to the culture she is in. She wants to seem comfortable and help make other people comfortable. Yes, she might be representing one culture (and want to be "true" to it) but she also wants to be a good diplomat, a good emissary. So she'll adjust. Learn how to do that.

Okay, let's move on with the assumption of "mainstream" American culture (I know that's harder and harder to define as we *are* a multi-cultural society)…

Know that just as with smiling, good eye contact takes practice. Just as we discussed with smiling, *practice* it with the people in your life—family, friends, strangers, co-workers—and you'll find yourself improving the length of time you can look someone in the eye and your comfort level with it.

Entering the Room

We'll assume for now that you are at a panel interview. As you walk in, smile warmly, and sweep (half slowly and obviously) the panel of judges, making brief eye contact with each if you can. If the panel isn't too big, your eye contact can linger a fraction longer to be more meaningful…a bit more of a true acknowledgement of the judge.

You'll take the person in for a moment and move your eyes smoothly to the next. If any of them are looking down, you'll just skip over them and maybe go back and catch them with a little nod when they do look up. Whatever you do, don't over-think this as it isn't that hard. It all happens quickly enough and is part of expected behavior (making eye contact is something folks look for consciously or unconsciously). It will become natural for you if you just practice even a little bit. So don't try so hard that it is over-artificial. Just remember they are nice people and you are happy to look them in the eye.

Panel Interview

It may seem obvious but let's say it just to be sure: If it is a panel interview, when a judge asks a question look at him or her while they are talking. Look like you are listening—because hopefully you are! Simply look them in the eyes, nod a little now and then as you listen.

Then you can keep your eyes on them at the start of your reply but be sure that you make eye contact with the other judges as well. It doesn't have to be perfectly even amounts of time for each judge and you may not be able to look at each judge on each question. But "even it out" over the course of the interview and be sure you catch the other judges on the next question, etc. No one likes to feel left out.

And to the degree you can, as you are wrapping up the response to a particular question, bring your eyes back to the judge who asked it. In other words, end where you started—come full circle—out of respect for that judge. Plus, you may get a sense of how you did on the question by how they react (though some judges are very hard to read, so don't try to figure it out).

If they happen to be looking down, look at them anyway (about where their eyes would be) or look at the judge next to him or her briefly and be ready to look back at the other judge when you see them move their eyes or head back up to you.

Sometimes people are shy so eye contact takes a bit more effort (initially) and practice. Others aren't shy but just haven't paid enough attention to the importance of eye contact or worked on the skill. Others don't want to maintain eye contact because they don't know what their eyes are "saying" or how it makes the other person feel. Well, just watch your expression and let that impact your eyes (the facial muscles all work together with attitude, etc.) First, remember to smile and/or keep a positive expression as we've discussed before.

That will go a long way but, additionally, don't "stare down" the judge or tell yourself you can never look away. If you hold eye contact *too* long or with a harshness in your eyes or expression it can come off as unkind or aggressive. Keep your expression and eyes interested and attentive and allow yourself to look away to another judge, etc. after a bit if it feels natural.

You don't need to look someone in the eye 100% of the time in most social settings. Just avoid looking away *too* often or you may communicate a lack of interest, focus, or stability. Shifty, darting eyes are distracting. Look at people in their eyes for a couple seconds at least as a start. Not just a series of quick glances (away, back, away, back too fast). You may find you look at other places on their face or in their general direction…that's better than looking some place else in the room for long periods of time. Gently work on it and you'll get better!

One-on-One Interview

Some pageants have you interview separately with each judge. For instance, at least at the time this book was written, the Mrs. International Pageant has you interview five minutes with each of five judges. If you are in a pageant with one-on-one interviews, adjust what you are learning to fit the situation.

You'd enter, smile warmly and extend your hand for a brief, firm handshake. All the while you'd be looking them in the eye and smiling. (In a panel interview, shaking everyone's hand would be time-consuming and possibly awkward so don't initiate it unless they do.)

During the rest of the interview, eye contact will likely come naturally to you as most of us have many one-on-one conversations in our life. But as more and more of those conversations are on cell phones—or while we are multi-tasking in some way—you still might want to practice sitting across from someone and getting comfortable with an appropriate amount of eye contact.

Start building that skill in the conversations you have with people each day. And if you don't have enough face-to-face conversations, you may want to create some opportunities for yourself to practice.

The eye contact pointers we covered above in the panel interview section also apply here too but now you'd not be looking away to other judges but just naturally in the process of talking you might now and then.

The key is to not stare down at your lap or anywhere else in an attempt to *avoid* eye contact with the judge. Doing that shows a lack of confidence, fear, or unfriendliness. (You may not feel anything of those things but that's what avoiding eye contact can convey in many mainstream U.S. social interactions.)

We'll cover more on eye contact later when we discuss on-stage interview considerations but, for now, let's stay in the personal interview frame of mind and discuss other aspects of starting the interview. Along the way, be aware that you will be engaging in eye contact during these other aspects.

Introductions

If someone else is introducing you to the judge make eye contact and *pay attention* to his or her name and any other information you are told (or read beforehand on that person). Say it over to yourself in your head or, better yet, say it right back to them as part of the introduction sequence. Saying it out loud will help you remember it.

As simple as introductions may seem, some people get tongue-tied in them waiting to see who is going to start or accidentally talking over each other. Just be a Sleuth and read the cues of whether the judge will begin or if he or she is waiting for you to do so. Go with the flow.

If a pageant staff person introduces you to the judge it might go like this:

Staff person
"Dr. Stephanie, this is Jennifer Smith, Miss Title."

Contestant
"Hello, Dr. Stephanie, I'm excited to be here!"

Judge
"Me too! Welcome, Miss Title, have a seat."

Or the judge might speak first and both may use first names without titles, etc. Just follow the lead and try to use the person's name right away to help you remember it.

If no one makes the introduction, it still works out pretty much the same. Here's how that might go if the judge starts off:

Judge *(extending her hand)*
"Hello Jennifer, I'm Dr. Stephanie Raye. Please have a seat."

Contestant *(shaking the hand)*
"Nice to meet you Dr. Raye. Or do you prefer Stephanie?" (taking her seat)

Judge
"Stephanie is fine; thanks for asking."

Or maybe the judge won't have your name at the tip of their tongue. (Although they'll have your paperwork, remember how many people they are meeting that day!) If he or she does not use your name right away, that's okay, they'll have it in their head soon enough. And you'll help them with that by using your own name when you introduce yourself:

Judge *(extending her hand)*
"Hello, I'm Dr. Stephanie. Please have a seat."

Contestant *(shaking hands)*
"Hello Dr. Stephanie, I'm Jennifer Smith, Miss Title. Thank you." (as you take your seat)

Or if the judge doesn't start things out, you may do so like this:

> **Contestant** *(extending hand)*
> "Hello, I'm Jane. It's nice to meet you."

> **Judge** *(shaking hands)*
> "Hello, Jane, I'm Stephanie. Welcome. Have a seat."

Or if you know or were told the name of the judge by the coordinator before you entered the room you might say:

> **Contestant** *(extending hand)*
> "Hello Dr. Stephanie, I'm Jane. It's nice to meet you. I've read your book!"

> **Judge** *(shaking hands)*
> "That's great, Jane, I hope you enjoyed it. Have a seat and go for it! Just be yourself and have fun. Let's see, you're Miss Title, right? Tell me about…"

Once the introduction is done and the interview is underway, remember to use the judge's name in the interview once or twice, if possible, but don't overdo it (or it may sound fake and like you are trying too hard).

Forgetting a Name

I say use their name "if possible" because if you have, for some reason, already *forgotten* their name, then you may prefer to not take a chance on using the wrong one. But if you do use their name and it is incorrect, just smile and apologize and make light of it in a professional way. Let's consider three responses:

Sleuth response, spoken with a smile in her eyes and in her voice:

> "Oh dear, and here I was trying to impress you! Sorry about that, I'm usually good with names."

Okay, a really good Sleuth will use the right name, but if she doesn't, she'll handle it well. And turn it into an opportunity to show her human side, good sense of humor, and work in a positive comment about herself (that she is *usually* good with names.)

Bungler response 1
"Oh, sorry."

...she might say, with a dejected expression, while getting agitated or otherwise "losing her cool."

Bungler response 2
"I know I shouldn't have tried to do that."

Again, she may show matching negative facial or body language.

Neither of these Bungler responses is as good. They both show that you get flustered easily. We will forget things from time to time; that's human. What the judges want is a Queen who can handle it if/when she forgets a name of the *many* people she will meet. And the second of the Bungler response shows the contestant puts herself down and suggests she gives up easily.

Remember that, generally speaking, judges (as with most people) are friendly and forgiving as we all make mistakes. Even though they take their job seriously, and some may be taciturn or firm, don't let a situation or one particular judge's personality throw you off your game. Recover the best you can and if it doesn't feel like it went well with one particular judge, be grateful you have several others to talk to.

Now it is possible that you've forgotten a name and want to admit it to the judge right away so that you then can work it into the interview later to demonstrate that you are actually and usually good with names. If that is important to you then try these approaches (again with a smile and a cheerful voice):

Contestant

"Oh, I know you just told me but my nerves slipped it right out of my mind: please tell me your name again."

Judge

"I'm Jack."

Contestant

"Thank you, Jack, for understanding. I'm usually good with names so we'll see if it sticks this time!"

Or if you prefer not to admit to any natural nervousness, you might try this:

Contestant

"Goodness, I've met so many people today I think your name just slipped my mind. Please remind me one more time."

Judge

"That's okay. Names slip my mind too. I'm Mrs. Smith."

Contestant

"Thanks, Mrs. Smith, I'm usually good with names but forgive me if I forget again!"

If it feels right, you could also try the "time out" technique which I'll discuss more fully in the "Damage Control" section of *Book 13: Ending with Grace and Ease*.

On a related note, it is not uncommon for someone to have an unusual name or one that is difficult to pronounce. Naturally, you'll do your best to get it right, but if what you say is wrong and someone corrects you just take that in stride. If you want to, try saying it the right way as soon as they correct you while it is fresh in your ears. Either way—whether you try saying it again or not—just say "Thank you." Or "Thank you, I'll try to do better next time."

Again, if you've used the *wrong* name (not just mispronounced) during the interview, then you need to fix it up as described above. But if you've simply forgotten a name (not used the wrong one) for most, I'd say that for the purposes of a short interview you can "let it go" and not bring it up just so you can use it later in the same interview. (Though it could be handy to know their names for various reasons later, so do pay attention.)

This is a personal choice, however, as some contestants may consider it a good strategy to clarify and use the name as it may help the judge remember her out of a long list of contestants because she cared enough to "get it right."

Finally, remember that as the Queen you'll be out at various appearances and sometimes spending time with people where you *should* know their name to help things go well for the appearance, the event, the day, etc. So if you happen to forget their name then just admit it gracefully as the examples above help with. Just imagine it is an event coordinator you are talking to rather than a judge and say what I suggested or your own version of "Oops, I forgot. Silly me. Please tell me again." And if they are "classy" they won't take it personally and will happily tell you.

Shaking Hands

We've mentioned shaking hands quite a bit in the above section as you are meeting a judge in a one-on-one interview. But what should you know about shaking hands? Does your handshake make a good impression?

You may think handshakes are easy and that you don't need to think about them at all. It is natural for us to think that about most everything until we *do* start thinking about it some more and realize we might want to approach it differently. Generally speaking, it's true: a good handshake is not rocket science but they do impact the "first impression" so it's worth a few minutes to consider how you do in that area. (That and my younger readers may not have had much handshake experience yet, and my international readers may benefit from knowing exactly how mainstream U.S.A. handles handshaking.)

So we'll go over a few basics that will help in the interview situation but then take it a little farther because if you win the title you'll be shaking *lots* of hands and there are a few things you might want to keep in mind.

A Good Handshake Is:

- Palm to palm – don't offer or grasp the fingers
- Firm not wimpy – don't be a limp fish
- Firm not painful – don't squeeze too tight! Think of a gentle squeeze two or three brief "shakes" – not forever. Just let go.
- At standard body distance – don't pull them in to you or stand so far away it is a "reach" for you both to shake.

What else to know?

Well, handshakes are usually right-hand to right-hand unless that's a problem because someone has a missing hand or other right-hand situation. If you see there is an obstacle to a traditional right-handshake from the start, offer your left. If you didn't see it and they offer their left, switch hands and accept their left-hand in yours without comment. (So practice your left-hand shake a little "just in case.")

If someone's hands are full, don't expect them to put their stuff down to shake hands if it is too inconvenient or awkward. Don't be offended. Just smile and nod or say cheerfully "It's nice to meet you! I'd shake your hand but your hands are full so let's not worry about that today." Of course, offer to help them with their burden if the situation calls for it (like they are about to drop something or you could open a door for them).

While *you* know what a good handshake is the other person may not. So if the person whose hand you are shaking just grabs fingers or is too hard or soft, don't draw attention to it. Just move on. But don't be the one to have or initiate a "weak" handshake. The whole idea of a customary handshake is to be friendly and natural and put people at ease. If you make a big deal about the handshake that works against what it was there to do in the first place.

If by chance the person you are meeting is behind a desk or table that is too wide for you both to comfortably reach across and shake in the middle, then a nod and smile is sufficient. Depending on the situation, the person behind the obstacle will come around to shake your hand anyway.

Tying back to our last section…if you can, use their name while you are shaking their hand.

Deeper Consideration of Handshakes

The handshake is the only part of an interview or pageant appearance that involves touch. Any time touch enters the picture there are all sorts of other things to consider.

The aspects of handshakes I'm about to bring up now aren't likely to come in to play during your pageant interview. They could, but it isn't likely because most pageant judges are pretty comfortable with this as they've had to shake lots of hands over the years.

But as a titleholder you may be meeting people from all walks of life in a variety of different places and settings and you want to be considerate of others. Not everybody does things or sees things the same way. It doesn't make them wrong and you right (or *vice versa*), it just means you learned different things.

Generational and Upbringing Differences

One thing to know is that there are generational differences in attitudes toward handshakes. What I mean by "generational" is that what is acceptable or common can differ depending on a person's age (and also where they were raised but we'll leave that aside for now).

So an older male might think it is polite to *not* offer his hand to a woman because there have been times when etiquette would dictate that the woman offered her hand if *she* wanted to. So if an older male (or classically trained and raised younger male) doesn't offer his hand, don't take offense. On the flip side, if someone offers his or her hand to an older woman and she does not accept it, do not take offense. If she smiles and nods that's all that may be appropriate based on how she was raised.

Physical Conditions

We mentioned before that you might encounter someone who is missing their right hand. Or perhaps the right hand is disfigured in some way. If the person feels comfortable offering their hand, great! Accept it. If they don't, just move on without comment or seeming otherwise surprised or uncomfortable. Usually you wouldn't bring something into the conversation about that unless they do. Whatever the case…

Older or younger, male or female, someone may have a very good reason for not offering or accepting a hand. They may have a rash, super sweaty palms, or painful arthritis or some other condition that makes it uncomfortable to them (or the other person) to shake hands. And this is true regardless of age—younger people can have "issues" too. So just be gracious whatever the situation and avoid jumping to any negative conclusions about someone too soon.

By the way, if you shake hands with someone with super sweaty palms don't let your words or face register any surprise or whatever. And don't immediately wipe your hand on your clothes. The person may or may not take offense at that. Put yourself in their shoes and imagine how you'd feel. Now they may be absolutely confident and fine with their sweaty palms and not care one whit how you react, but if they feel self-conscious about it you wouldn't want to hurt their feelings.

And if *you* happen to be a person with super sweaty palms, you can guess that I'd advise to not take offense if someone does react, wipe their hands, or the like. Some reactions are so automatic that folks don't think about it or mean anything by it. A titleholder would just take that in stride and use it as an opportunity to show her effortless ability to overlook such things or she might, depending on the situation, use it as an opportunity to share something about herself or educate on the matter.

For instance, if someone reacts poorly and then feels funny about their poor reaction, a gracious Queen would smile and say something like "Oh, don't feel bad about that. My hands have been extra-moist since I was a child so I'm used to people reacting to it. Unfortunately, there's not much I can do about it so I just get on with my life." Imagine how much better someone would feel to hear that if they were just moments before worried they'd just offended you or showed poor manners.

Finally, for those super-sweaty palm people out there…there might be help for you. Everybody is a bit different, of course, but if you worry about your sweaty palms (especially if you let it interfere with your enjoyment or experience of life), there is support for you and some products, etc. that might help. For more information about sweaty palms look for organizations and products that educate and help with that by searching the internet on "sweaty palms" and the like.

Psychological Preferences

For any of the potential physical conditions out there, some people may be fine with you shaking their hands and others might prefer to avoid hand shaking. It is all okay. But let's consider one last thing on the topic and, again, *if* this sort of thing comes up at all it might be out on appearances or events where you meet many strangers (not likely to happen at the pageant).

I know this is sort of a "deep and dark" subject to bring up, but if you are a future Pageant Queen you need to be strong and sensitive and be able to talk kindly and openly about a variety of things. So here goes: Sometimes if someone has been abused in their past, that person might be hesitant or resistant in offering or accepting a hand.

It may seem completely innocent to offer or accept a hand (and it usually is!) but put yourself in the shoes of someone who may have been grabbed by the hand at the beginning of what turned into a domestic violence situation. We should not avoid offering or accepting hands but we want to be sensitive if you get what seems like an unusual reaction.

Naturally, our wish for any abuse sufferer is that they eventually deal with those terrible emotions and memories in a way that lets them shake hands or accept hugs or whatever everyday "normal" stuff happens but that can take time and effort. Everybody heals in different ways and on different time lines so *if* someone ever recoils from an offered hand or innocent gesture that involves touch, just (as always!) take it in stride.

Avoid any defensive response, over-reaction, or temptation to make a "cute" comment or pry. Just gracefully adjust your approach and, if appropriate, say "sorry" or "oh, sorry, I didn't mean to make you uncomfortable." But you may not even need to say that if you just smoothly go on to whatever is next and that person may really appreciate your not drawing attention to their reaction. Sometimes those reactions are so automatic even if they have been trying not to do it! So it can be embarrassing to people. A good Queen wants the people they are interacting with to feel comfortable and safe so unless it is your platform or the situation calls for you to address something more directly, you "let it go" and move on.

Okay, let's move on. We've talked about several aspects to starting the interview and things to keep in mind. There are more.

Opening Statements

Some pageants will ask you to do a personal introduction (usually very brief), an opening statement (usually longer but not *too* long), or both. Some pageants will not ask for this. As with everything, just read the website or other materials and if it isn't clear, ask. But, in any case, it's good to be prepared for anything in case there's a change. (Queens are adaptable!)

Some introductions are very brief like "Hello, I'm Bonnie and I'm from the biggest little State in the Union—Rhode Island!" while others might ask for a little more. Some will occur at the beginning of the personal interview, others will be on stage as the contestants introduce themselves. Whatever it is, you can handle it. For a brief intro, just think through what you'd like to say and try it (preferably at home first so you can tweak it if need be). Remember, though, to keep it short and "light" or factual.

In contrast to a brief intro, opening statements are more involved. Opening statements (by whatever name they are called in your pageant system) remind me of what we call the "elevator speech" in the world of business. It has that name because if you are in the elevator with someone and have a brief time to make a positive impression or make a request, you need to be ready.

They also use these in "networking" groups where everyone briefly says their name, what they do, what they can help others with, or what they are looking for in a client, etc. Most professionals are encouraged to have a 30 second elevator speech ready (and they can cut it down from there if they need to).

The pageant version is similar in that you'll say your name, and usually add the title you hold currently (if any), and then something about your platform, or what you'd like to do with the title if you win, something relevant or outstanding about you, or the like.

Even though opening statements are still relatively brief (consult your pageant to see IF they have a time requirement), they take a little thought to put together well. Sometimes it is harder to give *short* answers than long ones as you need to be more precise and on-target. So let's spend more time using them as the focus of this section.

Why They Might Ask For an Opening Statement

Some pageants will require or invite an opening statement from the contestant. It can serve multiple purposes. It lets the judges see you, however briefly, in "public speaking mode" rather than "interview mode." As the titleholder may do some public speaking, that can be useful to them.

It also lets them see what sort of choices you make in selecting what to say. That tells them something about you. It can also give them a starting point for some of their questions.

Plan Ahead

So clearly the opening statement is something you'll want to have thought about in advance. If one is required or strongly suggested, they may also suggest a time limit for it. If they don't, choose a reasonable one for yourself as you don't want to go on too long and eat up valuable interview time.

Use your statement to convey your charming personality and a key point or two about who you are. Allow your choices to show that you are a good fit for the title and/or why the title matters to you (which might include something *brief* about your platform or career goals). Hopefully you will use it to guide the interviewers to start in a place that you know is one of your stronger topics.

Why You Want To Be Ready

Even if the pageant doesn't require or invite an opening statement, you'll want to have one prepared because you may decide to offer one on your own judgment (unless specifically told you shouldn't for that pageant). If you do, however, remember to keep it brief.

Or, and this can happen, a judge may spontaneously ask you a version of this classic pageant question:

Judge
"What would you like us to know about you as an opening note?"

You do not want to be caught off guard and say something like either of these Bunglers:

Bungler 1
"Er, um, where do I start? There's so much I could tell you...um, let's see...I guess I could tell you...."

Bungler 2
"Well, what do you want to know?"

You may not get that exact question or invitation but it is likely somewhere during your pageant experience you *will* get an invitation to "Tell us about yourself" which a classic pageant "question" worded as a statement.

In your mind, you can consider an opening statement as a version of that classic pageant "question" so be prepared for it. Choose a few key things that are interesting (and possibly unique) about you and relevant to the job as titleholder.

Why You Might Skip It

If it is not absolutely required (and if you've neglected to prepare properly) you might consider gracefully skipping an opening statement with a polite and positively toned:

> "I'll forego the opening statement so we can get right
> to the interview questions."

You might do that if, say, you are really uncomfortable with public speaking and worry you'll go into a "blank slate mode" which sometimes happens if you think you must deliver a little memorized speech perfectly. But just be aware that the judges may not follow your lead. Even if you want to skip it, you should be ready because a judge just might say in reply:

> "Oh, thanks for your willingness but we'd prefer you
> go ahead and do the opening statement as we consider
> it part of the interview."

You Don't Have To Be Perfect

I know. There can be a lot of pressure from society, or family, or friends, or *ourselves* to be "perfect" especially if you are in activities like pageants. But keep in mind that "too perfect" can actually be a turn off if it comes off as fake. So your opening statement does not have to be memorized perfectly and delivered 100% perfectly. If you focus on "perfect" you may pressure yourself into being extra nervous. Aim for competent and confident, professional and positive, not overly rehearsed.

Speak naturally and from your heart. For most pageants, you'll want to seem professional, yes, but also warm and inviting. You want to be easy to be around. Be yourself—and I don't know anybody who is "perfect" for real. We love people in spite of and because of their flaws.

And while we are on the topic of perfection…

An Aside—More on Perfection

As we've touched on before, for some the whole "be yourself" advice doesn't ring true in pageants. For some, the whole pageant pursuit—and documents like this—can make you *feel* like you have to be perfect. And you know deep down that none of us are so you wonder how you can "be yourself" and still do well. You can.

Perfection is not really what it is about, despite what some may say, think, or try to show. Again, we tend to love folks who are not-so-perfect because they are easier to be with, easier to believe. It's about being the best *you* can be within the framework of who you are! (Is that enough "you" for you?) ☺ Being yourself includes realizing the best parts that you want to share, the parts you want to work on, and the parts you are smarter to leave at home.

You can make mistakes, you can have flaws, you can disagree…it's all in how you handle it. And it starts with loving yourself for who you are when the make-up and gowns are off and it's "just" you. You are enough. Good pageants—or contestants with healthy attitudes toward pageants of any kind—appreciate that and use the pageants to grow, not to focus on faults. And we are all growing all the time. And we all make mistakes. If you make some, it's okay. Just learn from them and aim to not make them again. (And apologize if it is that kind of mistake.)

But Gently Practice

Ironically, seeming natural and easy does take a little practice! So back to the topic of opening statements…prepare for it.

Do so at home, leading up to the pageant so you can think it through, write it, edit it, practice it and then set it aside and let a little time pass. Practice it out loud now and then. Review it a couple times. Then see what you can *naturally* remember from memory. That's likely what you'll have to "work with" at the actual pageant.

Do you remember the key points? If so, great. You've got the outline in your head. Practice that now and then as you brush your hair or whatever. But don't over-worry or *over* practice. You know it, so now you can forget stressing over the details of delivery and just let it happen. That's the beauty of preparation.

If you can't remember the *key* points, then maybe they aren't really that "key" or important to you. Maybe you need to practice more or write a new opening statement! Remember, there is a balance to be had…you want to think of what may be of interest to the judges and think about what your strong areas are…but if that doesn't keep *your* interest then you need to figure something else out to say. (If you are in this bind, the upcoming Essential Pageant Interview Playbook would be a good investment for you.)

Pros and Cons of Memorization

Some people will choose to memorize their opening statement or other answers. While I do not recommend it as the *best* way to go—I understand that some do take comfort from doing that. And if you are good at it, maybe no one will notice. See what works for you. If you are going to try to memorize it then practice sounding like you haven't.

It may be a smart thing for you to memorize some things if you are very nervous (see other sections of this book and my website for help) or are very new to interviewing or public speaking. Have faith that after a little practice, experience, and/or some specific relaxation exercises you may not feel the need to memorize any more.

The downsides of memorizing include that you may sound "canned" like you've said it a hundred times already—because you probably will have! Your voice may sound flat and monotonous (losing its natural modulation). So you could sound all normal and then sound like a robot when you launch into your memorized bits.

Another downside is that you may get flustered if you start your memorized answer and forget part of it. Sometimes people who forget part of something memorized stop and pause for too long in their effort to remember "where they are at" in the statement or answer. Or they are tempted to start over, hoping that this time they'll roll over the bump that stopped them before. Either choice has a bit of a Bungler feel to it. Is it the "end of the world?" No, but better if you aren't so reliant on memorized stuff that you can't adjust on the fly.

Remember, this opening statement is about you so it should be do-able to have a little bit to say that comes naturally. But if you are going to memorize, then do it like a Sleuth so you *can* adapt more easily…

Memorization Advice

If you do choose to try the memorization route, I encourage you to structure your memorizing around "bullet points" or key clauses or sentences that you know you want to get out there rather than on fully formed, complete answers.

Why? Because you never really know what sort of questions you will get. Yes, some things are standard enough you might expect to get them, like you might memorize an answer to "Why did you enter the pageant?" *but* you may get something *similar* that doesn't quite fit how you memorized your answer, like "How did you decide to enter the pageant?" or "What do you hope to get out of participating in the pageant?"

Those are very similar questions but different enough that you'd likely need to adapt a memorized answer at least a little bit—if you don't adjust your answer it will be more evident that you memorized. So it's better to have key bullet points in mind that you can re-arrange depending on how the questions are asked. That way you won't worry if you lose your place in your answer or have to re-phrase it based on the slant they asked it in.

And whether you memorize full answers or use bullet points, keep an eye on making your delivery of your responses sound fresh! As an aside, sometimes we don't set out to memorize something but it just happens as we've said something similar to ourselves or others so often.

So even if you've accidentally memorized—or feel like "I've gotten that question before, I know my answer to that"—make sure that you don't *sound* like you've said it a hundred times before. Keep your voice lively and light, use natural volume and pausing, etc. to make it seem like it is the first time you've said it!

Having key bullet points in mind allow you to work them into *other* answers as the opportunities arise…that's how you will wind up being flexible and natural in your responses. What you are aiming for is to know things about yourself (and your platform, if applicable) that you want to work in as appropriate. If you think of it that way you may find you don't need to memorize. Working with this book (and other materials) will help you know yourself better and feel more confident.

"A woman whose smile is open and whose expression is glad
has a kind of beauty no matter what she wears."
~Anne Roiphe

Review

Let's review some key points in regard to starting the interview (and that matter throughout the interview as well!):

- *You've got to smile!*
  Smile, smile, and smile some more. And a "neutral" facial expression might actually look negative or unattractive so work on a variety of smiles and positive expressions. Build confidence in your smile, regardless of any imperfections, and your happy face, eyes, and attitude will be what shines.

- **Eye contact is important whether in a one-on-one or panel interview.**

  The judges, and others, want to get to know and relate to you. Making eye contact helps that along immensely. Understand that there are many cultural differences in eye contact expectations and learn what is appropriate for your pageant and culture.

- **Smooth and polite introductions are a good, safe start to an interview.**

  We covered the basics there.

- **We're all human.**

  Forgetting a name might happen. We talked about ways of handling that.

- **A good handshake helps with a strong first impression.**

  There may not be an opportunity to shake hands in all interview settings but if you can do so (more likely in one-on-one interviews), we've covered some obvious and not-so-obvious things to consider.

- **Opening statements—from brief introductions to something a little longer like an "elevator speech" is something you may be asked to do.**

  And you should be prepared with one anyway. We covered ways to approach them.

- **Memorization is something we can work on or that can happen automatically just through practice and repetition.**

  Whether you're trying to memorize or it happened naturally, there are some things to consider to come off as "natural."

Exercise 7.1: Practice Smiling

As I suggest in the book, practice smiling in all areas of your life to help build your smile muscles. Your face can get fatigued if you don't practice, so practicing at home will build your strength for when you are at the pageant and smiling more than you ever thought possible.

It may feel funny at first to smile a lot and a few cynical or paranoid people may look at you strangely but don't let that bother you. Chances are you'll be much more likely to find people smile back at you or just look at you with a curious "I wonder what she knows that I don't know" or "she must have just gotten good news!" look. Your smile will likely brighten someone's day so "just do it!"

Starting today set some do-able, fun goal for how you will work more smiling in your life. Smiling at other people is the best way to practice (and most fun) as you can also practice your eye contact at the same time so consider making the goal of smiling throughout your interactions with any friends, family, co-workers, classmates, or service professionals you encounter each day.

If you don't have many opportunities to do that on a given day, here are some other ideas; challenge yourself to:

- Smile while you are talking on the phone to people (notice how it often improves your attitude and the quality of your voice).
- Smile while texting; if you text a lot, you'll get lots of practice!
- Smile while waiting at a traffic light (or the like). Instead of just sitting in the car and staring into space, see if you can hold your smile for the duration of the light. Pay attention to how your face feels. Are your muscles cooperating? Do your lips get dry? If smiling all the way through a traffic light cycle is easy, then build up to smiling the whole time between traffic lights, etc. (In that case, you might rest your face at the traffic lights instead).

You get the idea. Whatever works into your world and routine, find a way to build in some smile practice time.

Naturally you'll want to do some of your practice in the mirror to yourself (and on video) so you can see what your smiles and other expressions look like. You might find you don't need to work so hard to hold a lovely smile if you play with it a bit.

Exercise 7.2: Practice Other Facial Expressions

Remember the value of practicing a variety of positive facial expressions from trying to look neutrally positive to interested and attentive, etc. Pretend you are an actress (some of you no doubt are!) and practice some gently different positive expressions until they are second nature (with and without smiles showing teeth or not).

So using the same ideas from Exercise 7.1, challenge yourself to work on other expressions. Indeed, in some settings it may be better to practice your non-smiling expressions. Here are a few other ideas. Challenge yourself to practice a positive (a little non-tooth smile is included here) expression in:

- A meeting at work. All the way through the meeting pay attention to the expression on your face (in addition to the content of the meeting!). Notice if your face ever goes completely slack. Don't let it. See if whether making eye contact changes the expression on your face.
- A class at school. All the way through the class, practice making eye contact with your teacher and looking interested and attentive. Nod at the right times.

Again, mirror and/or video work is useful because what you think looks positive or interested might come off a bit differently. Sometimes a small adjustment is all it takes. All of this requires *awareness* on your part and starting to build your ability to *feel* your own expressions and facial muscles so that you can improve your ability to control them and use them as an instrument. Don't over-worry about this but have fun with it!

Exercise 7.3: Practice Eye Contact

Re-review Exercises 7.1 and 7.2 for the natural opportunities to practice eye contact at the same time you are practicing your facial expressions.

Remember, if you are extra shy or inexperienced just start small. Challenge yourself to look right into someone's pupil for a second. (Say "one one thousand" or "one Mississippi" in your mind to approximate how long a "second" is.)

Do that with everybody for a week or so then bump it up to looking into their eyes for 2 seconds (one Mississippi, two Mississippi) before you look away. Work on that for a week and then move up to three seconds and so on.

You can also tell yourself "I'll look the person in the eye the whole time they look me in the eye" or "I'll look at them throughout this interaction" (like at the store, or the coffee shop, or whatever). Look at the clerks as people that you want to get to know (or as "friends" already) and that will help you look them in the eye.

To practice looking at a panel of people, you can do that with people at work, home, or school too. Or just sitting out at a coffee shop. Look at one person for a couple seconds and smile, then smoothly move your eyes to another. (Even if they aren't looking at *you*, you can do this. Just look at where their eyes would be if they were looking at you. It's just practice. You can practice with stuffed animals or your dogs or whatever.) As you get more confident, actually try to catch people's eyes and put yourself in situations where you can look them in the eye (rather than just looking "at" them in general for practice).

Exercise 7.4: Practice Your Handshake

You may think it is perfect "as is" but go ahead and practice it. Shake your mom's hand. Shake your dad's hand. Shake your spouse's hand. Shake, shake, shake. Get comfortable with how different people do it and how *you* can influence the quality of the handshake by how you offer your hand, etc.

Exercise 7.5: Practice Remembering Names

Even if you don't "need" to do it, start using your daily interactions as opportunities to practice remembering names and putting names with faces. If you do forget someone's name, try the suggestions from the book to gracefully admit it and ask their name again.

Exercise 7.6: Write and Practice an Opening Statement

Review the book on this (and your application materials and goals) and write out a rough draft of a couple potential opening statements. Read them out loud. Time them. What sounds natural? What parts are more important to you?

Re-arrange the statements and try again. Don't "rehearse" it. Right now you are just getting to know what's important to you and what you want to convey to the judges. Don't memorize it. You're just playing. (And you'll find you start remembering things anyway!).

Get something you like to fit in 30 seconds or less. Then ask yourself what you'd cut out if someone said it had to fit in 15 seconds. Then, every week or so, as part of your preparation (so maybe every day or so if you've *just* started to prepare and your pageant is soon!), get it out and read it over. Say it out loud.

Then see, just for fun, what you'd say out loud if you don't have the paper there. Try it at a street light or as you brush your hair. Before you know it you'll have confidence that you can deliver the key points in a variety ways to confidently present yourself and Sleuth in some key information.

"Believe in yourself! Have faith in your abilities! Without a humble but reasonable confidence in your own powers you cannot be successful or happy."
~Norman Vincent Peale

**Here I am in my swimsuit at my
national pageant.**

a pageant is just the beginning...

PAGEANT
*J*nterviewing
SUCCESS

———◆———

Being in the Win Zone

———◆———

Dr. Stephanie Raye, PhD
Former Miss American Petite

Book 8
Being in the Win Zone
Table of Contents

Pageant Interviewing Success:
Being in the Win Zone

We've actually already covered a lot of information that will help you be "in the zone" and knock the questions out of the park. But let's get to into more of the nitty-gritty.

Answer the Question

Generally speaking, you should *always* do your best to actually answer the question the judges asked you. Later in the book series we'll cover a few times where perhaps you cannot, or prefer not to do so, and how to handle that well. But make it your preparation goal to be prepared and willing to handle most any question. So let's spend some time going over some good information to help you answer each question. We'll also analyze examples as a good way to help us see what is more effective and what to avoid. As we do that you'll be learning the *key word* technique so watch how key words come into play.

Listen With Care

One of the biggest "turn-offs" that occurs in an interview is when the contestant does not answer the question! Don't get me wrong, it is okay if you don't know the answer but how you handle that is important so you still give a positive impression. Let's look at why this is important.

When you don't answer the question—when you give a partial or off-base answer, it is hard for the judges to know if:

- You don't know the answer and just don't want to admit it, or…
- You didn't listen carefully enough to answer the question.

Being able to listen with care and handle well what you do know and don't know are important Queenly attributes. A good Queen—and any good citizen, family member or colleague—is valued for listening with care and handling their occasional limitations with grace.

So listen. Really listen. Let the listening show in your face and body language. You don't have to stare them down and keep your face all serious and frowny, but do make eye contact (or at least look at where their eyes would be if they happen to be looking down) and keep your face pleasantly attentive if not in a full smile. The previous book goes into all of this in more detail so review that if need be.

Hearing is a biological event—sounds strike your eardrum and you "hear." Listening is a skill that takes practice…just because you hear and understand the words doesn't mean you take the meaning that was intended. That takes focus, intention, and attention.

To increase your skill in those moments of listening, resist any temptation to be thinking about something other than what that judge is asking. If you listen with care, you will not only hear what they are asking but, interestingly enough, what they are not *directly* asking but still want to know. Remember, a Sleuth is always listening for the "question behind the question."

If you listen with care, you'll increase the likelihood that you'll be able to answer their question and work in important information about yourself that is not only honestly representative of who you are but will also help them see why you are a strong choice to hold the title.

Example of Not Answering the Question

There are *many* examples of this. I could pull from just about any pageant (or any other interview setting), it is so common. That's why if you do better on this count, you'll stand out.

At the Miss USA 2009 pageant in Las Vegas, Nevada. The beautiful Alicia Blanco (Miss Arizona-USA 2009) was asked a question that she did not answer. Maybe I'm positively biased toward the Arizona-girl (being one myself) but had she "nailed" her on-stage interview questions better I think she could have walked away with the crown.

Here's how her final controversial/current event question went (you can probably still find the video online if you'd like to see it).

Judge, Keenan Thompson

"Do you think the US should have universal health care as a right of citizenship? Why or why not?"

Miss Alicia Blanco

"You know I think this is an issue of integrity regardless of which end of the political spectrum that I stand on. I've been raised in a family to know right from wrong. And politics, whether or not you fall in the middle, the left or the right it is an issue of integrity whatever your opinion is and I say that with the utmost conviction."

Let's examine this so we all can learn from it. The question, at its core, was a "yes or no" question (Do you think the U.S. should have universal healthcare as a right of citizenship?) followed up by a request for her reasoning (Why or why not?) and even *that* is telling her it is a *yes* or *no* question.

Yet she doesn't answer yes or no. If she'd prefer not to take a stand then at least she should bring up the issue or address one of the *key words* like "healthcare," "right" or "citizenship." As you go forward, in whatever interview you are in, *listen* for key words as they'll help you make choices about how to respond. (We'll expand on key word components in *Book 12: When You Don't Know the Answer*.)

Instead she rambles around saying things that don't really make sense. "Integrity" to or for what? Why is she bringing up "right from wrong"? What's her family got to do with it? Maybe they *do* relate somehow but she bungles making the connection.

Examples of Answering the Question

Let's try on a few different responses that may have worked better for her so you can prepare yourself to have a more productive response.

Let's say she wanted to work with the key word component of *health care*:

Judge, Keenan Thompson
"Do you think the US should have universal health care as a right of citizenship? Why or why not?"

Healthcare focus:

> "In an ideal world, yes, I do think universal healthcare should be a right because everyone—no matter what side of the political spectrum you stand on—cares about their health or the health of a loved one."

She could stop there or add:

> "That's what I believe. I realize others disagree or worry about how universal healthcare would be paid for, and I'm glad we've got committed people in positions of leadership working on this important issue."

What if Miss Blanco had focused on the key word component of *citizenship*? Then I could imagine her saying something that uses the concept of "balance" that we introduced earlier in the book series. Something like:

Judge, Keenan Thompson
"Do you think the US should have universal health care as a right of citizenship? Why or why not?"

Citizenship focus:

> "Citizenship is a great thing to have…we have people from all over the world coming here hoping to be U.S. citizens like us. Arizona is one of the states where many immigrants, legal and illegal, choose to settle and there are those that worry about whether some are making use of our healthcare system without being citizens. That issue aside, yes, I believe that U.S. citizens should have a right to universal healthcare. The U.S.A. is a leader in thought and innovation…somewhere along the line we'll figure out how to make this possible so we all live healthier lives."

I don't like that answer as well, it is *not* as simple and to the point. But I'm trying to mimic for you what could happen when you are on stage, thinking on your feet!

A Sleuth does her best but it won't always be perfect…you might start your answer in a place that you thought would be good and need to change directions to end on a stronger note. So in the previous example, starting with citizenship was leading to a controversy that didn't need to be explored so it was wise to turn it around.

The alternatives I just gave have to do with "yes" answers. What if she thinks "No" but wants to be tactful in how she says it? Any of these replies could be mixed-and-matched to some degree, certain parts would work well with a "yes" *or* a "no" answer.

But let's try a "No" answer, just for the practice.

Judge, Keenan Thompson

"Do you think the US should have universal health care as a right of citizenship? Why or why not?"

"No" focus:

> "This in an issue that is very complicated and I'm not sure where I stand, but my initial feeling is that "no," universal healthcare should not be a right. It would be a nice privilege but a "right" may be too strong a word. I think if it were as easy as saying "yes" we'd have done it by now."

What if she does not *want* to say "yes" or "no" even if that is what the question calls for? It would appear that her original response was intending to avoid taking a stand. That's fine, but she just didn't do it well. Let's see how else it could have been handled:

Judge, Keenan Thompson

"Do you think the US should have universal health care as a right of citizenship? Why or why not?"

Avoiding a stand focus:

> "This is a complex issue that I'd like to learn more about. On the one hand, I think everyone should have a right to healthcare—if you don't have your health what do you have? On the other hand, I know it has to be paid for somehow and there are disagreements on that. If I'm selected Miss USA, in addition to the fun and traditional duties that come with the title, I'll be sure to challenge myself to look into this further, especially as I interact with delegates from other countries as I believe other countries *do* have universal healthcare and maybe we can learn something from comparing our U.S. system to theirs."

Note how this answer:

- Admits the limits of her knowledge
- Shows initiative by saying she wants to learn more
- Demonstrates appreciation for two sides of the issue
- Outlines a simple starting place to learn more
- Sleuths in a suggestion of making smart use of the title

You may be thinking "Oh, it's easy to say what you'd do *after* the fact. Anyone can be a 'Monday morning quarterback' and maybe you'd not have done any better if you'd been in her shoes."

That's true. But here's the thing...I *have* been in a version of her shoes. I didn't get that question, of course, but I know what it is like to compete on a national stage and feel pressure. And, sure, *anyone* (including me) may have fumbled the ball and bungled away the opportunity the question offered her (as I've shown she did).

I'm certainly not perfect but I would probably be less likely to bungle it because of pre-pageant preparation for interview. And *you* probably will *not* either because you are starting to prepare and *think* in a way that will help you *see* the opportunities and *know* how to better handle them.

But what if you have trouble with the question? Or, what if you are worried that your answer is somehow "wrong?" Well, we've covered already that there really is no "right" or "wrong" if you express yourself well and diplomatically. And later we'll have a whole book on handling tough questions that you don't know the answer to (*Book 12: When You Don't Know the Answer*). Keep reading.

To Repeat (The Question) or Not to Repeat?

Don't Repeat the Question

Other experts may disagree. They may say that repeating the question is a good way to buy time to think. To me, it looks more like you are wasting time with filler, stuffing, padding, fluff. None of those words are Queenly. It is there if you are really in a bind but it is best to avoid it.

Now, let me be clear and make a distinction: consciously choosing to repeat part of a question to indicate to the judges which part of a long question you are focusing on is one thing. That can work nicely. As can using a part of the question to lead into what you will say as a "tag." That's different than repeating word-for-word much of the question—that can be just a yawn. Boring. Especially if it is a long question.

We may all repeat something once in awhile but that's different than over-relying on repetition as a strategy. Besides, a good interview is more like a conversation and how often do you repeat the question when you are having a conversation with a friend, co-worker, or classmate? Not very often, if ever.

Think Before You Speak

If you need time to think then—here's an idea—take time to think! Actually, pause for a moment and think. Not half-thinking and half-repeating back the question. Listen, pause for a few seconds as you think—maybe take a subtle deep breath while you do—then answer.

And, seriously, you may want to think before you speak even if you do *know* the answer to the question. A moment's thought may allow you to put your answer together in a better way, sleuthing in a bit more information to help them realize you're the best fit for the title.

Pause

A key word here is "pause" which means to stop talking. Don't fill your mind, or the room, with odd little sounds that you may not even know you make. In *Book 3: Personal Characteristics* we talked about how we sometimes mindlessly make sounds or use "filler words" so review that and work to overcome those habits.

And what about a "few seconds?" You may be thinking "that's not enough time…I'd get more time to think if I repeated the question." But a few seconds can feel like a *long* time if you are not busying part of your brain by repeating a question. When you are focused a few seconds is probably enough. Play with it and you'll see. It may seem too long!

And I'll mention one more benefit to pausing: you'll be sure the judge is done asking the question. It can be a bit annoying when the contestant is so eager to answer that they start to talk before the judge has finished. That's not good for two reasons. One reason is because it is like interrupting someone, which is generally considered poor manners. And, two, the contestant may not really know where the judge was going with the question so might answer something different; tempting the judge to say "Well, I was going to ask…" or just ignore her ill-directed answer. Either way, it isn't a plus for the contestant.

In the end, just remember that in an interview a judge will sometimes pause for a second to take a breath, think of how to phrase or rephrase something, etc. While you don't want to wait *too* long (awkward pauses are no one's friend), you do want to wait a heartbeat and watch for body language to see that the question is complete. Of course this sort of awareness is helpful in all conversations!

Breathe

And "subtle deep breath" means gentle and unobtrusive. In other words, don't take a loud deep breath that ends in a loud exhale and where your shoulders or chest go up and down too much. Just breathe naturally. It does not have to be perfectly invisible but it should not be distracting to watch you take a breath. But whatever you do, *breathe*. It is highly recommended! Holding your breath isn't good for your mind or body.

The good news is that if you use the tips on interviewing offered to you here you probably won't even be tempted to repeat the question because you'll be feeling more confident and be getting better at interviewing. You can do it!

Time

If you really get in a bind or feel like you are taking too much time thinking, you can always say "Hmmm...let me think on that for a second."

But, remember, you don't want to waste time thinking up a sub-standard answer about something you know nothing about. Only ask for a little time if you really are on the edge of pulling together a meaningful response. If you just don't know the answer or are too unfamiliar with the topic, it may be better to try one of the other responses or move on. Let's learn about those....

Paraphrasing

The only time I think someone should repeat a question is when they are *not* really repeating it but are paraphrasing it. There's a difference. Repeating is saying it back the same way, pretty much word-for-word. Again, that usually just comes off as a space-filler, time-waster (in my professional opinion).

In contrast, paraphrasing means that you've taken it in, thought about it, but aren't sure you understand something so you want to say it back in your own words to be sure you have it. So let's say the judge asks a somewhat scattered, rambling question, something like:

Judge
"The wars are in the media a lot lately, what do you think about our troops overseas and the mental health crisis and what the government should or shouldn't do there or here, then or later, and about the media coverage?"

Yikes! That question is all over the place. Some contestants can turn that into clarity, others will prefer to ask for a rephrase (we'll discuss this shortly), others may prefer to paraphrase the question to see if they captured the crux of what the judge was asking. Here's one potential paraphrase of that question:

> ### *Contestant*
> "Let me see if I can paraphrase that to be sure I understand what you mean. You're asking me about what the government should do about the mental health of the troops and what role the media plays? Is that the question?"

The judge could then reply with, for example, "No, I was really after…." And explain what he meant more clearly. Or the judge might say "Yes, that's it and you said it so much better than I did!" as you've shown your skill in listening, sorting out information, and getting to the heart of the matter.

Paraphrasing is a skill and takes a little time and practice. There's an exercise at the end of the book you might want to try. Trust you can build this skill into your life with relative ease. Still, let's say you aren't sure you want to try it in a given situation, then there are other response options that will arise as we move on.

Optimize Your Answers— Length and Content

Content of your responses is important. Much of this book series is aimed at supporting you in being on-target with your content. Length is something that relates to both content and delivery.

Two keys to remember about length and/or content is that:

- There is no "one size fits all" formula, and…
- The interview should generally feel like a conversation.

Some folks feel safer with formulas so if it makes you more comfortable to tell yourself that *every* response should be, say, 3 to 5 sentences, then go ahead and tell yourself that for awhile to get yourself started. It's a decent general "guideline" but I wouldn't consider it a "rule" as it may not work well in all situations.

Just know that someone more advanced in their interview skills will not artificially stretch out an answer to meet any particular "rule". Instead, a more advanced contestant will be a Sleuth and flex the length of her response with the question and the situation. Just like a contestant's voice should modulate (go up and down) rather than be monotone, it is more natural to have response lengths vary as needed (without ever rambling).

Put yourself in the judges' shoes. A judge or interviewer will notice if you are just fluffing up an answer with "filler" to stretch it out. Don't waste their time or yours doing that too much. You want to get on to questions where you can really shine; not stay on the ones where you feel you must use filler words or lists.

Also, a judge may not mark you down for it if you only do it a couple times, but they'll certainly notice if you rely too heavily on techniques like starting your response with "I like ___ because" and then ending with "And that's why I like ____." Using two sentences like that to bookend your response like that make it sound artificial (and again come off as filler). Just like in a Spelling Bee when we were little we stated the word, spelled it, then stated the word again. It may make sense in a Spelling Bee but it is fake sounding to format responses in that bookend way too often in an interview. (You may actually never need to do it!)

Still on that note, remember that a good interview is usually something like a conversation. So ask yourself if you would you ever start and finish a response to friend with such a rigid structure? If a friend asked you "Why do you like John?" Would you start with "I like John, the new guy at school, because he's cute, he's smart, he's nice…" and then end with "…And that's why I like John." No, you wouldn't say *both* of those sentences as it sounds too stilted. You'd just answer the question.

(As an aside, there are some that don't consider interviews to be "conversational" as they prefer to think of it more formally. Okay, if that describes you then just realize that press secretaries, public relations spokespeople, etc., don't start and end their responses with overly rigid or artificial sentences either. They may start with a good topic sentence and end strong but the ending sentence is rarely, if ever, the same or similar to the one with which they started the response.)

Now you *do* want to look at each question for opportunities to communicate you are a good choice for the title but there are way better ways to do that than answering each question along a rigid formula. You want to have more tools in your interview response toolbox than just one or two ways of responding. With what you are learning about yourself, pageants, and interviewing in this series you'll know how to answer things in natural, professional ways. Read on! We'll explore the extremes (too little and too much) and you'll learn how to find the balance.

It's Not a Race

Don't rush your answers as this isn't a race. Your answers don't need to be one-word answers or super short sentences. Though there may be times when such short answers do the job well, giving very short answers too often may communicate that you are nervous (or even unfriendly). So stay flexible to expanding a little here and there when doing so gives the judges a new appreciation for your depth, understanding, or personality.

You Don't Have All Day

The flip side is that you also don't want to ramble forever or suffer from "drooling words" that stopped adding meaning to your answer 3 sentences ago. Using the strategy of Thinking-Out-Loud-To-Find-Your Way-Into-What-You-Think-Is-An-Answer should be reserved for friends, family, or internal dialogues (talking to yourself in your head).

In a competition or press situation (when news reporters ask you questions), do your thinking in your head then translate that into something that makes sense to a listener. Don't ramble around if you can avoid it. It's boring and it can be confusing to you and to others. If you ramble, your listeners will be wishing you were "done already" so they can move on to something more interesting or more fun.

Lauren Caitlin Upton's much publicized response in the Miss Teen USA 2007 pageant is a fairly straightforward example of someone trying to ramble their way to a response. She's a beautiful and smart woman so I bet if she'd stopped to think for a second (instead of trying to think out loud to an answer), she'd probably had done much better. If you are "into" pageants, you've probably heard about or seen her response on video. Poor dear, the media was tough on her. But she did what a good pageant girl should do and bounced back well.

Hitting the Sweet Spot

If you've played certain sports, you know the concept of the "sweet spot." For instance, in tennis you can hit the ball with the racket in any number of places but when you hit it with the sweet spot, your performance is usually more powerful, your aim more on target, and your movement more graceful and elegant.

It can be the same with any one-interview response (and in how you feel about your overall interview). In the pageant world the length and content sweet spot is about two things:

- Answering the question they ask clearly and on-target *while*...
- Allowing them to get to know you a bit—your personality, knowledge, diplomacy, and fit for the title by what you weave into your answers.

If you answer *too* briefly, you'll miss that opportunity. If you go on and on and on—with either filler or trying to fit too much in any one answer—they'll stop paying attention and you'll lose the benefit of whatever you did right. Worse, they may think you are insensitive to when "enough is enough" on a topic or that you are trying to fill time (to avoid other questions).

Nervousness Versus Preparation

The funny thing is that being nervous can cause folks to do either, to be too brief or too lengthy (or both at different times in the same interview). That is, that sometimes when people are nervous, they clip their answers short—they just want to get through this and be done! Other times, nerves may lead them to go on and on, meandering around hoping they'll say something brilliant or funny.

Again, preparation is key—as preparation and practice reduce nerves immensely—but there are also other things you can do to reduce nerves and build confidence. (See other sections of this book series on "nerves" and stage fright. If you would benefit from more than that, check my website for other potential offerings.)

Use Good Judgment

But, whether you are nervous or not, the keys are balance and using good judgment about the length of your interview time. If your interview is very brief, you may want to keep your answers a little shorter so you can cover a few more questions. If your interview is longer, you can expand on your answers a bit more.

But length of interview isn't the only factor. If you have nothing to say or add to an answer—if you've answered it and can't add anything of true value or spin it to shine a little light on some other part of your qualifications—then stop talking. Smile. Make eye contact with another judge or two and get your next question. You don't have to say a paragraph in response to every question. Watch for the right opportunities. Be a Sleuth.

Time Considerations

As I've mentioned in various ways throughout, use your time wisely. Don't spend a lot of time on a dead-end or a low-value question (something that won't get you much for the effort you put in). Use your head and trust your gut on what to pursue (and how) versus what to gracefully let slide.

Ending the Question

In General

If you are following the tips in this book you will, with a little practice, feel comfortable with knowing when you've said enough. You may feel that way already. If you do, then remember that when you are done speaking, make eye contact with the judge who asked the question, smile, and sometimes you might give a little nod to help signify you're done.

In terms of your voice, as we discussed in a previous book, be sure your volume doesn't dwindle off to nothing at the end of a response. End strong, not fading away. Some folks will even increase their volume just a tad at the end of their response.

Remember that volume is just part of one's voice. So, matters of volume aside, you may find that sometimes your tone or the pitch of your voice may go up or down at the end of response as a way to emphasize. For example, think about when, say, a teacher or parent is telling you what to do and they sound just a bit firmer at the end of the sentence like "That's it. Don't even *try* to talk back to me." (It doesn't have to be angry but thinking of an example like that helps illustrate the point!)

That "done" sound is often because of the inflection at the end. If it goes down a bit it sounds like "this is final." If it goes up a bit, it can sound that way as well, sometimes, but it is trickier to accomplish. Why? Because when people inflect up at the end of the sentence it often comes off sounding like a question instead. So keep your voice tone even at the end or go down a bit to sound like "that's it for me on that." Whatever you do, don't sound like you are asking a question unless you really are.

In Terms of Content and Length

If you don't know when you've said enough yet, don't worry, you'll get there. You can and will learn how and when to end your responses. And when you do, you'll know how to end strong. Whether you think you've "got it" or are still working on "how much is enough" then know that…

This is one of those times when practicing out loud is invaluable. If you *hear* yourself rambling, you're more likely to realize it doesn't reflect on you well and start to notice it more readily. You'll start to build a sense of when you are going on too long which leads to a sense of when to stop.

Beyond practicing out loud by yourself, it will be easier to notice if you record yourself or work with a partner so you really *can* hear (or be told) when you are going on too long. I've had to tell people many times, as kindly as I can, "Stop now, you're rambling."

There could be several reasons a person might ramble, here are a few…see if any of these fit:

- You didn't briefly pause to think before beginning to speak.
- You aren't confident that you've answered the question.
- You are waiting for some signal from the interviewer that you've said enough.

Material covered elsewhere in this series will help you a lot with you taking a second to think, composing a decent response, and feeling confident that you've handle the question as best you can. With that understanding and experience, it will come more naturally to know when to stop talking.

But what about that last point? What about if you may—without even realizing it!—be waiting for some word or look from the judge(s) that signals you that you've answered it. Or, worse, that you haven't but that they are bored so it is time to move on. *Most* of communication is non-verbal so such subtle signals can and do happen sometimes.

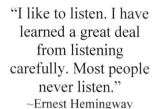

"I like to listen. I have learned a great deal from listening carefully. Most people never listen."

~Ernest Hemingway

If you think you may be doing that (even on accident), just tell yourself right now to notice it, break the habit, and stop waiting for permission to stop talking. *You* can decide when to do it.

Be sensitive to subtle signals you get, of course, but you usually don't want to wait until their eyes are glazing over.

On the flip side, as we've discussed, having too many super short answers isn't conversational or helpful to you or the judges either. They need information to get to know you (not filler, as that's not about you). Practicing out loud will also help you notice if you are too rushed or not offering enough of yourself.

Knowing ways to build answer content will help you find the balance between saying too much and too little. Remember the image and feeling of being on high heels? It takes balance, right? That's what you need in your interview.

Remember the children's story of "Goldilocks and the Three Bears?" Everything Goldilocks encountered when she went into the Bears' house was in sets of three. Usually whatever it was (chairs, porridge, beds) there was one too big, one too little, and one was "just right." Aim for "just right."

There are ways to help you find that balance. Let's move on to the next book and explore some of them.

Review

Let's review some key points in regard to "being in the zone:"

- Do your best to answer the question. That involves being generally well prepared, yes, but it also involves *listening* with care.

- You can learn to analyze responses—as we did with examples of responses that did stronger and weaker jobs of answering the question. You can still "be yourself" and answer "yes," "no," or give a "mixed" response while still answering the question!

- Remember the value of listening for key words as a way to help you choose how to respond.

- Avoid repeating the question. We went over a few basic tools to help you not "need" to repeat the question. We introduced the concept of paraphrasing and how that can be helpful.

- Aim to hit the "sweet spot" in terms of balancing length and content to optimize your answers and the time you have available.

- Nervousness tends to decrease with preparation. So do lots of other unflattering behaviors and patterns. So prepare as best you can, using ideas in this book, and you'll be better off than if you hadn't.
- End your responses well; don't dwindle off or sound like you are asking a question when you aren't.

Exercise 8.1: Practice Listening and Paraphrasing

Pick one or two conversations per day and try out your paraphrasing skills. Even when you *think* you listened carefully and understand what was said, go ahead and say "Do you mind if say that back to you to be sure I understand?" or "I'd like to be sure I've got it; do you mind if I paraphrase that?" or "If I understood you correctly, what you said was…"

However you start follow it with briefly, in your own words, saying what you think they said and ask if that was right. You may be surprised to find out sometimes that you were not right. Or, that you were right, however they meant to say something else! (You saying it your own way back to them may help them see where they didn't communicate as clearly as they'd thought.) Paraphrasing is a good thing for both people in the conversation as they usually want to be understood just as much as you want to understand them.

Exercise 8.2: Listen for Key Words

Whether you are at work, at school, at home, or from media sources, start listening for and identifying the key words in what people are saying. It sounds simple and generally is once you make yourself aware. Whether or not you find it easy or hard to do, just try it. If you do so a little now will help make it easier to do under the "stress" of an interview situation.

As with most of the exercises in this book series, just set a goal or make a game of how often or how long you will engage in this quick exercise. Most of the exercises don't take long…we just have to "do it" or plan it in somewhere.

Exercise 8.3: Practice How You End Responses

Say a short sentence out loud to yourself and play with different ways to make the end sound. Here I'll give you one with which to work…imagine you snowboard for a hobby and a judge asked you about it. You told him how you started, why you like it, and ended with this sentence:

"Everyone should try snowboarding once in their life."

Try saying that at least three ways where it sounds the same for most of it but you change the ending to sound like you are uncertain (like you aren't sure if you mean what you say, ending it almost like it is a question), are done answering with confidence, or are done but not confident. Now, just for fun, try sounding bored or indifferent, excited, bossy, neutral to positive (but not overly excited).

Start noticing how people speak and end their sentences. Start noticing how you do too! Then bring those observations into your awareness as you practice your pageant interview questions out loud.

Exercise 8.4: Self-Assess—Are You a Rambler or Too Brief?

Back in *Book 3: Personal Characteristics* we talked about qualities of the voice and things to avoid. You may want to review that and notice Exercise 3.1 where you were invited to self-assess your voice.

Do that again now but instead of focusing "just" on the voice, tape or video record yourself in a question & answer session (preferably with a friend playing the role of a judge). *Notice* if you tend to ramble on too much or if you tend to not say enough. Be sure to also catch yourself doing things right as I'm sure you do *many* or most things right...practicing just lets us get better regardless of our current level.

If taping is a trouble, you can start by getting the feedback of someone you trust who also will have a good sense about these things and be "honest" with you about whether you need to expand or reduce an answer. Remember that opinions differ but learn whatever you can from the situation you are in or person you are with, keep practicing, and before long you'll build your own sense of when enough is enough.

If you determine you have some room for improvement in this area, set about working on it. Set small goals and monitor your progress. Seek out the advice and support of professionals if that would help you.

"Bad human communication leaves us less room to grow."
~Rowan D. Williams

Here I am as the official Miss American Petite.

a pageant is just the beginning...

PAGEANT *Interviewing* SUCCESS

Answering Personal Questions

Dr. Stephanie Raye, PhD

Former Miss American Petite

Book 9
Answering Personal Questions
Table of Contents

Pageant Interviewing Success:
Answering Personal Questions

As you will recall from *Book 1: Build a Strong Foundation*, we talked about the five main categories of questions. One of those categories is "Personal" questions and as they come up to some degree in all pageants at all levels, we'll spend a whole book expanding on them. Let's start with some general things to keep in mind as you approach personal questions, then we'll expand on types of questions in more detail.

Personal questions are so wide-ranging they can include most anything. Truly, if you think about it, *all* questions are personal questions because they are asking *you* to answer! There are few areas from which the personal questions might arise, and a few things to keep in mind as you answer any kind of question.

"So when you are listening to somebody, completely, attentively, then you are listening not only to the words, but also to the feeling of what is being conveyed, to the whole of it, not part of it."
~Jiddu Krishnamurti

From Your Application Materials

We've already established that you want to know what's on your application paperwork and that you'd be wise and Sleuth-like to be able to expand on them in a meaningful way and anticipate some directions your interview might go. Nothing should catch you off guard there.

Anything in the paperwork should be well thought through so that the judges could ask you about most anything there (for example, your hobbies, service, family, or intended studies or career, etc.) and you'd be able to say something intelligent about it. Better yet, you'd be able to leverage—a form of sleuthing!—what you say about it into helping them see your personality or good fit for the title.

And remember that in some pageant systems (like Mrs. International and other divisions), the judges may get your material a month in advance and be encouraged to look up your websites and blogs. So the nature of "paperwork" has changed and often includes a "digital" component on the web. (Whatever it is, you'll handle it. You'll be a Sleuth and know what the pageant wants.)

Not From Your Application Materials

So we know the judges might ask you anything from your paperwork. But the judges might *also* ask random personal question that are *not* on the paperwork. They might ask you something that *does* catch you off guard. That's okay. You'll listen, pause briefly to think, then answer. And keep the following in mind…

It's Not Personal, It's Business

Never take a question "personally" in the sense that you think they are trying to make it hard on *you*—just smile and use some of what you've learned about interviewing skills to handle it with grace.

They (Typically) Only Know What You Tell Them

Remember, the judges cannot read minds so they only know what you tell them. Even if it is a "personal question" you don't have to give the *most* personal information or the most complete answer if it is embarrassing or hard for you. They are just trying to get to know you and, at the same time, see how you handle a variety of questions.

I'd generally recommend against volunteering information about anything illegal you may have done on accident or on purpose (unless you are legally bound to by law or by request of the pageant application or contract). Don't break any rules or laws but don't hang out your "dirty laundry" unless you must. And if you must, be sure to have positives you've learned from it.

Similarly, I recommend against bringing up on your own anything that is particularly controversial or questionable. Why? Because you *don't* want questions on that sort of thing, if it can be avoided. Just don't bring it up. If they do, handle it then.

Exception! If your platform or passion has to do with something controversial then:

- The judges already know about it from your paperwork and...
- You are prepared to talk about it so it is something you can bring up, as appropriate.

For instance, I wouldn't bring up that my friend committed suicide unless the tragedy had changed me for the better in some relevant-to-the-pageant way like that I now volunteer for a crisis line, or the like.

Unless you are trying to make a *personal* connection for something related to your *platform* (assuming your pageant requires one), it will not help the judges bond with you to hear you talk about what a troubled teen you were (or are), that you have a problem with speeding, or spending yourself into incredible debt, etc. None of that reflects well on you unless you've learned your lesson and improved or turned the "bad" into "good" through volunteering or whatever.

Even then—even when you've made the best of a bad situation—the judges may not need to hear about it (certainly not the whole history) in too much detail. Just share enough to make that personal connection and tell the key part of the story or relate a good "take home" point that you learned. Remember, be a Sleuth. If it isn't relevant, don't bring it up (unless asked directly and then be sure to answer wisely.)

And if the judges ask you about your romantic relationship (current or past), you can find something to say that you are willing to share that does not reflect poorly on you or the other person. Be selective. Be discreet. People will generally assume you have good morals and make good decisions unless you say something that tells them otherwise.

In the end, you *choose* what to say, so choose wisely. Sensitivity and relevance are key. As an extreme example, when you lost (or plan to lose) your virginity is not relevant unless your platform is about abstinence (even then such personal information is not necessary to volunteer). Along those same lines, how many partners you've had (or passed by) is not relevant.

You don't want them to think (or say!) "Whoa! That's too much information we didn't need know." Choose to talk about what a Queen would talk about. What would a titleholder say?

Leave the Drama at the Door

And steer away from dramatic topics unless it is relevant to your volunteer work, a theme of the pageant, or your platform. Even then, don't be overly dramatic in your delivery. Watch your language and the images you paint. Keep it G-rated. PG at the very most. (For those in other cultures, "G" is a movie rating meaning that it is appropriate for a "general audience" and "PG" means "Parental Guidance is Suggested.")

In a pageant interview, no one needs graphic descriptions to understand even difficult situations. Use sensitive language to convey your meaning. Even if your platform deals with some really tough stuff, you want to learn to talk about it in a way that will let people learn, understand, and support your cause without it being so uncomfortable for them they stop listening. If they get really interested, they can ask for more "sensitive" material as they are ready for it.

Your Web Presence

As I mentioned in the last sub-section title "They (typically) only know what you tell them." I say "typically" because…

These days, with the Internet, you never know what someone may know about your life. Or at least what they may *think* they know, as not everything written on the web or reported in television, radio, or news reports is *true*.

Be prepared for "random" questions to generate from something someone ran across about you on the web or in the media. Some judges have your application paperwork well in advance and they may take the time to get to know you better by "Googling" you or otherwise searching your name on the internet. What would they find on you? Will they be feeling positive about who they are about to meet?

And it is also possible that one or more of the judges just happened to run across information on you because a lot of you are "go-getters" who may have had stories done on you in various newspapers, etc. that show up on the web. (And they may have heard of you just through word of mouth as well.) So what would community members, other contestants, pageant directors, and others say about you? In person? Online? Would they be happy to have you show up and speak at an event? Be a role model for their little kids?

Maybe they see something from a preliminary pageant or from your volunteer work or around your family business (if there is one) or maybe you have "friends" in common, etc. Don't *over* worry about this, but also don't be surprised if anything you've ever done comes up in one way or another.

Social Networking Sites

You can't always control the media but you can control *yourself*.

So be careful in your words and deeds—just as a real Queen would be—and be extra careful for what you put on websites and social networks, in emails, etc. I'm not saying don't be social, but do be thoughtful with what you put on your social networking pages. (There are so many now and they come and go, like MySpace, Facebook, LinkedIn, Twitter, Instagram, etc.) Be thoughtful about what you share about yourself and be careful and kind in regard to what you say about others. "Just say no" to getting immersed in any negative message boards, or the like.

Common Sense

It just makes sense to reduce complications for ourselves when we can, yes? So consider that if you are serious about pageants and scholarship or achievement competitions—or maybe running for public office someday!—think through your choices and actions. What you do now can ripple into your future—resist the urge to allow friends or family to take pictures of you in compromising situations as they may wind up on the web. Remember, judges and others come from widely different age-ranges and backgrounds, you never know what might "offend" someone so err on the side of caution.

Even employers hiring for "ordinary" jobs (as opposed to being a pageant titleholder which is *extra*ordinary) may take time to see what you display on the web. I know one of my colleagues, also a professor, who goes to people's social networking pages as part of a lesson in class. Sometimes they feel angry, surprised or embarrassed to have their professor or classmates see their page but if they do, shouldn't they realize that they probably wouldn't want their *employer* or *pageant* to see it either? Maybe they wouldn't be impressed. (And don't think that they won't see it just because you've marked your page "private"—that's not 100% reliable.)

So if in doubt, take the time to start taking down unflattering information and photos about yourself from any pages you control. It can take a long time to get things fully off the web (some say you can never be sure it is really, fully gone). So if this sounds like something you'd benefit from doing, start sooner rather than later on cleaning up your web presence.

Of course, it is better to not even be engaged in "compromising situations." What is a compromising situation? Well, for instance, if you are underage and are at a party where people are drinking then take care. Maybe someone has a photo of you drinking something—

even if it was water, no one can tell that it is water in a "party girl" photo. Even if you've been following the rules innocent photos can be totally misunderstood or misperceived (again, just because you are at a party where people were drinking doesn't mean *you* were).

But maybe you did make a mistake or have a lapse in judgment that you regret. That happens. Many of us have made some not-so-good choices at some point in our lives. Okay, just learn from it. And maybe build your platform on it if it really changed your life. (That said, really think it through before you jump to decisions on your platform. Use *Book 2: How to Prepare* for help on deciding your platform, if you need or want one.)

In the end, a prepared contestant will have an idea of what's "out there on the web" on her and be prepared to answer spin-off questions from that and aspects of her past. Anything like this you can be reasonably prepared for (use my forthcoming Essential Pageant Interview Playbook if you need more guidance on this, on platforms, and more.)

Be Nice and Respectful

We've talked about using good sense in what you put up on social networking sites about yourself. But you may also find yourself on other people's sites or a variety of message boards out there. So the idea here is simple:

- Conduct yourself as a professional.
- Act like a benevolent Queen.
- In short: Play nice with others!

Even if you are upset or someone was unkind to you, take the high road. That is, don't go to a message board and bash anyone as a way to cope with your hurt feelings or jealousy. Really, it is not a particularly classy thing to do whether you are supposedly protected by an anonymous "screen name" or "handle" or whatever.

For instance, you can say "I feel rotten I didn't win. I'm worried my ___ is what's holding me back. Any advice!?" or "I'm so excited that I did win and I think it was because of my ___. Thanks to ____ for helping me with that." Such statements are about *you*.

But when you start saying what you think about *others*, keep it especially diplomatic. Remember to practice the skills this book talks about for *interview* in your *writing* too! Show balance and be sensitive to others. And avoid stating opinions as facts. There *is* a difference. Not everything we think is true. And even though we all have a right to our own opinion, it doesn't mean we need to try to influence others to have negative opinions.

So do some soul-searching and if you know that you are out there bashing people, ask yourself why you do that. And then ask yourself to stop. Tell yourself that there are healthier ways to express yourself and connect with people. Remember, at the start of this book series we talked about Sleuths, Bunglers, and Smugglers. Our emphasis has been how to be a Sleuth and avoid being an innocent Bungler. But a Smuggler is not "innocent" but carelessly or intentionally malicious or sneaky. Don't let that be you. Ever. It is totally *un*-Queenly.

It Matters

Now I know online communities are popular and a great resource for us all so I'm not saying don't go to them or don't participate. I'm just saying to use your head and know that what you put up there could come back to bite you in any number or unexpected ways. (Even if it doesn't it still isn't a happy habit.) And I'm saying to use your heart and not be unkind to people or talk trash about others. It is hurtful and entirely unnecessary.

If we want to learn from each other and analyze someone or their performance, we need to do it a respectful, constructive way that if they read it themselves they would feel like the good was seen as much as the bad. And when the "bad" is seen, it is framed in a way that is up-building and helpful, not destructive or hurtful.

Remember, we all have different strengths, levels of experience, etc. What seems silly or not-so-good to you may have been someone else's best effort! Let's respect that. Imagine how you'd feel if people said unkind things about you and there it was posted on the internet "forever." (Okay, everybody is different so *some* of you may have thicker skin than others and not care. Some folks can let things just bounce off them more easily than others. But most people would care, so put yourself in their shoes to see if imagining it happening to you doesn't help you see why this matters.)

Anyway, sites and boards change so quickly it can be hard to keep up with them. But you should always try to stick to those that make an attempt to stay positive, use neutral moderators, etc.

Just remember to be true to your *best* self (not the petty, hurt, or hurtful self that sneaks up on us sometimes!) and if a board doesn't feel right, don't join it.

Shine Your Best

Remember, *be* the Queen in what you do and how you treat people and that will ultimately come back to reflect well on you. If your attitude or approach to life is too much "me, me, me" and you feel like the way to build yourself up is to tear down others that is *not* the sort of thing we like to see in pageantry as it reflects poorly on us all.

There are some unpleasant (and largely inaccurate) stereotypes about pageant contestants because of a few vocal, overly dramatic examples played up on television reality shows. Some of these shows portray pageant girls as vain, unkind, shallow, stupid, selfish, and the like. Chances are they aren't *all* that bad but the magic of editing can drop out all the times the person was nice. But, of course, the fact that they have any footage of un-gracious behavior does say something.

We are all human and have our less-than-friendly, less-than-generous moments. (Let's hope they are the exception rather than the rule, eh?!) And, naturally, in any activity, sport, hobby, job, profession, etc., there will be a *range* of people in terms of skill, commitment, personality, motivations, etc. That's okay. Some will be more dramatic (in positive or negative ways) than others—that keeps things fun and interesting…but we *all* benefit if we keep our interactions positive. Each time we are gracious instead of selfish, assume the best about people (instead of the worst), etc. we help break down any negative stereotypes out there.

So, yes, pageants do have a component of "me" in them (as it is *you* that is being judged) but it shouldn't be at the expense of kindness, courtesy, and professionalism. So if you have something you feel compelled to say out loud at a pageant or to share on a message board or social network, keep it constructive and positive.

Take Control of Your Web-Self

So we've talked about what might show up about you from any number of sources. And we've talked about playing nice with others. But you can do more than "be careful" and take care with what you say in social network sites, etc.

But a Sleuth would take control of her web presence in a bigger way. One great way to do that is to get your own domain name and set up your own website. Building your own website doesn't have to be expensive—you can probably do it for less than most anything else you are doing as a part of your pageant experience.

Then you can tell people about your accomplishments, your platform, your activities, and perhaps collect donations for charities or for your pageant fees. Similarly, it could be a place to mention your sponsors. Certain pageants will want to see all this! So be sure your color themes, etc., matches your hard-copy paperwork color schemes. (Think about these things if you are competing in a pageant that invites or requires something different than plain text paperwork.)

It doesn't have to be hard to do. I assign building a website to my students for some of the university courses I teach (and these are not technical type courses) and they manage it in not much time at all so you can too. It doesn't have to be fancy or complicated. Simple and straightforward can get the same job done.

If you are of the "younger" generation you may have grown up with a computer in your hands and find the whole idea easy to imagine. If you didn't (or are not of the "younger" generation) that's okay! You've probably brought yourself up to speed and can do this (my students' ages vary and they all manage) or have someone in your life who can do it (or you can pay someone to do it).

Take a look online for other sources relating to website hosting, getting domain names, etc. As long as you are doing it properly and safely, it's a great idea to boost your web presence!

But whether or not you build a simple website for yourself, the key is to be a Sleuth about what's out there on you and be prepared for interview questions about it.

One more thing: If you happen to be competing in more than one pageant, be sure to change your webpage to reflect the competition you are aiming for *now* and the title you hold now, as appropriate to the situation. Stay on top of such details so that you convey a consistent, professional image. (You want to make a favorable impression on the judges, sponsors, the public, etc.)

Types of Personal Questions

We've discussed that personal questions are about you and your life and they may come from anywhere but would usually generate from your application materials (your fact sheet, bio, resume, etc.). Let's go into "personal questions" in more depth. And you'll see toward the end of the book how what seems like strictly a personal question can actually reflect on other women or the country you represent.

Personal questions can be just about anything but tend to fall along the lines of:

- School and Studies
- Career or Community Services
- Hobbies and Activities
- Platform and Passions
- Family and Relationships
- Age or Division related questions

We'll cover more on Age/Division related questions later (and work some examples in along the way). But let's stay more general for right now. Personal questions can be either:

- "Classic"
- Spin-off
- Demonstration
- Comparative
- Age or division

Classic Pageant Questions

These are the sort of question that come up very often—in one form or another. Examples of "classic" questions that any one may get would be:

- "Tell us about yourself."
- "What three words best describe you?"
- "Tell us about your platform/career."
- "What are you studying in school?"
- "What would your friends say is your biggest weakness?"

"Your only obligation in any lifetime is to be true to yourself."
~Richard Bach

Spin-Off Questions

There also could be deeper personal questions that *spin-off* of basic information that get more at *why* you do something or *how* you do it. Questions like these get to know you more (and more quickly) than just asking you to tell about *what* you do or brief questions to describe yourself.

We covered some of these in *Book 4: Question Types* so you can review more about this there. Remember, some examples of "spin-off" questions would be:

- "How did you get started in _____ ?"
- "What does it mean for you to be able to ____ ?"
- "What is your favorite and least favorite thing about _____?"
- "Why are you studying _____?"

Demonstration Questions

Demonstration questions, also introduced in *Book 4: Question Types*, are those that ask you in some way to *show* how serious you are about something you said is important to you. Or, put another way, they want to see how well you "know your stuff."

Examples of "Demonstration" questions might be:

- "You say you are studying broadcast journalism to be a television reporter, pretend we're the camera and give us a 30 second report on the pageant."
- "You say you are studying vocal performance, give us a few bars of your favorite song."
- "Give us an example of when you ____ ."

Comparative Questions,
With Response Examples

Comparative questions, as the name implies, ask you to make comparisons though it may not be obvious. The judges probably won't use the word "compare" in the question but that is still at the root of what they are asking in this type of question.

For instance, perhaps the question implies to compare yourself to other contestants, your pageant to another pageant, or your kids (or spouse) to some ideal or some high standard. The comparison could even be comparing yourself to yourself in some way, like comparing the past to the present or your strengths to your weaknesses.

Often comparative questions are a tempting invitation to be negative about yourself or others. That is a temptation that is best avoided. Handled well, however, comparative questions can highlight your diplomacy and good fit for the title.

Here are some examples of Comparative questions with what they are essentially asking you to compare. I also offer you examples of potential Bungler responses (things you *don't* want to say) and Sleuth responses so you can see how to avoid the tempting trap to diminish others. Yes, I've exaggerated some of the Bungler answers to really drive home the point so you'll get the idea of how to avoid being negative (or, if you must, how to be negative more gracefully).

Oh, and while I've give a variety of examples that you can imagine being said equally as well in Teen, Miss, Mrs., and Ms. pageants, just remember that whatever the example is you can pretend it is a Bungler or a Sleuth in your pageant. That is, if I use the word "mom" you can substitute "husband," "daughter," "friend," or whatever and make other imaginary adjustments to imagine how it might sound in your division or category.

Comparing Yourself to Others

Here are a couple examples of how you might be asked to compare yourself to someone else.

Example 1

Judge

"Why should we choose you over the contestant that was just in here?"

Bungler 1

"Her? She's my roommate and I can tell you that you do *not* want to pick her. I mean really…if you only knew!"

Bungler 2

"Because I'm better than the others. Have you seen what some of them are wearing? And a few aren't very pretty, in my opinion."

Bungler 3

"Oh my, seriously? The contestant that was "just" in here?! I know her. Our kids go to the same school and she's on the PTA and I've seen her at the grocery store. Anyway, she's so rude and I don't like how she talks to her kids. You should pick me because I'm a better parent and nicer and would be better on the appearances. You just never know when that lady will go off!"

Sleuth

"If you select me as titleholder, it will be because you see how good a fit my qualities and experience are for the position. I'm sure there are many strong contestants here but what I know about myself is that I have worked hard for this and I would continue to do so as the titleholder. I would make you proud for having chosen me!"

Judge

"What qualities make you better than the other contestants?"

Bungler

"I'm generally smarter than other people. I'm as pretty, if not prettier than the rest. I've shown I'm really committed to the pageant because from the look of their gowns I suspect I spent more on mine."

Sleuth

"Oh there are so many great women here I would hesitate to say I'm "better" than anyone else. But I can say that I do feel well prepared to be the titleholder and am excited and hopeful you will select me. I've spent a lot of time building my public speaking skills, I'm well-informed about my platform, I've got great time management skills to handle all the duties and I really enjoy people—I'd welcome every minute of all the appearances."

Example 2

Judge

"Is there anything you really regret doing or not doing?"
(comparing your past self to present self)

Bungler

"I really regret experimenting with drugs in high school. I actually got caught and have a juvenile record. But I never got hooked and don't experiment with drugs anymore. I don't even drink alcohol that often."

Sleuth 1

"We are human so we all make mistakes! Fortunately, I haven't made any that have been too negative or life changing. There are no skeletons in my closet! So I guess there's nothing I really regret doing. But is there anything I regret *not* doing? Well, I wish I'd gotten involved in volunteer work earlier in my life. I was nervous but when I finally started it really helped me build confidence at the same time I'm helping others. It's a win-win experience I wish I'd started sooner.

Sleuth 2

"I did make a mistake that I regret. You may have noticed that my platform is to build awareness about eating disorders and encourage sufferers to get help. When I was in high school I had an eating disorder and I regret not trusting anyone and getting help with it sooner. Thankfully, I did learn to trust, overcame a lot of obstacles, and now I let that experience help me help others. So, on second thought, maybe I don't regret it for the long run because a lot of good has come out of it!"

Comparing Yourself to an Ideal

Judge

If you could change one thing you did wrong, what would it be?

Bungler 1

I know better than to admit anything I've done wrong. In fact, it drives my husband and family crazy because I always have to be right.

Bungler 2

Oh that's hard. I make so many mistakes and am so moody I'm like a ticking time bomb. I guess I wish I could change one thing that would be making my mom cry the day we checked in for the pageant when I yelled at her for closing my evening gown in the car door. I thought it was ruined! But it was okay and I shouldn't have yelled at her anyway.

Sleuth

Hmmm…I try not to do wrong things. I try to be careful and accurate in my tasks and to be sensitive to others. But one thing I did wrong was I got so busy with school, work, and community service that I totally forgot my mom's birthday—which of course I know but I forgot! She was so nice about it but she does *so* much for me I really shouldn't have let that slip. To prevent that sort of thing in the future, I've put everyone's birthdays in my planner right next to my homework assignments, pageant appearances, and everything else—my time management skills have just gotten better because of it.

Comparing Yourself to Yourself

Example 1

Judge

"What's your biggest weakness?"

Bungler

"I'm vain. I am always worried about how I look to the point that I'll be late for appointments because I'll change my clothes so much or keep re-doing my hair or touching up my make-up. But that's okay, right? I mean I'm a pageant girl after all!"

Sleuth

"I try to improve in any areas in which I learn that I'm weak. Right now I'm working on my web skills. With technology changing the way we communicate and do business, I feel like I could stand to understand even more about the web."

Comparing Other People to Ideals

Example 1

Judge

"If you could change one thing about your spouse (or your kids or your parents), what would it be?"

Bungler

"My spouse works too hard. He really could stand to make more time for me and the kids. I know he's working to support us but, wow, if I win this pageant I doubt I'll ever see him between his work schedule and my appearance schedule. Thank goodness the kids are pretty self-sufficient. I guess I raised them right!"

Sleuth

"My husband is great. He works hard to support our dreams as a family. He and the kids are supportive of my pageant goals and are excited about the appearances I've been doing for my local title. If I could change one thing, it'd just be that we would have even more time together. We have regular family time together but who wouldn't want more!?"

Example 2

Judge

"What qualities make for a great husband and does your husband have them?"

Bungler

"A great husband is sensitive, handsome, rich, and smart. My husband was handsome and sensitive when I met him but he's not aging well. I wish he'd take care of himself like I take care of myself! And he's more stubborn than sensitive now. And mom was right, he's not as smart as I thought he was but that's okay. I was young and in love. And I'm smart enough for both of us."

Sleuth

"My husband does have the qualities that make for a great relationship! He's kind, funny, supportive, creative, and dedicated. Those are the qualities that help you through the tough times and make the good times even better. He's a great role model for our kids too as he has a great work ethic but always finds time for the family."

Comparing a Thing to an Ideal

As with any of these examples, you can imagine substituting any number of "things" in the question. You'll still get the idea of how to avoid unnecessary negativity.

Judge

"If you could change one thing about the pageant (or your school), what would it be?"

Example 1: Pageant

Bungler

"Well, I didn't like how much it cost to enter the pageant. If I could change something, it would be that the pageant finds more of its own sponsors so the fees to contestants are lower and we don't have to find so many of our own sponsors."

Sleuth

"I'm not sure I'd change anything about the pageant. Everyone has been great. I guess I just wish it was an extra day or two because I'm having so much fun and the days wouldn't be quite so long! We're all working pretty hard and keeping very busy. We can't wait for the big night!"

Example 2: School

Bungler

"I hate my school. The teachers think they know everything and aren't very good. The cafeteria food is tasteless. And our sports teams lose most of the time. I can't wait until I graduate!"

Sleuth

"School is okay overall and I enjoy learning. But I do know our school could use more computers and art supplies...there never seem to be enough to go around. Hopefully the budget situation will turn around as all areas of learning are important!"

Comparing Two Things

Example 1: Comparing Pageants with Other Activities

Judge

"What are the downsides to being in a pageant?"

Bungler

"Well, having to look perfect all the time isn't always easy. But I manage. And the costumes and other clothes can get expensive, but I don't mind—my parents pay for most of it. Besides, I love to shop."

Sleuth

"Downsides? I'm not sure there are any that are unique to pageants. *Any* activity we participate in, whether sports, hobbies or pageants, takes time, energy, and money. But we wouldn't do it if we didn't love it, right? At least speaking for myself, I enjoy pageants. They are fun and allow me to develop into a better person for both myself and the community."

Example 2: Comparing Winning with Not Winning

Judge
"Are there any drawbacks to winning the title?"

Bungler
"Sure, there are drawbacks to everything. Like I'll probably have to keep dieting for a whole year. I'll probably have to get up early more often than I want to for appearances. I'll probably have to break up with my boyfriend. But, don't worry, I'm willing to do all that."

Sleuth
"None are coming to mind. I mean, I know it is like a job and I want to win the title because I look forward to the kind of work I'd be doing for the next year. I'm sure there could be some surprises but I think I know what I'm signing up for. So maybe the main drawback would be that the year would come to an end!"

You can see from those examples that questions that ask for comparisons can let the judges see you at either your best or your worst. Okay, maybe not as "worst" as some of the Bungler examples I just gave! (I know, some of the Bungler examples were "over the top" but it was a more fun way to make the point. That said, some contestants do say things like that—one of the reasons this book (and practice!) can be such a help.)

But even if you aren't the sort to bungle that blatantly or be that insensitive or arrogant, *do* aim to approach comparative questions with the intention to find something neutral to positive to say. Even if you choose to share something negative find a positive way to frame it. A good frame can make any picture look better.

Age/Division Questions

Let's expand on that last general kind of personal questions (which encompass the other kinds). In this case, "division" means roughly which "type" of pageant in terms of age and/or marital status. So teen and junior contestants will likely get some questions that differ from the type that a Miss, Ms., or Mrs. contestant may get.

Across division, personal questions will occur but the *focus* of them will shift according to what makes sense for that group. For instance:

Teen/Junior

Younger contestants will likely get more "classic" and "spin-off" questions. Given the age level, the questions could center around school in general—what they like least and most about it, various subjects in school, their teachers, etc. They may get questions about how they get along with their friends at school, parents or siblings (brothers and sisters).

The questions, especially in preliminary pageants, might stay "easier" in that they may be more informational (facts) rather than "analytical" (designed to show more advance thinking skills). In other words, it is less likely that a teen will be asked controversial or current event questions. But as you never *really* know what you'll be asked, you'll want to be prepared. The teen or junior contestant that is a bit better prepared than the others and can handle a surprise question with grace leaves a strong positive impression.

Along those lines, a teen that is clearly more "mature" and in control may be asked "harder" questions because she can handle them! If she is that strong in interview it will help her shine there and the glow will carry over to other areas of her judging categories.

Miss

A Miss contestant may get questions about her education as well, depending on the situation, but the focus would likely be more on how what she is studying relates to her current career or life or what she wants to pursue once she finishes school—generally college or graduate school at this age.

A Miss may get questions that are more about how they work with others and about relationships other than their parents and siblings. If it is a platform-based pageant, questions related to that would come in more seriously at this division too. In a Miss pageant (depending on the pageant) the judges will expect to see more comfort and awareness with questions that require more thinking. It is unlikely that all the questions will be simply informational.

Mrs.

As you'd suspect, with a Mrs. contestant the personal questions may very well include something about her attitudes toward marriage and family. Instead of questions on friends or school questions, the focus may be more on husband and children. That said, many Mrs. contestants also have a career so those questions are fair game. Of course, your application materials will tell the judges whether you are working outside the home or not.

Either way, they may ask questions about your experiences and choices. Questions might also include topics and concerns from the community (education system, crime, drugs) or larger society (war, debt/economy, healthcare) matters that impact families.

Someone mature enough to be married (and possibly have children) will be expected to have thought through some of life's choices and grappled with some of the more controversial issues out there—whether in regard to balancing family with career (if she works) or in community service. A Mrs. contestant should be prepared to show how she thinks by answering questions more thoughtfully and analytically.

Ms.

Depending on the pageant, Ms. contestants age range can be broader than for other pageants, and she could be married or single. (For instance, the Ms. United States Pageant includes married, divorced, widowed, or never married.) So the Ms. contestant would get questions appropriate for her situation, but imagine the options as blending what we talked about for Miss and Mrs., above.

Senior/Elite

In the pageant world, most use the word "elite" to mean the "top notch" and/or long-standing pageants with strongly positive and consistent reputations. (Clearly Miss America and Miss USA are in this category but there are many others.) Or, as you'd guess, the word "elite" may be used to refer to the contestants that compete to win in those pageants.

But, just so you know, there are few times where the word "elite" is used as a respectful term to mean someone who is perhaps older than the standard Mrs. or Ms. contestant. There is nothing wrong with the word "senior" but some prefer "elite" so if you hear that in certain circles, just know that may be what is meant.

Anyway, if you (or someone you know) are competing in this sort of senior division or pageant, just remember that it is much like the Mrs. and Ms. categories combined because whether marital status comes into the questions or not, there is an expectation of mature thinking.

So the questions may be like those for Mrs. and Ms. but, again, the judges would adjust them for the particular contestant (remember to make your applications meaningful) so if the contestant had grandchildren they might ask about them. And the community and societal issues (both of which can sometimes be controversial) would include the same sort of things but could also include more on, say, attitudes toward aging, efforts to increase longevity, and quality of life, etc. Be prepared.

Broader Concerns:
Women and International

While this book is on personal questions, it should be clear that the "personal" winds up rippling out to and including others.

Representing Women (Not Just Yourself)

Remember that in all cases, you are representing not just a certain title area (like your state) or a certain division but you are representing *women*. Being a titleholder is a relatively rare opportunity and you want to remember to be a strong, effective woman that helps empower other women.

Some people feel negatively about pageants—saying they aren't good for women or are outdated. As you gather from this book, I disagree (see my website for more on this over time) and find some of the attitudes out there are based on assumptions and incorrect information.

That's not to say *every* contestant has a good experience or healthy motivations for entering, just as not every pageant may be as well-run and empowering as others. Each person needs to use her own head to determine if a certain pageant, or pageants in general, are supportive of her personal growth.

All that said, as a potential titleholder you have the opportunity (perhaps even the responsibility) to show through your actions, deeds, and words that pageants can be good for women. As a contestant you can show that pageants aren't just about being pretty but that they help in personal development for years after the pageant.

And as a representative of women, you'd be a Sleuth and look for ways to tie your answers back to women's issues and rights…you'd look for ways to honor other women by knowing their achievements.

Not that you can't honor men as well but be especially aware of women's issues.

Using the Miss Universe pageant as an example, a couple of contestants left some invitations to speak up for women laying on the table. Let's see if we can learn from them how we might have approached the question differently.

For instance, judge Valeria Mazza asked Miss Australia 2009 something like:

Judge
"Tonight you were judged in how you look in a swimsuit. In some countries women can't wear them, how does that make you feel?"

The lovely Rachael Finch responded along the lines that swimsuit allows the contestants to show their form and the beauty of the female body to the world. She focused on how she felt in *general*, not on how she feels about the fact that other women can't do it.

To me, she missed the mark. She did okay, but bungled away an opportunity to really shine and show more of her intelligence and sensitivity. She did not take the big hint in the first part of the question that she could have (some would say *should* have) included something that addresses the difference between her country and those that don't allow swimsuits, or something about women's rights. Some *balance* would have been nice.

"A woman is the full circle. Within her is the power to create, nurture, and transform."
~Diane Mariechild

Rewind: Be a Sleuth

So something like this would have been a more complete answer:

Sleuth

"The swimsuit competition is a great opportunity to show our fitness level and celebrate the beauty of the female body and I'm grateful that I live in a country that permits it. At the same time, I feel badly that in some countries women cannot be seen nearly at all— let alone in a swimsuit. I respect cultural differences but do hope that there will be increasing freedoms for women."

Maybe not perfect but not a bad answer if you are thinking on your feet and taken off-guard by a potentially controversial issue. Of course if an international level contestant is well prepared this is exactly the kind of question for which she'd have been prepared! Without being "preachy" or "judgmental," this response doesn't ignore half of the question and acknowledges there are cultural differences that impact women's rights.

By the way, if you are trying to place what category of question this is, I'd say it is a hybrid. It is a controversial question that asks for a comparison (your country to those countries that don't allow it). The contestant's actual response did not address the controversy or implied comparison…she pretty much just said why she thought it was great there was a swimsuit category. She could have spoken up for women a bit better.

Miss Australia 2010, Jesinta Campbell, interestingly enough, was also asked a clothing question at the following Miss Universe pageant and I believe she offered a more thoughtful response than her countrywoman's response the previous year. Let's take a look.

Judge, Niki Taylor

"Legislation banning certain kind of religious clothing has caused controversy around the world.

What role should a government play in determining such a personal preference?"

Jesinta Campbell

"One of the greatest things we have is the freedom of choice. And tonight we wore our swimsuits, which were designed by Tala, and she said that "Fashion is freedom." I don't think the government should have any say in what we wear because we can all make our own personal choices."

You might say that she could have brought in another element or two but it is still a good answer. What she did do was bring in something other than beauty; she brought in a connection with women, she mentioned a sponsor, and she answered the key part of the question. Her countrywoman, you'll recall, skipped the controversial part.

Miss Campbell was generally effective and direct and, if you saw the show, you'll note she paused to let the audience respond to her initial statement. That's good because it honored the audience, and you do not want to raise your voice to be heard over a crowd.

One other example along the lines of remembering to, where appropriate, consciously represent women is also from the Miss Universe 2009 pageant. Judge Andre Leon Talley asked Miss Venezuela a question that started with "In many parts of the world...." and finished by asking about obstacles women encounter in the workplace.

The gorgeous Stefania Fernandez's answer glossed over the comparison. She said that women have overcome many obstacles and reached the same level as men and it is time we realize there are no barriers between us. *But* she seemed to ignore that his question already communicated that the gender inequality problems *do* still exist.

She was a general cheerleader for equality but didn't answer as strongly as she could have if she *really* addressed what he had asked.

Preferably, she'd have taken on the challenge of responding to the fact that it isn't all rosy for women in the workplace in all parts of the world.

Stefania did win the title but I doubt it was on the strength of this response. And now that she will get to travel the world as Miss Universe, maybe she will see how the countries *do* differ in what women can achieve and why the judges ask comparative questions like this.

There's one last thing on this topic to remember, however. While I encourage you to remember to "represent women" in positive, empowering ways through listening with care and thoughtful responses, don't portray yourself as if you are "the voice" of all women. Avoid saying something like "Women everywhere would agree…" or "Women don't like it when…"

You can't know what *all* women would think, like, or say so don't come off as "speaking for all women." Surely many would agree with whatever you say but many other women wouldn't. You don't want what you say to make the judges (or half the world's women) think "That's what not what "all" women" think!"

Remember to think diplomatically not just about issues and controversies, but people in general. Speak what you know to be personally true for you, and speak in ways that are empowering for women, but phrase it in a way that keeps the line clear between what's your opinion and experience separate from what "all" women might think or experience.

Representing the Country (State, City, Etc.)

As mentioned before, whatever title you hold, you are something of a representative or ambassador for that town, region, state, etc. What you say can reflect, directly or indirectly, on your country in positive or less positive ways. So just keep an eye out for that and endeavor to reflect well on the area you represent.

Taken to the extreme, we'll focus on the international level—if you win a state pageant, you'll then compete to represent the nation. So what you say will reflect on your state as well as, indirectly, reflect on your whole country as people all over may watch certain national U.S. pageants.

And some pageant systems don't stop at the national level but send that Queen on to an international level pageant where the national titleholders vie. For example, if we look at what the beautiful Miss USA 2009, Kristen Dalton (previously Miss North Carolina-USA), said in response to two of her video interview questions at the Miss Universe 2009 pageant, we'll get a sense of this.

Judge
"Tell us something interesting about your country that people might not know."

Kristen Dalton
"There are a few different interesting things about the USA that some people may not know. One is that we have 4 time zones, pacific, eastern, mountain and standard. Another interesting fact is that in just one small city, Queens, New York, there are roughly 192 languages spoken."

She delivered the answer in a calm confident voice and you can't help but like her. Not bad. In fact it is a "diplomatic" response in that she at least tried to acknowledge the breadth of the country she's representing and nods to its diversity.

But, unfortunately, both parts of her answer have something inaccurate in it (check your facts, ladies) and there could be some expansion that would show both her and the U.S.A. in an even more positive light.

Let's take the wrong part first. If I had been coaching her, and if she'd run that answer past me in practice, I'd have pointed out to her that she either needed to modify her answer to say the "continental

United States" or realize that the residents of Hawaii and Alaska may not appreciate her answer very much since the U.S. actually has *six* time zones, not four. And some would accurately say that U.S.A has *nine* time zones. Let's take a look...

If we just count the time zones of the 50 states then there are six:

- Hawaii-Aleutian Standard Time (HST)
- Alaskan Standard Time (AKST)
- Pacific Standard Time (PST)
- Mountain Standard Time (MST)
- Central Standard Time (CST)
- Eastern Standard Time (EST)

But you get to nine with Puerto Rico and the U.S. Virgin Islands which are on Atlantic Standard Time (AST). Then there's American Samoa and Midway which are on Samoa Standard time (SST). And we have U.S. holdings in the Mariana Islands (Guam) and Northern Mariana Islands (Saipan) that are in the Chamorro Standard Time (ChST). That's the official count for USA time zones.

So if a contestant thinks time zones are interesting and wants to use that as her answer, I'd coach her to get her facts right and expand a bit on *why* she is mentioning time zones as interesting or important. Is it because it shows the size of the U.S.A? Or, since she's at the *Miss Universe* pageant, she might frame her response in a global way.

Rewind: Be a Sleuth

Let's try a couple alternative responses instead of:

Miss Dalton, Part 1

"Um, well there are a few different interesting things about the USA some people might not know. Um one of them is that we have 4 different time zones: Eastern, Pacific, Mountain, and Central."

Let's see how this may have been a more accurate and interesting (and sort of cute) answer:

Sleuth

"I think it is interesting how many time zones we have! A lot of people think the U.S. has just four— Pacific, Mountain, Central, and Eastern—but we also spread to the west far enough to have Alaska and Hawaii, which brings us up to 6 time zones. And if we count U.S. territories and such we have 9! Getting to meet contestants from all over the globe here at the pageant has really helped me appreciate the impact of time zones—and some of the girls are quite jet lagged!"

If she were really into it, she could actually mention some of the other time zone names, etc. But, personally, I think there is probably more potential in the second half of her response to remember.

"Tell us something interesting about your country that people might not know."

After her time zone response she added:

Miss Dalton, Part 2

"And then the other interesting fact is that in just one small city, known as Queens, New York, there are roughly 192 languages spoken."

Here she has a real opportunity to expand in a way that shows her knowledge and the U.S.A.'s history and largesse. If she'd mentioned this "fact" in a practice session with me I'd have encouraged her to expand it but, first, we need to clear up inaccuracies.

For instance, I'd have pointed out to her that the many, many residents of New York (and the U.S. too) might prefer she be accurate and realized that Queens is not a separate small city. It may feel like its own city in many ways but it is actually one of the five boroughs of New York City.

Given the prominence of New York City on the national and international stage, I would expect a Miss U.S.A., a Miss America, and Miss anyone at the national level in any U.S. based pageant to know this basic fact about this iconic U.S. city. A little fact checking and changing how she talks about is all it would take to make a better, more informed impression here. With that out of the way, I'd have encouraged her to expand and perhaps try something like:

Sleuth

"While English is most widely spoken in the U.S.A., it is an interesting fact that in just one area of New York City—the borough of Queens—there are roughly 192 languages spoken which I find exciting as it shows what rich cultural diversity we have! And I've gotten a new experience of cultural diversity meeting all the great Miss Universe contestants from across the globe. If I win the title—and I hope I do!—continuing to learn more about the other cultures during my reign will be the best part."

Let's consider another example in considering her reply to the question:

"What would your 3 wishes be?"

Miss Dalton's first wish was about health for her and her family. A lovely wish! Her second wish didn't, in my opinion, reflect well on the U.S. when she said:

Miss Dalton, 2nd Wish

"Um the second one would be uh for me to be able to pay back my parents everything they've helped me out with, especially in this uh horrible U.S. economy."

It is sweet and shows responsibility and maturity for her to want to pay her parents back. It's a good answer in that she does not come off like it is "all about me" or with a sense of entitlement.

That said, she could have gotten the same point across without emphasizing to an international audience that the U.S. has a horrible economy! (At least at the time her answer was given.) For instance, she could have said something like.

Sleuth

"My second wish would be for a great career that provides both rewarding work and a great income as I look forward to paying my parents back for everything they've helped me with. I appreciate their believing in me and helping make this all possible."

If she were to give a response like that she could modify it to briefly include *what* kind of career she'd like. That would tell a little more about her and fit in with the "wish" theme—two wishes tucked into the one!

For instance, based on her bio she might say "a career in theatre on Broadway" (as she sings and dances) or "a career that utilizes my education in Psychology and Spanish." If the latter were true for her (no Smuggling!), it would be a stronger answer at an international pageant as it shows she appreciates more than the English language or culture. Either way, the alternate answer reflects better on her and on the U.S.A.

And in considering her third wish, she makes the point for me that contestants do represent their countries and it is a great opportunity. She could have worked on her filler words (she's got a handful of ums, uhs, and repeated words, etc.), true, but people don't notice them much if you don't use them *too* often or if they fall in the middle of sentences. Your eye may even skip over the repetitions in this transcript. But the key here is I like where she was heading with the content!

Miss Dalton, 3ʳᵈ Wish

"And uh the third one would be that um all all women around the world would have a chance to represent their country here at the Miss Universe pageant because it is such a once in a life time amazing uh growing and learning experience. Um we get to you know find out know so much about each other, about different cultures around the world. And to me it's just it's sad that that there are countries and women out there that don't have the opportunity to even represent their country or have an opportunity like this. So that would be my third wish."

This is good in that she shows sensitivity to women's issues (representing women), different cultures (important in general and at an international pageant), and implies she's happy being a citizen in a country that allows these opportunities.

Review

Let's review some key points in answering a variety of personal questions:

As we've emphasized, know your application materials as they can be what the judges rely on to generate a number of questions. Sometimes they'll just be the sort of questions the judges start with to warm up to other kinds of questions. Other times, depending on the pageant and length of the interview, the judges may intend to limit themselves to questions that at least start from those materials.

- Personal questions can also come "out of the blue" or from something someone's heard or learned about you from any source—with the internet becoming a more and more common source.

- Personal questions may be about you but be sure you don't take any questions "personally." Always keep it professional. Only share deeply personal or private things if asked directly (even then show discretion). If you are in a platform-based pageant, it is absolutely appropriate to make a personal connection about why that platform matters so much to you—then you may find in sharing a bit of your story or connection that you do get personal or private. Just remember to share what is relevant in a brief and sensitive way.

- Social network and message board sites can be great or harmful. We discussed keeping it positive and suggested taking control of your web presence.

- "Personal questions" include the following: classic pageant questions, spin-off questions, demonstration questions, and comparative questions. We went over several examples of these questions with an emphasis on how to avoid being overly negative when asked questions that are essentially comparative in nature.

- Personal questions are common in all pageants, though the focus of them may change depending on age category, division of pageant, and the like. We covered how the questions may change between Teen/Junior, Miss, Mrs., Ms., and Senior pageants.

- Titleholders are representing not just themselves but, in some way, they are representing women—so being thoughtful about how what you say reflects on women's issues is worthwhile. And titleholders must remember that they are also representing their *area* (the locale, city, state, or country). Using national contestant's responses at an international pageant, we examined the importance of listening with care, being accurate, and phrasing responses in a way that reflects well on your country. (Those examples, while broad, can help you think about how to best represent your city and state.)

Exercise 9.1: Find Yourself on the Web

If you have never done it (or haven't done so lately) go "Google" yourself. Go to http://www.Google.com and choose a couple other search engines (http://www.Yahoo.com is another popular one—there are many). Put your name in and search. Try different versions of your name and/or put your name in quotation marks to potentially increase the focus of the search. What do you find?

Whatever you find, know that other people can find it too. Does it reflect well on you? If you were a judge, what sort of impression would it make? What questions might be inspired from what's out there on you?

Exercise 9.2: Self-Assess Your Self-Authored Web Presence

Not every contestant will have a web-presence that they created for themselves—that's okay. Some contestants are of an age (young or less young) where they may not be "into that" or at least not into it yet (unless someone else does it for them). Again, that's okay...unless your pageant is expecting it, you can do as you wish on that front (but just know you may be missing some opportunities.)

In Exercise 9.1 you were looking at what is out there on you in general. Now I want you to focus on the part you can control. What I mean by "self-authored" is what *you* put out about *you*. If you have a website, a blog, a Facebook page, a MySpace page, or whatever sort of page is the next new thing, look at it with care and see if there is any content or any photos that it would be better for you to change.

And while you are at it, if you post on others' social networks and/or participate in any message boards consider if you are being Queenly and constructive. (Think about it, whether you think it anonymous or not.) If you haven't been playing nice with others, challenge yourself to do so. Before you know it, it'll be second nature.

Exercise 9.3: Practice a Range of Personal Questions

If you haven't done so already, go back into this book and practice responding (out loud!) to each of the sample questions (or a version that would be appropriate for your pageant or situation). Think through how the questions might play out based on your age/division. Try a variety of responses and build your skill at being a positive Sleuth.

It may help to review your pageant paperwork first. Review the exercises from *Book 4: Question Types* too!

Exercise 9.4: Think About the Bigger Picture

Whether you are in a pageant for the fun of it or to build life and career enhancing skills, think about what your participation means to you. Then reach beyond you and think about what it may mean to others who watch you—little girls in the audience, family and friends, coworkers and classmates, sponsors and community members.

Remember that in some ways—as a titleholder—you represent more than yourself and you reflect on all pageant contestants, women, and whatever area, city, state, or country is on your banner. Think about this and see if it enriches your pageant experience. Be proud of yourself—we are all proud of you! Allow this perspective to enrich the content and quality of your responses.

"Just as your car runs more smoothly and requires less energy to go faster and farther when the wheels are in perfect alignment, you perform better when your thoughts, feelings, emotions, goals, and values are in balance."
~Brian Tracy

**Here I am in my interview outfit at
my national pageant.**

a pageant is just the beginning...

PAGEANT
Interviewing
SUCCESS

Handling Silly and Tough Questions

Dr. Stephanie Raye, PhD
Former Miss American Petite

Book 10
Handling Silly and Tough Questions
Table of Contents

Pageant Interviewing Success:
Handling Silly and Tough Questions

Everything we've covered so far will help you be (and do) your personal best in the interview but wait: there's more! Let's expand your Sleuth skills as we explore more kinds of questions and winning strategies.

Whether it is in response to personal questions or more conceptual or topical questions, remember, to be a Sleuth. We covered how to approach several current event and controversial questions already, with more to come. We also covered some basic pageant questions and delved into personal questions in depth in the previous book.

All that together should already help you knock it out of the park—for most every ball (question) that gets thrown at you, you'll be able to hit it over the fence! Remember that what you learned in considering one kind of question transfers to all sorts of other questions. To start this book, we'll spend a little time on another kind of question, explore another "tough" question and how it could have been approached from different angles, and then talk a bit about judges.

Be the Sleuth

Any question isn't just about you or an opportunity to repeat exactly what you already said in your application materials. The judges want to see your personality and ability to connect with people. You can also tie in information that shows your depth and connection to important issues.

Hidden Value in "Simple" or "Silly" Questions

One category of questions we haven't spent much time on yet are those that may seem a bit silly at first. They seem simple at first glance. A certain judge may ask each contestant their favorite goofball question just to see what they do with it, or a silly question could come up spontaneously. Why or how a judge asks it isn't as important as how you answer it.

Some examples of simple or silly questions might be:

- "Why did you choose that nail color?"
- "What's your favorite color?"
- "If you could meet anyone in history, who would it be?"
- "If you could be any animal, which would you choose?"
- "What's your favorite food? (or song, movie, etc.)"

Once in awhile a simple question like that will be on your pageant application so you'll have at least thought about it a little (more than that, hopefully). But sometimes a simple question will be totally "out of the blue" and might catch you off guard.

So build a little skill with this sort of question. Every question has potential to be more than it appears and a Sleuth will watch for the "question behind the question" and for opportunities to deepen questions to highlight her skills and goals. Why? Not just to "win" but to help the judges make an informed decision on who to select. So even if a question seems simple or silly like:

"What's your favorite recipe?"

…it provides an opportunity to show how whatever they are asking about makes you special, connects to your title, or possibly your next title.

For instance, if you are from Georgia and a judge asks you about your favorite recipe, a Sleuth might reply:

"I love to make my Grandma's peach pie. I don't know if I will ever do it as well as she does but it makes me happy to honor her with the effort and continue the family tradition. And, with Georgia being the Peach State, I have to say, our peaches really do make the best peach pies!"

If you are from Florida, you might remember key lime pie would be a nice choice. What sort of foods are your town, county, state and country known for?

Be Honest But Also Use Honest Opportunities

Don't say anything that isn't true but if there is the opportunity to say truthful things that shine a nice light on you or your title (city, state, country) or platform, do it. You'd be a bungler if you were a Miss Georgia and said you like making grandma's meatloaf if she happens to also make a good peach pie! (Now mentioning grandma's fabulous meatloaf would make more sense if you were a Miss Texas or lived in another state where cattle is a big industry.)

If we can think that way about a question about food, imagine what you can do with a question with more substance! Don't force-fit references that are awkward or artificial but *do* keep your eye out for when they really, authentically, can work for you. That's something with which thoughtful advance preparation can help.

If you want more ideas on what sorts of things to know about your city, state, country, etc., please consider using the forthcoming Essential Pageant Interview Playbook as there's lots in there to help you prepare in different ways.

And what if you don't cook? Well, remember, to always listen to the question! In this example, the judge didn't ask "What is your favorite recipe *to cook*?" The question was more open than that. So you could say the favorite dish you like to eat, what you like about it, etc. Just remember to keep your Sleuthing opportunities in mind.

Keep a Sense of Humor
and Stay Flexible

And if "simple" questions teach us anything it is that not all of your preparation has to be "serious." And there is time and space for you to be light-hearted and funny in an interview—even while you are professional, you should still be human!

Have fun with it and think through how to make even the goofiest question more fun or how to turn it into something that tells the judges something more about you than what the question initially asks. Just as you can take a potentially serious question and turn it into something funny.

For example, I heard one interchange like this:

Judge
"What are you most afraid of?"

Contestant
"Spiders!"

Everybody laughed and she could leave it at that. And she did. The judges moved on to something else. This was not a bad answer and every interview—even if you have some serious-minded judges—can use a little levity. It shows your light-hearted side.

It also would have been fine if she had talked about a more serious fear (perhaps about war, education, something about her platform or in her community), and that *may* have been what the judges were expecting. We don't know. But it is also fine that she took the question in a different direction.

Rewind: Turning a Bungler Into a Sleuth on "Simple" Questions

Still, as I watched I thought she had bungled away an opportunity as she left a rich, inviting question laying there when there was more she could do with it.

She could get the laugh *and* do more with the question—if she had been a Sleuth. This is what I'd like to have seen her say:

Judge
"What are you most afraid of?"

Contestant
"Spiders!"

(Judges are laughing as she starts to speak again, still with a smile in her voice.)

Contestant
"Yes, I am afraid of spiders and would like to get over that. But, on a more serious note, I'm really afraid of what's happening in our schools these days. I'm happy to face that fear, though, as my platform focuses on issues in education. Being your next titleholder would really help me bring attention to the issues so we can turn the fear into positive action. I know it won't be as straightforward as dealing with a spider might be, but creative, committed people working together can help us keep making improvements in this area."

Notice how she could have uncovered the opportunity in that question—that's what Sleuths do. She can keep it light by bringing the spider back in at the end (and by keeping her voice positive in tone).

Are You Ready to Optimize Your Interview?

As we continue to consider the previous example, had she utilized the question to unfold a bit more of her potential—on top of the personality and sense of humor she already showed—she'd have shown more of her multi-dimensional nature. That's a good thing.

And it would have opened the door for the judges to ask her to expand on what she introduced. Now, the judges may not go down that path as they may be happy with where she stopped and move on to something else. But they also may have had their interest aroused and taken the opportunity to ask her more on something she clearly wants to talk about.

For instance, they might ask her what, specifically, she's worried about in schools. Or maybe they'd ask her if she has any concrete (specific) ideas about how she'd use the title to bring attention to the issue. They might ask her what she's already done on this issue like what her personal experience with it is, if she's volunteered, if she is studying education in school, etc.

If you were asked questions like that about anything on your application paperwork, would you be prepared to respond? If not, don't panic…now you know to start thinking about it. (And if you need help, there is plenty out there. Please reach out to knowledgeable others, practice, and use some of the other supports I offer.)

Different Pageants, Different Questions?

But what about everything else? There's a big, wide world of information and issues out there. You're right! You never know what you'll be asked.

Pageant System or Focus

And while local and preliminary pageants may focus on personal sorts of questions, state and national (and international) pageants probably won't stop there. "Bigger" pageants, and those focused on scholarship and achievement, will likely, at some point, ask you about issues in your community, your state, the nation, or the world.

And while you might think that pageants that focus more on beauty—over scholarship or achievement or performing talent—will only ask you "simpler" personal question, that's not always the case.

Even in a primarily "beauty" pageant, the judges are still looking for the person that stands out from the rest. An interview is where that usually happens! Even if the competition is more about glamour, remember that the titleholder usually still has duties, so her showing she can think on her feet matters.

Take, for example, the Miss USA pageant which is typically considered a "beauty pageant" system whereas the Miss America pageant system is a "scholarship foundation" where the girls are competing in an achievement contest. They are both great pageant systems (as are several other systems) and *both* sets of contestants and their Queens are beautiful and accomplished women.

Still, the two systems do have different judging categories and requirements that might lead a young woman to believe that she doesn't need to prepare as much or in the same way for one versus the other. I'm here to tell you that preparing for your *interview* matters in *both* (and in any system that has interview on- or off-stage).

Any Pageant Contestant Might Get a "Tough" Question

For instance, someone might mistakenly think that since the Miss USA pageant doesn't require a platform, and may focus on beauty, that interview skills won't matter as much. And some Miss USA materials say things that are there to make you feel less nervous, yes, but might *accidentally* make it seem like you don't need to prepare, like this quote from the Miss Arizona-USA website at the time I was writing this:

> "*Interview*: preliminary interviews are personal one-
> on-one style. You will have interviews with each of
> the five judges. It's very comfortable and
> conversational. Contestants are scored on their
> communication skills, and personality. They are *not*
> scored on their opinions or personal beliefs."

So it may make you think you won't ever be in the position to offer an opinion or belief but, naturally, most responses include a bit of your opinions and beliefs in them. They are just saying that whether you are "for" or "against" something isn't the basis of the score. Being sleuth-like in how you respond is important.

And, as we've covered, I do believe you should approach interviews as conversations with new professional friends. I do believe that your communication skill and personality matter tremendously. But I *also* believe that your skill and level of comfort increase dramatically by your planning ahead a little bit and following some of the user-friendly suggestions in this book.

No matter what the title (pageant title or job title), your ability to interview well will help you secure it (or lose it). Let's take Miss Carrie Prejean (former—she lost her crown—Miss California-USA 2009) as an example.

She was asked about gay marriage for her on-stage question at the national Miss USA competition. She did okay (depending on who you ask), but she wasn't being a Sleuth or she'd have done even better and avoided all the trouble her "okay" answer caused her and her pageant organization. If she'd knocked it out of the park, instead of being "okay" she may very well have won.

As you know, I emphasize that you can and should have your own beliefs—that you can be yourself. But how you communicate it is important. In this case, I believe this lovely young woman bungled the response (no matter what her beliefs) when she could have sleuthed it to great advantage. Some may call it being "politically correct" but I call it being smart and sensitive to alternate views.

Let's take a look at what she said and how it is *okay* for her to be for *or* against gay marriage—she has a *right* to her opinion—but *how* she expresses it is what matters when you are vying to win a title.

Judge, Perez Hilton

"Vermont recently became the fourth state to legalize same-sex marriage. Do you think every state should follow suit, why or why not?"

Miss Carrie Prejean

"Well, I think it's great that Americans are able to choose one or the other. Umm. We live in a land that you can choose same sex marriage or opposite marriage. And you know what in my country and in in and in my family and I think that I believe that a marriage should be between a man and a woman. No offense to anybody out there but that's how I was raised and that's how I think that it should be between a man and a woman. Thank you."

On the surface, you may think her answer was great (regardless of whether you are for, against, or neutral on the issue). You may admire her for "taking a stand" and speaking for the "majority." Like I said, in my opinion, her response was "okay" so that's like "average." But where her response was *not* so great was that it:

- Accidentally implied that *her* family is smarter than everyone else's (who might believe differently)
- Incorrectly implied that the entire U.S. agrees with *her* ("in my country")

- Neglects to acknowledge that *four* U.S. states (at the time) disagree with her showing insensitivity to "minority" voices
- Didn't really answer half the question
- She contradicts herself saying "it's great you can choose" in the beginning and then says the equivalent of "no, it shouldn't be that way" by the end

As her country was a little bit divided on the topic, it shouldn't be a surprise that this question was out there to be asked. A Sleuth should know what's been in the headlines, know the judges, and expect questions from any current or controversial event during an interview—even in a pageant where you might not expect it. We'll get to judges more in a moment, for now, let's see how this response could have been improved.

Rewind: Turning a Bungler Into a Sleuth on Tough Questions

So let's still work with some of her own words, to start with, to see how she might have handled it better. Then we'll branch out to see how it is okay to take a stand if you do it well.

Here are a few things she could have done to fix to her answer:

Judge
"Vermont recently became the fourth state to legalize same-sex marriage. Do you think every state should follow suit, why or why not?"

(Shorten it)
"Well I think it's great that Americans are able to choose one or the other. Umm. We live in a land that you can choose same sex marriage or opposite marriage."

Sometimes "less is more" and if she'd stopped there, she'd have been ahead of the game. Even though it is *true* that she still wouldn't have *fully* answered the question. At least she'd have avoided the problems I outlined above. (So remember, sometimes saying less is better! Especially if you are uncertain or super nervous.)

Judge

"Vermont recently became the fourth state to legalize same-sex marriage. Do you think every state should follow suit, why or why not?"

(End it better)

"Well I think it's great that Americans are able to choose one or the other. Umm. We live in a land that you can choose same sex marriage or opposite marriage. I don't know whether every state should follow suit or not, that's up to each state to decide, but it is an interesting time to live and see this great example of U.S. democracy where some states have adopted this and others haven't and we can all still get along."

Maybe not "perfect" but we don't need perfect! This is still a reasonable answer under pressure. It starts with something she believes (or at least said) and ends it stronger than her actual answer because there is no self-contradiction. Add to that in this version she answers the rest of the question about state laws. (She skipped that part before.)

There's been a lot of controversy about her answer. Some have said the judge(s) may have scored her lower because of her personal view, but *if* she was scored lower (she was still *first runner-up* for goodness' sake) for her answer it would be because she contradicted herself in her answer *and* didn't show a diplomatic nature. (At least not in this answer. She may be a very diplomatic person. I don't know her personally.) Remember, a national titleholder like Miss USA will interact with people from all over the world, she needs to be tactful.

This topic is controversial enough that I'd recommend she'd have taken one of the middle-of-the-road approaches above. *But* you have to do what feels right for you and I support you in doing that as long as you do it sensitively. So let's say Miss Prejean felt strongly about wanting to come out clearly against or in favor of gay marriage.

Judge

Vermont recently became the fourth state to legalize same-sex marriage. Do you think every state should follow suit, why or why not?

(Against it)

"I think it's great that Americans can choose same sex marriage or opposite marriage. I was raised to believe that marriage between a man and a woman is the way it should be, so that's how I personally believe (no offense to anyone!), but what I love about America is that no one family gets to make the rules. I'm glad we have the voting system and the courts to help each state decide."

Judge

Vermont recently became the fourth state to legalize same-sex marriage. Do you think every state should follow suit, why or why not?

(Generally for it)

"Well I think it's great that we live in a land that you can choose same sex marriage or opposite marriage. I was raised to believe marriage should be between a man and a woman, and I love my family for who they are but I also respect that my family doesn't run the country. I've learned that love is love no matter who shares it so I'm now okay with it if a given state wants to approve same-sex marriage."

Those are just ideas to illustrate that even though you may not have time to think, you *can* teach yourself to say things in a way that is honest *and* doesn't offend too many people. We've covered a lot on this in this book series. Re-review it with a fresh eye and you'll see it again. Balance in your answers, Ladies, as much as you do in those high heels!

To come full circle with where we started this sub-section…no matter what system in which you compete, remember that just about any sort of question is "fair game." They just might ask you about politics, or current events, or cultural differences (like religion). They aren't trying to trap you; they're trying to get to know you and give you a chance to shine. If you become a Sleuth you will *welcome* tough questions because you know you'll do a fine job!

So don't over-worry but start (if you aren't already) paying more attention to the world around you and the implications of what you hear and read about. Think through your beliefs, values, etc. (The upcoming Essential Pageant Playbook will help here, if you need it.) We are all better citizens—and definitely better interviewees—if we have a basic knowledge of as much as we possibly can.

Judges: Each Has His or Her Own Style

No matter what sort of pageant or contest you are in, the judges will bring their own fingerprint to the interview. There are serious judges who only ask serious topical questions on controversial issues. Other judges may only ask light-hearted questions on personal information. Others may ask "quirky" questions just for fun. There might be a judge who, for instance, asks every contestant the same thing (regardless of what the pageant suggests or the other judges do) in order to have one "constant" in mind and see how each person handled that one tough or silly question!

Some pageants or contests will have a list of questions that the judges will try to stick to for each contestant (with little or no room for divergence or variance). Some contests won't—anything goes.

Some judges are quite experienced and may have judged at many pageants or otherwise really appreciate what goes into competing in a pageant or being a titleholder (they may be former contestants or directors, etc.). Other judges may be very experienced in interviewing and evaluating but from some other professional field that helps them ask clear questions. And there could be some judges who are less experienced or less articulate and ask you poorly worded questions.

You never know; the judges may be from the pageant world, from local businesses, from national sponsors, or they may be celebrities (from whatever level or locale is appropriate for your pageant.) That's okay! A Queen is comfortable talking with anyone.

Usually there are enough judges on any one panel that you'll have a mix. When there is a good mix, they tend to balance each other out. But you could wind up with everyone being more "serious" or everyone being more "fun." You won't know if that's the tone they always have or if they are all in a certain mood because of what was said in the previous interview.

And you don't have to know *why* they are that way at that time. Whatever sort of judges you have, adjust to fit their tone while you stay generally positive and professional. At the same time, as we've discussed, you can look for ways to shift the tone or at least open little windows into the other side of yourself that may not show if the judges are on a particular trajectory. That is if they are all serious you'd adjust to that but look for a window to show a lighter side and get them smiling or chuckling at something.

"I always try to believe the best of everybody—it saves so much trouble."
~Rudyard Kipling

Conversely, if the tone is more light-hearted, you'd adjust to that but create a little window to "get serious for a minute" and bring up your serious platform. And if your platform is really dark and dramatic in nature then you may want to have practiced some ways to find something positive to turn the dark into light so that you don't permanently dampen the mood after talking about heavy stuff (like drug abuse, domestic violence, etc.).

In the end, the key is to appreciate the judges as people, and appreciate the time they are spending with you. Adjust to them, within reason. Appreciate what a tough job they have, and do your best.

Know Your Judges and Sponsors

It won't always be possible—a lot depends on your pageant—but if you know the names of the judges in advance, learn about them. Sometimes judges' bios will be in the program or on the website. When you learn who they are, take note of basic information about them and let it inform you.

Going back to the 2009 Miss USA pageant, if the contestants spent a few minutes reviewing who their judges were they'd be better prepared for what sort of on-stage question they'd get. For instance, Perez Hilton is openly gay and is known for his openness and gossipy blog. A Sleuth-like contestant should then expect that if he's given the opportunity to ask, he might ask something about gay marriage. Which he did. It'd been in the news a lot and he no doubt follows the news. It probably seemed like a very fair question to him.

Miss Prejean was Miss California and they'd just passed a huge gay marriage proposition event that took gay marriage rights away from folks who'd gotten them from a court ruling about six months earlier. So just from following the news in her own state, she might have expected a question on this topic whether Perez Hilton was on the panel or not. (As it is, he'd have asked any contestant that question who drew his name or question from the fishbowl).

But knowing about your judges doesn't just help with potentially "controversial" issues.

Yes, a Sleuth will, for instance, keep in mind if the judges are "known" for anything in particular (like Perez Hilton). An example of this might include knowing if you have a particularly conservative or liberal person on the panel. If they are a celebrity, politician, or local business owner, you might know this from the kinds of things they've said to the media (or has been reported on them). If they aren't in the public eye in any way, you'll just have to go without knowing (and remember you can't believe everything in the media). If you have the judges names, you still might do a simple "Google" search on each to see what surfaces.

If you don't know who the judges are until the last minute, it's okay. A diplomatic potential Queen will be balanced enough in her responses that she won't offend anyone, so knowing if the panel leans heavily in one direction or another won't make or break you. And hopefully your pageant has looked for a balance of viewpoints and judges, so what else might you like to know?

It'd be good to know about your pageant sponsors—especially if you have a pageant sponsor on the panel. Know a bit about the history and scope of that business. I remember that I impressed the judges when they asked what I thought about petite fashions and I was able to answer it well. The interchange went something like this:

Judge

"Since this is a pageant focused on petite women, what can you tell me about petite fashion?"

Me

"I can tell you there is some out there but there could stand to be more. It's so great when I can find styles proportioned for my height! I really appreciate that JH Collectibles, one of our national sponsors, has such an extensive petite line that include classic separates that really are "collectible" so a petite can build a nice wardrobe over time. Labels like theirs and Liz Claiborne giving petites that much attention is encouraging the department stores to give petites more floor space and selection."

That was a good answer because it showed I'd done some homework and would do a good job answering similar questions of petite women, store owners, the media, etc. as I made appearances at events and educated the public about petite fashion.

At that same pageant, one of the contestants was sad after her personal interview because she knew she'd "missed something." From what she said, the conversation went something like this:

Judge
"Since this is a petite pageant, tell me, what can you tell me about petite fashions? Like can you name a clothing line or designer that carries petite fashions?"

Contestant
"Nothing is coming to mind. I just hope to find them but most the time I have to buy out of the girl's department or buy from the normal department but just get it adjusted for me."

Judge
(trying to give her a hint)
"Perhaps you can think of a clothing line that is headquartered in your state?"

Contestant
"Not that I can think of! Is there one? Maybe I should shop there!"

Judge
"What about a clothing line associated with the pageant?"
(Trying to give her another big *hint since this was listed right in the program!)*

Contestant

"Oh, I know someone provided the outfits for our opening performance but I can't remember who they are."

She left knowing she'd missed something because the judge looked a bit disappointed or a couple judges exchanged silent glances so another knew to pick up with a new line of questioning because this wasn't going anywhere.

And the reason they'd given her the hint about her state is because that's where a major pageant sponsor was from. They had a judge on the panel and supplied all the clothes for the opening number…but she didn't know any angle of who they were, where they were from, what they did in general let alone for the pageant.

Don't worry if they aren't available, but *if* you know the judges in advance learn their bio and maybe do a little homework on them (just like some judges will do on you). And if the judge also works for one of the pageant sponsors, then know about that company that is so generously donating time, products, money, clothes, or whatever to your pageant.

"We hear only those questions for which we are in a position to find answers."
~Friedrich Nietzsche

You don't want to talk about the judges or the sponsors in the interview *too* much. It takes time away from you and/or your platform. (And it could seem creepy if you know *too* much about them!) But *do* use whatever you learn as a Sleuth who will adjust her answers to include information when it matters. You may never need or use the info but you'll have it in case a question comes up that relates to it.

Review

Let's review the concepts in this book:

- Don't let simple, silly questions throw you off and don't let them go to waste. Every question you get has potential to let you show your personality and good fit for the title.

- Even on questions that may seem less important, look for opportunities to show your sense of humor and knowledge. Know basics about your city, state, region, or country. Learn new things as you prepare for new pageants.

- Different pageants may focus on different sorts of questions but a Sleuth will be ready for all categories of questions. Don't be afraid of tough questions. Follow the news in your area and practice balance in your responses.

- Judges will differ as individuals and a panel of judges may have a certain "feel" or style to the questions they ask. In general, adjust to their tone but also look for appropriate opportunities to change the feel if it serves your purposes.

- To the degree you can, know the backgrounds of your judges. That may help you understand what sort of perspective they have or questions they might ask.

- Know your pageant sponsors. A Sleuth will work in connection to the sponsors when it is genuinely appropriate—but you can't make those connections if you don't know about them!

Exercise 10.1: Practice With Simple Questions

Practice out loud responses to the simple and silly questions offered as examples in this book. (And you can find more in pageant interview question books.) Record yourself if possible.

Listen to what you say. Is it average or interesting? Do you sound at ease and intelligent? Or do you ramble around looking for an answer or use filler words? Are you able to find something "deeper" or more interesting or fun to say about your favorite color or animal? It's just practice—those questions may not come up but if you start thinking about the "why" and "how" behind simple things, you'll likely find you have more meaningful things to say. Practice connecting to information about yourself and/or your platform, your goals, your community, etc.

Exercise 10.2: Practice Your Balance

Pick a "controversial" issue and pretend a judge just asked you a question about it. No matter what you really believe—just for this exercise—try answering it out loud three ways: one that supports it, one against, one neutral. See if you can show sensitivity and balance in each answer. Watch that you don't contradict yourself in your effort to be diplomatic—you can acknowledge both sides without contradicting yourself or sounding wishy-washy.

If you need to learn more about the issue to do this successfully, then research it a bit (just remember to get neutral sources and/or a wide range so you actually learn about both sides).

Exercise 10.3: Look in to Your Judges

Whether you are thinking about entering a pageant or preparing for one for which you've already signed up, see if you can find out anything about the judges.

Start with the website. If they don't mention who is on deck for your pageant, see if they mention the ones from previous pageants. If you have the video from a previous year, watch it and pay attention when they introduce the judges. All or some of the judges will be different, yes, but at least you will get a sense of the types of judges who might be on the panel. If you find names, look up their bios and learn about them.

If you can't find the judges' names, don't worry. You may find out closer to the pageant. You could ask the director if they have the judges lined up yet but do *not* be a problem to them. They are probably busy trying to get the judges lined up! If you bring it up with them, as always, don't have a demanding attitude. Ask nicely and if they don't know yet, just move on to one of the many other great things you can prepare.

Exercise 10.4: Look in to Your Sponsors

As in Exercise 10.3, look up the pageant sponsors. Not every pageant will have them, but see if yours does. Sponsors usually pay some money or give something to the pageant to help it function. Sometimes some of those goods are given to the contestants to use (or to keep!). Every situation is different. But start learning about the pageant sponsors just because it is good to do in general but also in case you get an interview question where it makes sense to connect some bit of that information into the response.

"If we knew what it was we were doing, it
would not be called research, would it?"
~Albert Einstein

The group swimsuit shot at my national pageant. I am standing 5 to the right of Minnie Mouse.

a pageant is just the beginning...

PAGEANT
*I*nterviewing
SUCCESS

Four Strategies to
Build Answer Content

Dr. Stephanie Raye, PhD
Former Miss American Petite

Book 11
Four Strategies to Build Answer Content
Table of Contents

Pageant Interviewing Success:
Four Strategies to Build Answer Content

This book is filled with ideas on how to answer your questions directly on-target in ways that put your best foot forward. And, just as important, to help the judges have the information they need to know if you are a good choice for the title.

If you practice being a Sleuth in your approach to questions, you'll find building answer content and thoughtful delivery become increasingly natural for you. As we've discussed, that includes:

- Listening for the "question behind the question" (Book 1)
- Listening carefully, in general (Book 8)

We know that careful listening is important—how can you know what to say or when you've said enough if you didn't really hear or understand what they asked? So always listen carefully as that will help you build the right type and amount of content for your response. That, coupled with knowing yourself, are the best tools.

We also have talked about using *balance* as a content building technique, especially for controversial topics. We introduced "balance" way back in *Book 1: Build a Strong Foundation* and used it in several examples.

But for here, let's go over a few more content-building strategies for your tool box that'll help with all kinds of questions. Here we'll discuss three techniques:

- Deepen/Specify
- Reporter
- S.T.A.R. Story

And then in the next book, we'll spend a whole section on building content for questions for which you think you don't know the answer.

Deepen/Specify

Deepening your responses and adding "specifics" is something you'll see in several examples throughout this book, but let's draw our attention to it more now.

As we've discussed (see *Book 1: Build a Strong Foundation*) there are different categories of questions you may be asked: Personal, Pageant, Simple or Silly, Current Events, and Controversial. Any of those questions can come in a basic "What do you think about...." form or in an open-ended "Tell us about...."

Whenever you are asked a basic "What" or "Tell" question, consider turning it into a "Why" question or a "What you like best about" question. Expanding a shallower question by deepening gives you natural content and lets the judges get to know you better. It is part of looking for (or creating!) a "question behind the question."

Usually Current Event and Controversial questions are "deep" enough on their own. So let's work with an example from the Pageant question category which includes inquiries that get at your motivations to enter; your knowledge of pageant, title and area; and knowledge and motivation for your personal pageant platform (if relevant), or if the pageant itself has a platform.

Such questions might include versions of:

- "What qualities would make you a great titleholder?"
- "Why did you enter the pageant?"
- "If selected as Ms. ___ , what would you do during your reign?"

Another classic pageant question is "Tell us about yourself" which some contestants struggle with because they feel it is too open. They might stumble for words thinking "Well, what do you want to know?" They may say too much or too little or just be confused. We've talked about being prepared for this (as a version of an opening statement) but let's use it for another example.

Judge
"Tell us about yourself."

Teen/Junior
"I'm a freshman at Freemont High School where I get good grades and am on the track team. I have 1 brother, 1 sister and 2 cats. I love cats."

Miss
"I attend University of Arizona where I major in Broadcast Journalism and am active in my sorority. We have so much fun."

Mrs.
"I have been married 5 years to a great man. We hope to have children one day but right now I'm busy with my career and community service."

Ms.
"I'm a nurse at a hospital and am active in sports and volunteering after work."

There's nothing wrong with any of those answers. But they are "shallow" responses in the sense that they don't use the opportunity to help the judges see how they would be a good fit for the title. They gently Bungle away an opportunity where they easily could have been more of a Sleuth and added, or at least changed, their content in helpful ways by adding some "specifics" about, for example, themselves or their pageant goals. Let's see how.

Sleuth Teen
"I'm a freshman in high school with my eye on college. I'm delighted to be competing in this pageant because even though my good grades or other activities might earn me a scholarship, it'd be great to get a scholarship through the pageant as well."

Sleuth Miss

"I'm majoring in Broadcast Journalism and am happy to be involved in this pageant because the appearances and working with the media are helping me build my skills from a different angle than I can in the classroom."

Sleuth Mrs.

"I'm happily married and active in volunteer work for the community, especially with the American Red Cross. My part-time "day job" is as a fire department dispatcher and every time there's a serious fire, I know one or more families will need some help to get back on their feet—or even just get through the night with someplace to shelter after having lost their home. The Red Cross is often involved in providing that sort of help right after the fire and it feels good to be involved on that end of things. If I win the pageant, I'd like to raise awareness around fire prevention and volunteerism."

Sleuth Mrs.

"I'm happily married, work part-time, and volunteer at our children's school. Education is so important; I want my children to see that we value it as a family by not just what we say as parents but what we do. My participating in this pageant is also good for the children to see as my husband and I encourage them to take risks to grow and be involved in the community—the pageant shows my kids that I'm willing to do the same!"

Sleuth Ms.

"In my free time you can often find me involved in activities that raise money for different health causes or charities. For instance, I might do the Susan G. Komen Race for the Cure and other events. I am a nurse and I know firsthand how important it is to raise awareness and money for these causes—whether it is to help the patients' morale or raise funds for research. That and I know how important physical fitness is to health. So I can help others and help myself through these sorts of activities. Were I selected as titleholder, I'd hope to inspire others to get involved!"

Reporter

Beyond thinking like a Sleuth to deepen and get more specific, you can also build content by imagining yourself as a reporter. Think about this: in a short news story—whether in text, audio, or video—the reporter usually starts with the most important information and then offers more detail after that. That's because they know that the reader, listener, or viewer may only "stay tuned" briefly so you say the most important thing first (in case that's all they hear) and hope that captures their attention so they'll stay tuned longer.

Thus, a reporter doesn't save the best information for last. When you are trying the reporter technique in your interview preparation, *lead* with the strongest information or a sentence that tells the main point. In this case instead of telling a story and saving the best for last, a reporter gives away the ending up front (as they aren't writing mystery novels!) In fact, if a reporter doesn't start with the best information first, they might be told by their editor or boss that they "buried the lead" and told to re-write their article or audio/video story.

Another way to think of this is to imagine yourself starting with something like a "headline" so that the reader or viewer can decide if they even want to listen to this story and are prepared for what comes next.

In a pageant interview, the judge can't change the channel or turn the page—they are there in the room with you! But they can stop listening and let their mind wander away if your answer doesn't capture their attention by starting strong and on-target to what was asked. So lead with a clear, relevant piece of information, then provide additional relevant details to enrich your response. You don't have to provide *all* the information (we've discussed making choices and not rambling) but definitely use some of it to help support your answer to help the judges understand and know you better.

What would a reporter add to their initial clear statement or headline? They'd offer information to answer the fundamental questions of:

- Who?
- What?
- When?
- Where?
- Why?
- How?

"The ability to simplify means to eliminate the unnecessary so that the necessary may speak."
~Hans Hofmann

Let's go through an example where I'll interrupt the flow a bit by pointing out the 5 Ws and 1 H (more or less) in a response for both a Bungler and a Sleuth. But we'll start with a slim answer to show how you can build content if you remind yourself to expand a bit on the 5 Ws and 1 H.

Examples

Judge
"I see you've been in several pageants. Why do you keep entering? What's the high point for you?"

Bungler 1
"Pageants are my hobby because they are fun! The high point is the excitement of the big night and waiting to hear if I won or placed."

That response has a little of the what (pageant, hobby) and the who (the contestant) and the why (fun, excitement) but it's rather thin on content. We learn a bit about her but not much and it makes her sound a little shallow. Let's see how to build content first, and then we'll work on the Sleuth Factor.

Bungler 2

(What)

"Pageants are fun. Yes, they are a lot of work too with getting ready and appearances and all, but it's fun work."

(Why)

"And why not enter?"

(Who and Why)

"My parents and boyfriend really like to see me on stage and are-"

(How)

"-happy to pay my entrance fees and buy my pageant clothes."

(When and Where)

"The high point is every new dress and the applause when I walk across that stage because-"

(Who, What, and Why)

"-I know I'm doing my best and getting recognized for it. And who knows? Maybe I'll place or win!"

So that has more content, yes? And while that isn't a terrible answer in that she addresses the question fully and acknowledges that pageants do involve work it still sounds a little self-centered and pampered. Let's try a different approach and imagine a contestant who thought more about why she got into pageants and how they've helped her.

Judge

"I see you've been in several pageants. Why do you keep entering? What's the high point for you?"

Sleuth

(Why)

"I enter to do my personal best and I enjoy helping others."

(Who, When, and Where)

"When I was in junior high school-"

(What)

"-I was very shy."

(Who)

"One day Miss State came to speak to our school and-"

(What)

"-she was confident, friendly, and really passionate about her cause."

(Why)

"I wanted to be like her. So I started to enter pageants and-"

(How)

"-they really helped me build my people skills and get in touch with the community through volunteer work."

(Why)

"So I keep entering to keep improving myself and-"

(What)

"-the high point is every time I make a little difference in someone else's life. I'd love to win this title and-"

(Why)

"-be an inspiration to others like Miss State was for me."

(How)

"I'm really grateful my parents and friends have supported my involvement in pageants."

She more or less answered the question in her first sentence—why she entered and what's the high point. That's her *lead*. If the timer for the interview rang right then, they'd at least know the "take home point" of her story.

But she uses the Reporter technique to build content by laying out the rest of the 5 Ws and 1 H. And we could have left off that last "how" but it is nice to show gratitude and I included it to show a better way to express gratitude to our family than saying "they pay for my fees and clothes." (Compare this to the Bungler 2 response above.)

Your answer would be different, of course. You might have entered because a friend or your parents said you should. You may not have ever been shy but still saw pageants as a way to build on the skills you already had. Whatever your reason, think it through. And then think about what you've learned and what you get out of it. (I've got worksheets to help you on this in the upcoming Essential Pageant Interview Playbook.)

The point of this section is that you can build content if you think like a reporter. Oh and don't stress yourself out trying to sort out "Is this really when? Or where? Or what!?" Just get the general idea in your head and play with it. Just remembering that there are those angles will help you build content. (It isn't crucial that you label the pieces just right as you won't be sharing those labels with others anyway!)

How to Remember

And speaking of remembering things, the way journalists are often taught (or used to be!) to remember this was, again, "Remember, the Five Ws and One H." But here's how I remember it:

I tell myself there is one W for each of my fingers and thumb and the H is for the palm of my hand (H for hand!). Then I remind myself I have two hands and that I should always seek balanced information and perspectives so my answers will be sensitive and diplomatic.

As I said, depending on the question and what you have to share, you probably wouldn't try to provide specifics on *all* of those in an interview response, unless you could do so briefly and succinctly.

Remember, any one response in your interview *isn't* a full news story so you don't need to feel obligated to give every detail. What you'd do instead is start your reply with the most on-target part— which may very well cover one or more of the 5 Ws and 1 H. If that doesn't feel long enough or strong enough or if, as a Sleuth, you see it could be useful to share a specific about another of the 5 Ws or 1 H, then do that.

You do not have to do the reporter technique on *everything* but keep it in mind and use it as a base from which to build. There are exercises at the end of this book to help you build your skill with this.

S.T.A.R. Story

You always have choices. *You* get to choose what to say (and how) to everything you are asked. I hope you will always be a Sleuth about what to include, yes, but your style may differ from someone else's so it is good to have multiple ways to build content.

For some contestants or some questions, approaching it like a reporter may feel just right, other times it might not. So I'll share another strong strategy that will seem on the surface as the *opposite* of the Reporter approach. In one way it is, but you'll see that both techniques help you develop content effectively. With a S.T.A.R. Story you get the same result in the end—an on-target answer that shows who you are and what you can do—you just approach it a little differently.

As you'll recall, a Reporter *starts* with the "take-home" point and has more of a "just the facts" feel (even though you'd be friendly, warm, and smiling while you delivered your response). A S.T.A.R. story is different in that it sets the stage a little bit and *ends* with the strongest point. How do you do that? Let's look at what the letters S.T.A.R. represent.

Situation
A sentence or phrase that gives the
general setting or context

Task
What the challenge, problem, or
opportunity was

Action
What action *you* took to address it

Result
What happened in the end

A good S.T.A.R. story could be told in one or two good sentences or it could take a couple more—it just depends on the question, what you have to say, and if it is a good use of your time to expand or contract what you share. Think like a Sleuth as you decide what to include.

Let's say, for example, a judge asks:

Example 1: Longer

"Can you tell us about a time where you had to think on your feet?"

You can be sure you've got a decent, complete answer if you use the S.T.A.R. story technique. You might say the following (I've inserted the S.T.A. R. words so you can see how it works):

S.T.A.R

(Situation)

"I was working on the yearbook committee and we were about to send the book to the printers. Unfortunately there were still a few blank pages here and there because a couple clubs hadn't turned in their pages and other issues."

(Task)

"We tried to help them and waited as long as we could but we'd go over budget and ruin the rest of our time line if we didn't get it to the printers *that* day. We couldn't just pull those pages out because it would mess up the pagination of the whole book!"

(Action)

"So I quickly put a nice border and the word "Memories" at the top of a page. "Five years from now…" on another, and "If I only knew" on another, etc. We inserted pages like this wherever we needed to and got it to the printer."

(Result)

"The budget and time line worked out and the students *loved* these pages because there's never enough room to sign yearbooks inside the covers and sometimes you don't know what to say so these pages gave extra space and ideas."

That may seem sort of long but it isn't too bad (if you read it out loud it is really only around a minute) but I included that as I wanted you to see all the parts of the S.T.A.R. story clearly. Using this framework gives you a beginning, middle, and an end. Knowing how to end can save you from rambling! Let's try to imagine a shorter version, though, as another example for you.

Example 2: Shorter

Judge
"Can you tell us about a time where you had to think on your feet?"

S.T.A.R.

(Situation)
"One time, I was coming home from school and I saw a car run into a tree!"

(Task)
"No one else was around and I knew I needed to help."

(Action)
"As I ran to the car, I dialed 911 to report it and then I stayed on the line while the operator walked me through helping the man in the car until the paramedics arrived."

(Result)
"It was scary but I didn't panic. I stuck with it and the paramedics said what I did helped save his life. I really hope I don't have to witness another accident but now I know I can think on my feet and handle it. And I've taken a CPR class since then too—just to be better prepared!"

Let's try a different example. Let's say a judge asks you:

Example 3

Judge
"What are you most proud of?"

That may seem like an easy question but if you have *lots* of things you feel proud of it may be hard for you to choose. Just as hard as it might be for someone who feels unsure of what they feel proud of. If you are on the spot, you might be tempted to say:

> "I'm proud of my grades because I worked hard for them. I've really improved my study skills this year."

Or:

> "I'm proud of my body because it was hard to get in shape after having children. Now I bet no one can tell I have 3 kids."

Or:

> "I'm proud of my marriage and children—our good marriage has led to well-behaved, enjoyable kids. I couldn't be prouder of them!"

Or:

> "I'm proud that I just got a promotion at work…it shows my boss and peers really respect me."

There isn't really anything wrong with those answers. They may not be Bungled but they aren't optimized either. A Sleuth would choose something that will show her ability to be a good titleholder or otherwise reflects well on her. Let's see how she might use a brief S.T.A.R. story here:

S.T.A.R.

(Situation)

"My teacher wanted each student to find a way to help in the community."

(Task)

"I decided to focus on a friend whose dad had just lost his job."

(Action)

"I organized a community wide bake sale/auction and food collection. It was a lot of work but it was-"

(Result)

"-worth it as the bake sale/auction raised $325 dollars for them *and* two carts worth of groceries were donated. And I got the local grocery store to donate a gift card so they could get some fresh meat and produce too. I'm proud of many things but that has to top my list right now because it was so great to see so many people contribute in whatever way they could, big or small. And the family really appreciated it."

How do you remember the S.T.A.R. Story frame work. Just use the letters we've already laid out: one letter for each main piece. The word STAR will be easy to remember because you *are* a star in the making (if you aren't one already!).

"If you can't explain it simply,
you don't understand it well enough."
~Albert Einstein

Balance

I keep coming back to this because it is so important. We introduced the concept of balance earlier and have demonstrated it through many examples in the book already. So I won't spend much more time on it here except to remind that "balance" helps you build content for your responses too.

Building balance into responses helps with having good content especially for questions that might be considered "controversial." Again, you can still be yourself and have your own opinions, practicing "balance" just helps you be more gracious about it. So remember to consider multiple sides as you compose your responses but usually limit what you actually say to two sides (three at most!), for the sake of time and clarity.

While there are additional examples in the book, you can start with these to refresh yourself on what "balance" does and doesn't look like. Go back through the book and review the example responses to the following questions:

- "Do you believe that taxpayer's money should be used to bailout struggling U.S. companies, why and/or why not?"
- "What do you think about the scandal going on in your state right now?"
- "What are your thoughts on smoking?"
- "Do you think the U.S. should have universal health care as a right of citizenship? Why or why not?"
- "The wars are in the media a lot lately; what do you think about our troops overseas and the mental health crisis and what the government should or shouldn't do there or here, then or later, and about the media coverage?" (Remember, this was worded poorly on purpose to help you sort through it when a judge asks a scattered question!)

- "Tonight you were judged in how you look in a swimsuit. In some countries women can't wear them, how does that make you feel?"
- "Vermont recently became the fourth state to legalize same-sex marriage. Do you think every state should follow suit, why or why not?"

As these are from books earlier in the series, take a second to revisit them now. If you found those questions challenging when you first encountered them in the book, hopefully you don't find them quite as challenging anymore because you are already changing how you look at them. And don't worry, not all questions are as "deep" as universal healthcare and citizenship.

Conclusion

You've come a long way! When we started this book you knew to be like a Sleuth, you knew to listen with care and let that guide you to your response content. But now you have more specific approaches to use to build content. Just raising your awareness about them will help you improve but if you actually do the exercises and practice out loud, you'll be amazed at how your confidence and performance can change!

By the way, if you liked those exercises and enjoy worksheets and questions to help you get to know yourself, your interests, and your title better, be sure to check out the forthcoming Essential Pageant Interview Playbook I've been working on. I know I've mentioned it before but I can't emphasize enough that it may be "just the ticket" for some of you to really get comfortable with who you are and what you know.

And that will help you not just in pageant interviews but other career and life interviews down the road. Lots of good experiences await you. Remember, the name of my materials is "Pageant To PhD" because a pageant is just the beginning!

Review

Let's look back for a moment in review on creating good response content!

Listening with care was emphasized again. It is the foundation of creating good content that is on-target (as you cannot answer what you didn't hear or understand).

- One strategy to build content is to Deepen/Specify which involves turning "What did you do" and "Tell us about" questions into "How you did it" and "Why you did it" questions. Making that transition in your head expands the original question which, in turn, encourages you to say more in your response.

- The Reporter technique is effective in that it gives you a list of things to consider including in each response. You don't *have* to say each of the six parts in each response if it gets too long but you should at least consider them and allow yourself to choose the best information to share (as a Pageant Sleuth). With this technique you generally aim to start with the most important information first.

- The S.T.A.R. (Situation, Task, Action, Result) Story technique is helpful to building content as it gives you a structure to follow as you tell about something you did. It helps you stick to the main points of the story. In this technique, you usually end with the most important point.

- The importance of being balanced was mentioned again. Recognizing that there is usually more than one side to anything helps you see there may be more to say. And the beauty of balance is that what you have to add will likely be more meaningful (and show your thoughtfulness and diplomacy).

Exercise 11.1: Tell Us About Yourself

Practice out loud a couple responses to "Tell us about yourself" or other versions of that request or question. See if you can share more relevant and interesting information about yourself that shows your skills, personality, or that relates to the pageant. Review the material on opening statements in *Book 7: Making a Strong First Impression* if you need additional guidance.

Exercise 11.2: Noticing the 5 Ws and 1 H

As a practice exercise, start noticing the 5 Ws and 1 H when you listen to, watch, or read the news. If you are reading a newspaper, write in the margin "who, what, when, where, why, how" next to what the sentence is addressing. If you are listening or watching, challenge yourself to note the elements as you listen.

Exercise 11.3: Including the 5 Ws and 1 H

Start practicing building the 5 Ws and 1 H into your own practice answers. At first it may feel awkward and artificial to "dig in" to your memory to provide that information. That's okay because this exercise is just for practice to help you "get the point" that such information *is* available to you to expand your answers with.

Challenge yourself to provide all 5 Ws and 1 H a time or two during each out loud practice session, even if it makes your answers too long. Notice what information enhanced your response versus details you didn't really need. If that doesn't come easily at first, keep trying! Try recording yourself, so you can hear yourself. It helps if you are working with a friend or a coach as well, since we never really "hear" what we sound like in real time.

Do that for awhile and then consciously stop trying to provide all 5 Ws and 1 H. Let the exercise go and allow yourself to answer with just what feels right, which will usually be fewer of the 5 Ws and 1 H but now you'll be better able to make choices about what to include while you are "thinking on your feet."

Exercise 11.4: Practice Writing S.T.A.R. Stories

Go through your application paperwork (your fact sheet, resume, bio, etc.) and challenge yourself to write a S.T.A.R. story for each key fact, entry, hobby, etc. Don't worry about being perfect, just start! You may need to come back to it a time or two as you remember details. Just write some for fun—no one has to see them. You don't have to memorize them. Just write them to help jog your memory and build your skill with the S.T.A.R. approach.

Exercise 11.5: Practice Speaking S.T.A.R. Stories

Practice responding out loud to a variety of questions and use a S.T.A.R. story as often as you can. Even if it feels funny at first, just do it. Practice is *practice*, you don't have to be perfect in your practice when you are trying something new. Perfection" comes over time (if ever!).

Trust that you'll build your skill and know when it feels right to use a S.T.A.R. story and when to leave that tool in the box. It would really help if you taped yourself and/or worked with someone. That will speed your progress in recognizing what is actually interesting to share and what isn't, what is too much, too little, too personal, and so on.

"One of the basic causes for all the trouble in
the world today is that people talk too much and
think too little. They act impulsively without
thinking. I always try to think before I talk."
~Margaret Chase Smith

a pageant is just the beginning...

PAGEANT
*I*nterviewing
SUCCESS

When You Don't Know the Answer

Dr. Stephanie Raye, PhD
Former Miss American Petite

Book 12
When You Don't Know the Answer
Table of Contents

Pageant Interviewing Success:
When You Don't Know the Answer

Despite your good intentions and preparation, you may get a question that catches you off guard or you think to yourself "I don't know the answer to that!" That's okay, it can happen to any of us. We cannot possibly know everything and be prepared for every possible question we might get.

Remind yourself that the amount of preparation and practice you *did* do, however, will serve you well in artfully handling it if (when!) you get a surprise question. You may not be able to be a gold-star Sleuth on every question—in fact, if you don't know the answer, you may feel like you bungled an opportunity. It's true, there may be a bit of bungle to it, but if you handle surprises well, you can minimize the Bungle Factor.

We have already covered some things that will help with "not knowing the answer" earlier in the book, especially in discussing whether to repeat questions and strategies on handling personal questions. But wait! There's more! Let's go over some ways to deconstruct the question to find what you *do* know as you may surprise yourself! We'll also cover ways to handle it if you find you actually *don't* know the answer.

Forms of Knowledge – Fact Versus Concept

We've discussed five categories of questions in this book—Personal, Pageant, Simple/Silly, Current Events, and Controversial. Regardless of which category of question you get, they can pull on different forms of knowledge—any question can be phrased to be either, generally speaking, factual or conceptual.

Factual questions are asking for something more precise and you either know the answer or you don't. Sometimes they are phrased in a way that appears "closed-ended" meaning the answer is either "yes" or "no" or a specific fact. In short, you either know the answer or you don't.

Conceptual questions usually have more open-ended kinds of responses that show that you can analyze or apply information so the answers usually combine knowledge, analysis, and opinion. There usually is no "right" answer—no simple fact that answers it—but these show more how you think and what you value.

Put another way, we can have "factual" knowledge—this is along the lines of memorized dates, numbers, places, and names. This could apply to your life, career goals, area of study, platform, title, etc. and could be your stories or memories.

And we can have "conceptual application" of knowledge—which is more how you apply the facts, think about an issue, solve a problem, or frame a debate. This comes from understanding what things mean and then developing your own informed opinions and connections to that information or knowledge. It can involve facts, of course, but goes beyond them.

Let's use this framework as a way to explore how to handle it when you get a question for which you don't really feel like you have an answer.

Factual Questions

Most factual questions have a specific answer or could be "yes/no" questions at their root—so there *is* an answer to these questions.

The sorts of facts you should know include, as we've discussed, anything that pertains to your life and what you put on your fact sheet and application materials and to questions that spinoff from there. Similarly, you'll want to be reasonably well-informed about your pageant, title, the area you represent, and your platform and passions.

If it is a factual question that you don't know the answer to, like:

- "How many counties are in your state?"
- "How many women have been appointed to the Supreme Court?"
- "Who was the first female presidential candidate?"
- "Who is the current titleholder?"

…then that's pretty hard to hide. If you don't know the answer to a factual question you have four choices:

- Guess
- Try to fake it
- Admit you don't know
- Switch to something you do know

The latter two are the only choices I'd recommend—admit you don't know or switch. But we'll still talk very briefly about guessing and faking, before we get to the other choices.

Guessing/Faking

Guessing is more or less a Bungler move. Trying to fake it is more or less a Smuggler move. Either way, these are approaches to responding you shouldn't need to make if you prepare and learn good answer strategies from this book and other materials. Even if you didn't prepare, I don't recommend guessing or faking. This book will help more with figuring out how to handle tough questions you don't know the answer to or do your best to gracefully handle it without figuring it out.

Sure you could take a guess but, of course, you could be wrong. And depending on the style of the particular judges you face, you may not even *know* you were wrong. Right or wrong, they might just move on to the next question to help you save face.

That'd be a blessing. Because if you guess or fake it and you *are* wrong it would be an unfortunate waste of time—not to mention a poor reflection on you—to have the judge tell you that you're wrong, ask you why you guessed, or otherwise explore why you don't know. So, in my opinion, it's better to cut to the chase with a more reasonable choice which is…

Admit You Don't Know

You can do this gracefully and everybody will be happier if you do this, rather than guessing. The judges may still wonder why you don't know something that they might consider "basic" or "important" but we can't know everything, right? The judges know that and are interested in how you handle it when you don't know something because as Queen the media and the public could ask you anything!

That said, as I have emphasized, you really should know things like how many counties are in your state and how many women have been appointed to the Supreme Court, etc. After all you may be representing your state and you are certainly a representative of women! Questions like these may not come up but they also aren't hard to learn or remember "just in case."

(This is why I keep stressing preparation and using tools like the upcoming Essential Pageant Interview Playbook that will really support you in developing both basic and advanced knowledge, and help you figure out what to value and believe in lots of key areas. It will help you not only with personal areas (like goals) but also assist you in figuring out your opinions.)

But in this book, I'm assuming you are already there in the interview chair—at whatever level of preparation—and they have asked you some sort of factual question that you simply don't know.

Here are a few ideas to work with to admit gracefully that you don't know something. I offer you a little "stage direction" below but you have to do what is natural for you and fitting to the situation. But, for example, depending on the question you don't know and your personal style you might say:

(Thoughtful look)
"I'm sorry but I'm drawing a blank on that right now.

(Smile)
Could we please go on to the next question?"

(Slightly apologetic look and tone, but tone still confident)
"I admit I feel like I should know that, but I don't.

(Starting to smile and nodding that you will fix this for the future)
I will study up on it and know it from now on, but for now, *(smile)* can we please proceed to another question?"

"You know, I don't know that right now. I refreshed my memory on some other facts, but this particular one has slipped away. Can we go on to a different question?"

(Note: if you say something like this last response, be prepared for them to follow up with "What sort of facts did you refresh yourself on?" So only say it if it is true and you are prepared to come back with something interesting that, say, relates to your community service or platform, or some other interesting thing about women or your State, etc.)

Switch Via Substitute and Side-Step

If admitting you don't know doesn't sit well with you and you really want to answer in some other way (or if you've already admitted you don't know once and feel it would reflect poorly on you to do it again) then you can try to switch to what you do know. In essence you are switching the question they gave you to one you can answer! There are three primary ways to switch:

- Substitute something different (like a movie for a book)

- Substitute something similar (like a child's book or text book for a novel)
- Side-step

Sometimes you'll get a question that you don't know the direct answer to because you haven't done it or can't remember. But you can substitute something directly (or indirectly) for the key part of the question (listen for key words). For example:

Judge

"What's the last book you read and what did you think of it?"

If a judge asks you that, the "question behind the question" may be to get at how you spend your free time, how "cultured" you are, what your taste in books is. Or they might be asking it "just because" they are generally curious!

Whatever the reason they asked it, if you haven't read a book lately (and can't remember the last one you did read), you can answer it with something closely related and maybe be a Sleuth to work in something else that will help you shine or help them appreciate what you have to offer the pageant.

So even though you know the judge is asking about, say, a novel or non-fiction "how-to" book (like this one!) you haven't read one lately. Let's go through a number of ways you could switch. You might say, for instance:

Example 1 Responses

"I've been so busy with appearances and preparations that I haven't read a book lately, but I did see a great movie and I hope to read the book it was based on. I saw _____ and it was very powerful. I realized I need to learn more about _____ so I want to read that book and another on the topic soon."

That directly substitutes a movie for a book and connects to a future book.

> "I read quite a bit—I usually have more than one book going at once. So the last book I read doesn't stick in my mind, but I can tell you that my favorite book is *Gone with the Wind*. I know, it may be a bit old-fashioned in ways (and it is certainly a thick book!) but there's a lot in there about family, hope, values, and had a strong female lead character."

That substitutes a favorite book for the last book and shows a few things the person values.

> "I read a lot of news so I haven't taken the time to read a book lately. But I tell you one I'm looking forward to starting soon is _____ . I hear it is both good entertainment and full of information—the best of both worlds!"

That substitutes a future book for a last book.

> "I've been so busy with school that I haven't had time to read a book just for fun for awhile. But I have been learning a lot in my textbooks, especially in my communication class. It's really helped me understand more about how to be a better public speaker that will help me better represent my platform and the title."

That substitutes in a textbook and works in important title-related content.

> "My family and community service activities haven't allowed me to read books for myself lately. I will again one day but for now I can tell you about the book my youngest son likes me to read him at bedtime. It's 'Goodnight Moon' and I love it as it

> helps him settle right down and go to sleep with a
> smile on his face. My platform is "Adult Literacy" so
> I know how important it is to help children appreciate
> reading from early on—most of the adults I've helped
> learn to read wish their parents had done the same
> with them."

That substitutes a child's book, emphasizes family and platform—a great Mrs. response!

You can see how this approach could be adjusted even if the question was more simply put, like "What's your favorite book?" Or favorite movie. Maybe you can't remember it under pressure or maybe you don't have one. Either way, you can substitute or side-step.

Side-stepping is really very similar to substituting. I just separate out the idea because you'll find that some factual questions that you don't know the answer to may not be right for a direct substitution—not everything is as simple as swapping out a movie for a book, or the like.

If the question is a little more involved than that, you might find something that relates to what they are asking that allows you to side-step a little but stay along the general lines. For instance, they might ask you something specific you might not know so you could say:

> "I don't know *that* detail about the situation but what
> I do know about it is __"

Then you'd continue with some information that you do know and can tie in. It wouldn't be a fact for fact substitution but a re-direction and expansion.

So let's say they ask you a detail about your platform or volunteer work (or whatever else) and you don't know.

Example 2

Judge

"I see your platform is to raise awareness about early detection of breast cancer. So how many women die of breast cancer each year?"

While you *should* know this if it is your platform, let's say you don't. Here are three responses…which would you model yourself after?

Bungler

"Oh darn, I knew someone would ask me that and I meant to remember it but I forgot to look it up. It's a lot of people. We have to stop cancer."

Smuggler

"2 million. (A number she just made up! The annual estimate is closer to 40,000 a year in the U.S.)"

Sleuth

"I must be a little nervous as I can't recall that exact number but what I can tell you is that if breast cancer is detected early, the survival rate is 96%. Much better than if it is detected at a later stage. So my focus is on how many we can keep living rather than how many have died."

(You could fill in any fact you know rather than the 5-year survival rate. If you don't know a numerical fact then you could offer something more general on quality of life or something more personal like a story on how it affected a family.)

Let's try a couple more:

Example 3

Judge

"I see you've done volunteer work at a women's shelter. Do you know any domestic violence statistics for this city or state?"

Bungler

"No, I don't know that. I probably should but I really just bring them some used clothes and help watch the kids at the shelter now and then. You know, like when the mom has to go to court or the doctor or something around the abuse."

Sleuth

"I hear different numbers and they are hard to keep in mind because it seems to depend on how you count it. And one of the problems is that so many abuse victims don't report abuse. Part of my hope is that my platform will encourage people to report it or at least get the help they need. This problem impacts men, women, and children and cuts across generations as elder abuse is more and more common."

Example 4

Judge

"You've said on your paperwork that you are interested in studying heart and cardiovascular disease in women and maybe going into medicine. Tell me more about that, for instance, how many women die of heart disease each year."

Bungler

"Well, I don't know that but I do know that heart disease runs in my family and I don't want to die from it. And maybe what I learn will help others too. Of course, I don't want others to die!"

Sleuth

"I have to admit the actual number has slipped my memory at the moment but I do know that, incredibly, the number of women that die each year is twice the number of women who die of cancer—including breast cancer! I know we have to fight cancer too but there is so much fundraising and research on it already. I'd like to study heart disease and raise awareness so it gets the attention it deserves too. I lost my grandmother to heart disease. I miss her and it was preventable. I'd like to see other women and families spared from what my family went through."

This Sleuth didn't know the answer but she did know something! And even if she hadn't known the fact about more women dying of heart disease, she could have admitted she didn't know the number and skipped to why she wants to study it.

So we've covered a simple personal question and some on platform types of facts around which you don't know the answer. But what if it is a factual current event (potentially controversial) question that comes up?

Let's say you were asked a factual current event question like:

Example 5

Judge

"What do you think about your city's plan to raise money during this economic downturn?"

Chances are if you are asked that there is some *specific* city effort they have in mind—like, say, an increased sales or property tax that has been in the news. But maybe you've not heard much, if anything, about it.

You might say:

Sleuth

"I've not heard details on the plans to increase money coming *in*, but what I do know is that there have been many programs and services planned to be cut to save some money from going *out*. Economic challenges can be scary but I think they can also bring the best out in our leaders as they hopefully work together to find creative solutions. It is unlikely that everyone will be satisfied at the start but they might be when they see it worked out."

You didn't substitute anything directly but you picked up a lead that allowed you to sidestep the original question and offer what you could on something related. Along the way, you showed that while you may not follow the news all the time, you follow it enough to say something. And you ended with something positive and hopeful which, if it doesn't sound fake, is usually appreciated.

Notice how that question actually was a combination-question; the judge asked what you thought about something as well as assumed you knew a fact (about what was going on in your city). We focused on the factual side but let's dig into "harder" questions that are more topical and don't have as much plain "fact" involved in them.

Conceptual Questions

By "concepts" what I mean is ideas and matters that might involve *how* you think and why, rather than just your ability to remember facts.

In reality, there is often overlap. If the judges ask you a question about your thoughts on a current event or potentially controversial topic, it is like they are asking you a combination-question in that it is about *you* (it is your thoughts, opinions, beliefs) and it could be about some "fact" (in that it is a fact that there *is* abortion, euthanasia, gun control/rights, gay marriage, etc.) but they aren't really asking you about the fact or for details. They are looking to see how you think about and handle ideas and deeper concepts.

It would be very rare, if ever, that you'd ever be asked directly by a judge if you are "for" or "against" abortion, gun control, gay marriage, or whatever. So don't worry about that. The judges usually aren't interested in that and you aren't judged on your opinions or beliefs. So questions that deal with these deeper philosophical issues usually are not phrased to be closed-ended questions—there isn't one answer and it usually isn't as simple as yes or no. (And even if that is what it boils down to underneath—as we'll soon talk about— you'd be wise to expand on it.)

So you don't necessarily need to know dates, names, numbers and places for every event or issue out there, unless it is about your platform—you should know some facts about that. But you *do* want to know a little something meaningful about a lot of things so you can understand a variety of questions and be able to answer them intelligently. That's why watching the news and doing personal exploration is important.

But there's a lot to know out there so if you don't happen to have an answer to what they are asking, you first have to know *why* you don't have an answer.

Regardless of your reason, you have four basic choices—ask for help, try to make it work, fake it, or try to pass. Those are the basic choices but that's an over-simplification so let's also examine some of the options that relate to them more closely:

Ask for some help.

- Ask for a rephrase.
- Ask for a definition or clarification.

Try to make it work.

- Avoid the question but make a statement.

- Figure out what you can; answer part of it, taking it in a direction you can comment on.

Fake it.

- Take a stab at it and hope for the best.

Try to pass.

- Admit what you don't know and imply you want to move on.

We'll try to consider them in roughly that order but, as you'd guess, there'll be a little overlap. Let's get started.

Ask for Some Help

If there is a word you don't know take a second to see if you can figure it out from context. If you understand the rest of the question, sometimes one word that was unclear can come into focus. But if it doesn't, then consider asking the judge to rephrase the question.

WHY DON'T YOU KNOW THE ANSWER?

Here are a few possibilities...

- You have *no* idea what they just asked you. Maybe you weren't listening! But assuming you did... You've never heard of what they are talking about. You have no clue. Or what you think it might be about is so vague you are likely to be wrong.
- You have an *idea* of what they are talking about but don't really know much about it. At least not enough to answer the question as confidently as you like.
- You know a little about the topic they've asked you, but you aren't sure you understand the question.

- You know a little (or a lot!) about the topic but you don't know what one of the words the judge used means and that's what's confusing you.

There's a good chance that when the judge rephrases the question, he or she won't use the word you had trouble with or will expand on the topic enough to help you understand what it meant. A compassionate judge might realize you are struggling with some part of it and intentionally say it in different or simpler words or give you a little direction.

Speaking of "expanding," you can simply *ask* for them to expand on it with something like:

> "Would you please expand on that a little so I know better what you mean?"

If it is a particular phrase or word, you could ask directly about that saying:

> "I'm not familiar with the word _____. Would you please use a synonym or define it?"

Or, if you understand all of the words in general but aren't *sure* what one of them means—as some words have multiple meanings or the concept is complicated—you might ask for them to be more specific. But you can do it in a way to demonstrate that you are keeping up by sharing that you do know a little bit. For instance, you could say:

> "When you say _____, do you mean _____ or _____."

In this case you are showing you appreciate distinctions and being clear. The judges see that you know a couple meanings but are trying to zero in on which aspect they meant.

Any of the above might be the way to go if you do have some knowledge on the topic but aren't certain. Or, remember, judges aren't perfect so you may need to ask for clarification if the question is just poorly worded or confusing.

Don't spend a lot of time clarifying a question on something you know nothing about. (Some would argue not to spend any time clarifying even if you *do* know something about it.) Don't nitpick details. Get the gist of what they are asking, clarify if necessary, then answer best you can and move on.

(Remember that back in *Book 8: Being in the Win Zone* we also talked about "paraphrasing" which is saying back the whole question in your *own* words to be sure you understand it. Paraphrasing is another way to ask for help or clarification but is more handy when you know all the words and/or if the whole question is worded in a confusing way. If you just don't understand one word, you might as well just cut to the chase and ask about that word.)

Try to Make it Work— Get to the Key Components

You may know more than you give yourself credit for. Sometimes questions sound scary and when you're a little nervous on top of it, the question may seem "too hard."

But even with a long, scary-sounding question you can always get to the core and break it down into its component parts. When you see the parts, you may realize that you do have some knowledge or opinion on one or more of the parts. With that in mind, you'd then focus your response on that part.

For instance, let's say you get a question something like this:

Judge
"What are your thoughts on women's rights and the Constitutionality of abortion and partial birth abortion?"

Yikes. Unless you studied it in school, are a lawyer, or your platform or community service work, etc., has something to do with family planning, pro-life, or pro-choice, no one really wants that question! It is at once "too broad" and "too specific." It can feel overwhelming or too personal.

But you're a Sleuth! So you take it in stride. You'll be prepared for questions like this because you will have read at least a little about it (you don't have to be an expert) as one topic that could possibly come up. (More on those topics in my forthcoming Playbook). But, for now, let's assume you aren't prepared for such a question so you need to use your Sleuth skills in a different way—you need to figure out how to handle the fact that you don't know.

"Insight, I believe, refers to the depth of understanding that comes by setting experiences, yours and mine, familiar and exotic, new and old, side by side, learning by letting them speak to one another."
~Mary Catherine Bateson

Let's take this apart, step by step. It may take a lot of words for me to explain this effectively but, believe it or not, when you go through the process "live" during an interview it'll happen in just a second or two!

What's the Core?

The core of every question is, deep down, getting at a "yes," "no," or "maybe." I know, the judges didn't *ask* you a "yes" or "no" question and they aren't invested in whether you are for or against it. But, underneath all the words, you do probably lean one way or another and you can use that to inform your answer in a *balanced* way. Even if they do want to politely find out your leaning on any controversial issue, remember that how you lean isn't as important as how sensitively you handle the answer.

No matter how strongly you feel (or not!), in reality, there isn't a "right" or "wrong" answer to these sorts of tough questions—that's what makes them tough and why they are "controversial."

So if you don't know what to say, start with just this: feel it through and think it through. What's your core feeling? Yes? No? Or maybe? It is often wise not to *say* your core feeling but get in mind and think about the components before you answer.

What Are the Components?

Remember how I emphasized listening for "key words" back in *Book 8: Being in the Win Zone*? The components of the question usually include key words. In this example they are:

- Your thoughts
- Women's rights
- Constitution
- Abortion
- Partial birth abortion

If you don't feel strongly that you know all five parts, what *do* you know?

You can at least take a quick read on 1) your thoughts. Imagine if you weren't in the interview chair but were instead talking to friends over lunch and this topic (in this case, abortion) came up. What would you think? Feel? Say?

If you aren't clear on your deep down feeling, what's the general tone? Positive, negative or neutral? What sorts of words will diplomatically convey the tone you have in mind? You're going back to the core here and then expanding a bit.

Now ask yourself that about each of the other components—have you ever heard anything or thought about 2) women's rights? Let's say you know that they matter to you, that you value them, and that you know women didn't always have many rights.

Okay. So what's your sense of the role of 3) the Constitution? What do you remember? Let's say you know that lawyers argue over it all the time, that it is generally there to protect rights, and that you don't know much about the constitution.

And maybe it just doesn't matter, in this particular moment or setting, to sort out the difference between 4) "abortion" and 5) "partial birth abortion." Let's say you decide to set this distinction aside and not ask for any definitions. (Good choice, don't spend too much time on a question you don't know much about.)

It may seem like a lot, but all that thinking I just wrote down can happen in the space of a breath. It can happen as the question is being asked and you pause for a moment to collect your thoughts. (Or it can with a little practice.) And then the time comes to form your answer. So, again, the question was:

Judge
"What are your thoughts on women's rights and the constitutionality of abortion and partial birth abortion?"

So you might say something like:

Contestant
"In general, I don't feel good about abortion. I don't think most people *like* the idea even if they are "pro choice." But I try not to pass judgment on people. As this is a serious thing I imagine if a woman did it we'd hope she had a very important reason. It seems like an individual decision. I know women haven't always had as many rights as they should and that the Constitution is there to help protect rights. At this time, as I'm not an expert in any of this, I'll have to

> leave it to well-meaning people and the lawyers to
> work out the details."

That's okay. The response may be a little long but good under the circumstances. This contestant tried to be balanced and her response is way better than a blank look, faking it, or trying to pass. If you came up with something like that after initially feeling scared by the question, you did good!

Remember, though, we can also practice shortening our answer while still keeping the content strong. Let's try that. You could drop off the first part and shorten it to:

> "It seems like an individual decision. I know women
> haven't always had as many rights as they should and
> that the Constitution is there to help protect rights. At
> this time, as I'm not an expert in any of this, I'll have
> to leave it to well-meaning people and the lawyers to
> work out the details."

The part we just edited out was your internal response to the core of the question. We didn't offer the judges a leaning but still answered the question!

What should you do if you don't know what the Constitution is there to do? Then you leave that component out or admit you don't know that part. In that case, you focus on the part you *can* answer, which might be something like this:

Judge

"What are your thoughts on women's rights and the constitutionality of abortion and partial birth abortion?"

Contestant

"In general, I don't feel good about abortion. I don't think most people like the idea even if they are pro-choice. So I assume if a woman does something like this—at whatever stage of pregnancy—they probably had some very important reason. It seems like an individual decision."

If you feel too uncertain about the components, you might consider another form of trying to make it work…

Avoid the Question, But Make a Statement

If you just can't deal with the question, or some key component that seems critical, then maybe try something like:

Judge

"What are your thoughts on women's rights and the constitutionality of abortion and partial birth abortion?"

Contestant

"Abortion of any kind is a sensitive topic that I suspect most people prefer not to talk about. Just as I expect most women would prefer not to ever think about having one. But I'm glad I live in a country where people can discuss their rights around this issue if they want to."

That doesn't really answer the question at all, in my opinion, but it may be enough to show that you can gracefully sidestep something you aren't prepared to answer. That's good to show! At this point, the judges would likely move on from this topic. But if they don't, and ask you a follow-up, start the thinking process again or try one of the other approaches.

Faking It

As I mentioned before, I don't recommend this. Let's talk about it. It may be hard to admit you don't know something, but better to admit it than to say something that reveals the truth of it (that you don't know) in an unflattering way. I would not recommend taking a full out guess on something. That sets you up for a major bungle as the odds are against you guessing correctly.

If you feel like you do know a little about the topic but only in one area, you could try:

> "I'm not an expert on this but my opinion on this part of it is _____"

Some might recommend you take a chance and answer the question, guessing at the part you don't understand. That's a risk only *you* will know if you should take, based on what the rest of question is and your chances on getting it right based on the rest of the conversation.

I recommend against that and suggest, instead, that you try one of the other options we've covered. And remember, if asking for clarification, working through the components, etc. isn't working for you, you can still admit what you don't know and/or focus on what you do.

After all, the pageant wants a Queen who knows what she knows and what she doesn't. That reflects well on herself and the title. Pretending you know things you don't rarely works out as we'd hope! Don't let pride or fear of looking bad get in your way of being a genuine person who knows she too has some limits.

Try to Pass

Depending on what you know (or don't) about the topic and how much time is left in your interview you may prefer to move on as quickly as possible. Time is precious, you only have a few minutes together so you don't want to get bogged down on anything. (Even if it is a positive thing staying on one topic too long may not be wise as there is so much of you to highlight!) Also, if possible, you want to end on a strong note.

If time is getting away from you, or something else in the situation makes you think or feel you should try to do this, you can consider trying to pass on a question. Gracefully, of course. You probably would not say bluntly "Pass!" but you could say something like:

> "I'm sorry but I'm not familiar with that topic."

Said with a smile and a note of finality (like saying "let's move on" without really saying that!), they may take the hint and move on.

But be prepared that if you say "I'm sorry but I'm not familiar with that topic," the judges may not move on. They might tell you a little bit about the topic, rephrase it for you and ask you what you think. Or they may ask you why you wouldn't know about _____ or ask you if you think it is important to learn about _____ .

To avoid that, you might prefer to say something like this:

> "I know a little about that but not enough to speak with confidence. But you can trust I'll be looking into that more carefully very soon!"

Or:

> "I've had that on my list of things to look into more deeply—it's a pretty complex topic from what I can tell so far—so I'm not sure I'm ready to comment on that just now."

Do your best to only attempt passing on a question once in a while. For instance, if you did it more than once in a given interview, they may start to wonder if you are "just a pretty face." That's a nice thing to be but it is rarely enough. (And is why interview is important to decide between all the contestants' pretty faces!)

Also, be sure that if you say you were planning or are going to look into a topic, be sure you do! Do it before your next interview—even in the same pageant, if at all possible. Learn a bit, think it through. Why?

Because you could get a question on that topic on-stage or you could get the same judge in another interview or pageant. It would not reflect well on you if they remembered you promising to look into a topic and then finding that you didn't follow-through. Always follow through.

"The art of being wise is knowing what to overlook."
~William James

Time Considerations, Again

As I've mentioned before in various ways throughout, use your time wisely. Don't spend a lot of time on a dead end or a low value question (something that won't get you much for the effort you put in). Use your head and trust your gut on what to pursue (and how) versus what to gracefully let slide.

Review

As always, it is good to review a little to help us remember what we learned.

- While there may be some overlap, questions are generally factual or conceptual in nature.

- Factual questions have to do with numbers, dates, what happened, time, specific people, etc. Conceptual questions are more about ideas and interpretation of events and facts. They want to know how you see and apply what you know, or what's your personal perspective on something. The "something" might be anything. The reason these questions are interesting and sometimes "controversial" is because there is no one right or wrong answer (whereas with a "fact" there often is).

- With facts you either know them or you don't. If you don't know the answer to a factual question, you could try to guess or fake it but that's not recommended. There are better choices. We went over examples of how to gracefully admit you don't know something and ways to substitute or side-step in your answer which, basically, switches the question.

- With conceptual questions, you generally know something. But if you feel like you don't know enough, we covered several ways (with examples) to handle the situation including asking for a little help, deconstructing the question in your mind to find what you can say, avoiding the question, and trying to pass.

Exercise 12.1: Practice Noticing Facts Versus Concepts

Since you have this book handy, take a few minutes to go back through the earlier books and look at the example questions. When you look at the question, notice if it is basically a "fact" question or a "concept" question.

There may be times when it may be a little of both but don't be too quick to just say "both" to them without taking a second to think through what part of it is fact and what part is concept. This won't take you long to do and it will help you start recognizing this in your own interview questions. When you do that, you'll be more at ease about how to approach any question even when you don't know the answer!

Exercise 12.2: Practice Admitting You Don't Know

Sometimes when people don't know something, they are too proud to admit it! You may have seen a version of this when a friend says something and then if she fears it is incorrect (or someone tells her it is) she'll quickly say "just kidding," like it was a joke or she didn't mean it when, in reality, she was just wrong.

Being wrong is okay—none of us are perfect. But in the pageant interview, you don't want to pretend you know something when you don't or say "just kidding" when you realized you made a mistake.

Prepare for when you might not know something in an interview situation. Actually practice out loud saying the examples in the book about how to gracefully say "I don't know" and try to pass. Hearing yourself say it will help you feel more comfortable and confident doing it when/if the time comes. You do *not* want to hang your head and seem embarrassed. Look at the "stage direction" I gave you. And practice in your non-pageant conversations too…if you don't know, admit it. (Unless you are going to try to switch to what you do know!)

Exercise 12.3: Practice Switching and Key Word Components

Go through the questions in the book (and with any other practice questions you have) and practice out loud answering them. If there are any that you have trouble with either use the switch technique or practice listening for the key components as a way to build your answers. You can do it! Start with the examples in the book and see what *you* would say in response to those questions. (Rather than what I wrote…what are your thoughts and feelings?)

Exercise 12.4: Practice Asking For Help

Everybody is different. Just as some folks have trouble admitting when they don't know something, others have trouble asking for help. A good titleholder knows her limits and isn't afraid to ask for help if she needs it. She just needs to do it in a classy, professional way. So review that section of the book and practice asking for help by yourself as you do the review and, of course, when you are doing your out loud pageant question practice.

But remember that my materials are called "Pageant to PhD" because everything we learn in pageants can be helpful to other areas of our lives if we are mindful to *transfer* the skills. So just as it is good to admit what you don't know during your pageant interview, you may also find that it is useful to admit what you don't know or ask for help in other areas of your life.

In this case, practice asking for help, when appropriate, in all areas of your life like in school, at work, with your parents, with your spouse, with your kids, etc. If you don't know what someone means when they say _____ then try paraphrasing (from Book 8—saying it back in your own words) and/or ask for clarification. Asking for a little help via clarification saves *so* many misunderstandings, hurt feelings, and fights if folks are sure they are on the same page.

It can be a little scary to ask especially if you think the other person isn't friendly or will accuse you of not listening. But, *in fact*, you asking shows you are trying hard to listen well. And, in reality, most people are nice! Most people would rather have you ask and know what they mean. Things don't work out as well when one person means X and the other means Y (but they both think they are talking about the same thing!). And, naturally, if anyone ever asks you for clarification, be nice about it.

"Remember, if you ever need a helping hand, it's at the end of your arm, as you get older, remember you have another hand: The first is to help yourself, the second is to help others."
~Audrey Hepburn

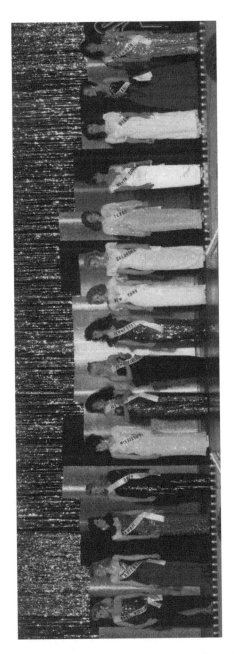

The 15 semi-finalists at my national pageant. I am second from the left.

a pageant is just the beginning...

PAGEANT
*ℐ*nterviewing
SUCCESS

Ending with Grace and Ease

Dr. Stephanie Raye, PhD
Former Miss American Petite

Book 13
Ending with Grace and Ease
Table of Contents

Pageant Interviewing Success:
Ending with Grace and Ease

You've prepared, you've waited. You've walked in confidently, smiled, and made eye contact. You've listened; you've talked. You've been a Sleuth and watched for opportunities to share key information about yourself in a way that shows your enthusiasm and good fit for the title.

Things might have gone well (yes!) or, despite all your best intentions something might have gone "wrong." Let's talk a bit about handling unhappy "surprises" in the interview as well as aspects of wrapping up any interview.

Damage Control

Everything we've covered in the book helps you shine and avoid damaging your own reputation or that of the title you hold (or aspire to hold). But the best laid plans can still go awry. Chances are slim that anything "bad" will happen but let's chat about this side of things a little bit.

- Accidents can happen. You could trip, knock something over, or miss the chair when you go to sit! (Hopefully not. Practice sitting down.)
- Mistakes crop up. Errors in paperwork or scheduling, something you say is actually "wrong" somehow and someone confronts you on it, etc.
- Distractions occur. One of the judges may have an annoying visual or verbal habit, there could be construction noise or other loud sounds coming from nearby, you may have an itch or be in some pain.
- People can be unkind or surprising. You may have just had a bad interchange with another contestant (or staff person) that's still on your mind; someone (even a judge) may try to get you off guard to see how you handle it, etc.

Whatever happens, roll with it. A Queen is graceful and forgiving to herself and others. I've used phrases like "take it in stride" and "roll with it" in the book before. Let's be clear on what I mean here...

That expression—"roll with it"—comes from the physical side of life but we can apply it to the mental and emotional side of life as well. One source for it is "roll with the punches" from when a boxer moves in such a way to decrease the impact of his (or her!) body getting hit. Or, imagine when someone physically falls or is thrown; if they allow themselves to roll into or with the force that threw them they usually fare better than if they resist it.

So, in the interview setting, if something "throws" you, roll with it. Just take a breath, smile, and handle it appropriately.

If an accident happens, try to laugh it off. That relieves the tension for everyone. Apologize if you damaged anything. Keep it genuine but light (unless it is truly a serious matter).

If you damaged yourself, for instance, if you snag part of your outfit on the door as you walk in or the chair as you sit down, you can ignore it like it never happened (and the judges will likely do the same, being polite people). But you can also make a joke out of it if that fits your personality. Showing good humor is important so even if you "ignore it" do it with a smile, not a frown.

If you make a mistake, apologize with sincerity and explain how you'll avoid that in the future. Make it right if you can. If there are distractions, keep focused and adjust to them best you can. If you really need help, ask for it. For instance, maybe you ask nicely for someone to speak louder, or maybe you ask if the window could be closed.

If something upsetting has happened, try to shake it off for the brief time of the interview. Don't let something or someone outside your control dictate the quality of your performance. When you're in that room, set the rest aside as best you can.

You don't have to be a doormat to hope people like you, and you don't have to be a superhero and solve every problem. Just respond appropriately—and as kindly as possible—as a confident, capable Queen would. (And I don't mean a drama queen!)

Why do I mention this all here, in the chapter on "Ending the Interview," when something odd could happen at the beginning or any other time? Because depending on how you dealt with the "bad thing" when it happened, you may want to deal with it (again) at the end of the interview.

It is usually better to handle things right when they come up but if you made a little joke about something you did awkwardly at the beginning (not all of us are naturally graceful) you might refer back to it to get another laugh.

"Smile. Have you ever noticed how easily puppies make human friends? Yet all they do is wag their tails and fall over."
~Walter Anderson

Or, if you realize you misspoke or misrepresented somehow in something you said, you might decide to set the record straight before you leave. It may be better to just leave it alone but if you think a disparity between something you said and something that is on your paperwork will stick in their craw, you might do some damage control and say something like (depending on your situation):

> "Oh, and sorry to back track but I wanted to apologize and correct something. I think I said I'd volunteered for the National Cancer Institute but it was really the American Cancer Society. I sometimes get those important organizations mixed up—especially when I'm a bit nervous as I am today. Anyway, I just wanted to be accurate."

Said with a smile, the Judges will likely appreciate that you care to be accurate. And *if* any of them noticed the disparity, they'll certainly realize and appreciate that you caught your own mistake.

"If you have made mistakes, there is always another chance for you. You may have a fresh start any moment you choose, for this thing we call "failure" is not the falling down, but the staying down."
~Mary Pickford

Closing Statements

As discussed in the section on Opening Statements (please review that if it has been awhile as I won't repeat it all here), you'll want to be ready with one. But you'll want to be more flexible with any closing statement as it may need to shift based on what happened in the interview.

Why They Might Ask For One

A pageant is less likely to require or invite a closing statement than an opening one. But, as we discussed with opening statements, an individual judge may give you the opportunity to offer one. They might do that because they don't think there's time to ask anything else specifically but there's a little time for you to wrap it up. Or maybe they simply wonder what you'll do with the opportunity.

If they offer you this opportunity, it might be phrased, for instance, like:

"Is there anything you'd like us to know as we wrap up?"

Or:

"If there's one thought you'd like to leave us with, what would that be?"

If you are asked something like this and you know that key thing or two about you has yet to be brought to their attention, then be a Sleuth and share it with them at that time.

Whatever you do, it is wise to use the opportunity rather than to let it pass. To the first question you could just say "No" but I wouldn't recommend that. I'd say something! Tell them something you haven't had the chance to say yet or reiterate (say again but in a different way) something you mentioned that you want to emphasize.

Create Your Own Opportunity

If they do not offer you the opportunity but you want it, then try to make it happen. For instance, if you know you are getting to the end of the interview and haven't been asked something to which you were hoping to reply. Or you wanted to highlight something important but haven't gotten to yet. If that happens, as you are wrapping up another response to one of the questions near the end of your time, you might look for a way to say:

"And I wanted to share briefly that _____"

Or:

"And that reminds me, I wanted to mention _____."

But that should only be used *if:*

- It makes sense. That is, if it is a believable connection to the "This reminds me…." statement,-

- You really need to say what it is you feel you must work in, and-
- You keep it *brief*. Don't go on too long if you are tacking on an "and…"

You can make the interview "yours" in a number of ways that this book details. And none of those ways involve hijacking control from the judges. Wresting control in an awkward way (or ever interrupting someone) is never a good idea.

If it doesn't feel right or if you haven't built up your skill or comfort level with gently redirecting like this (you will in time!), then let it go for now and just be happy you had a great interview. You may not be able to employ every tip in this book in every interview. As you develop as a Sleuth you'll be more aware of when the time is right. Along the way, just trust the process and have fun.

Do You Have Any Questions For Us?

This doesn't happen often—schedules are tight and this is about them asking *you* questions (not the other way around). It can happen, however, if one of the judges has interviewed a lot of job candidates for non-pageant jobs because it is a pretty standard way to end a traditional job interview. (So they might ask it accidentally or automatically). It's unlikely, but it is better to be prepared "just in case" it does, so let's talk about it briefly.

So if you are asked and you do have a question, you could consider asking it. Put on your Sleuth hat ahead of time (or in that moment, at least) and consider if it is an appropriate question for the judges.

Really, most questions about routine matters should be handled between you and the Director or other pageant personnel (*not* with the judges). So you'll want to consider if the question you'd ask of the judges is the sort of question they'd know the answer to (or be free to say). You don't want to ask something that is going to be awkward for anyone or take a lot of time.

What this question is really doing, in my opinion, is offering you an opportunity for a closing statement, if you want to take it. So if you are asked, the interchange could go like this:

Judge
"Do you have any questions for us?"

Contestant
"No questions come to mind right now…but I want to thank you for your time and add that _____."

And, as before, keep it brief. Add *only* the key thing that is important for them to know. You do not want them internally rolling their eyes at how long you are going on or feeling sorry that they asked.

If it fits with your personality and confidence level, you could consider asking a question like "If you had your way, what one thing would you want the titleholder to keep in mind for her great year ahead?"

That question is related to the title's reputation and future and may also tell you more about what they value (which could be useful in on-stage interview). This sort of question is also *quick* in that it asks for *one* thing, not a whole list. It doesn't invite long responses that will drag out the time.

Ask For the Job

Yes, the judges know you are interested in being the titleholder to some degree or you wouldn't be in the pageant. But some contestants are just in it for fun and aren't as invested in whether or not they win. Even if everyone is in it to win there will still be differences in each person's potential "fit" and preparedness for the title as well as how much tasteful enthusiasm each shows.

One way to show enthusiasm is to, in essence, ask for the job. I don't mean to say "Are you going to choose me?" Or "How'd I do? Do I have a chance?" or "Can you please pick me for the title?" Clearly those are all a bit tacky and imply that you want a response. You do *not* want to ask in a way that puts them on the spot. It has to be done adroitly and with tact.

"Asking for the job" is really more about making a statement that indicates your sincere intent and interest. I've shown you examples of doing this in several of the sample responses you've read in the book so far. Basically, it is simple—I suggest that sometime during the interview you communicate that you do want the title! Don't assume they know. There are generally three ways to ask for the job:

- Assumption
- Direct
- Indirect

"If you don't ask the answer is always 'no.'"

Assumption

An assumption looks like this "When I win the title, I'll _____." You have to be careful with assuming you will win. Done well (which include the right sort of smile and twinkle in your eye) it comes off as confident and charming. Done poorly it could come off as arrogant or haughty. You'd have to decide if you have the personality and style to pull it off well.

Using an assumption with humor can work. For instance if you've entered the pageant a couple times before and not won (but now you are super-prepared and have a stronger chance), you might get away with "When I win the title, and as you know I keep trying!, I'll _____. I'm ready and I hope this is my year." You've softened the potential edge by being a little self-deprecating (pointing out you've not won before) and turning it into a "hope" at the end.

Direct and Indirect

You can also ask for the job more directly. For instance, you might say toward the end: "I've enjoyed the interview. Thank you, and I hope you choose me for the title."

Or, anywhere during the interview in a response that it works with you might say: "I'd ask that you choose me for this title because I'm so eager to do both a good job as the titleholder and I welcome the doors it will open to get the message out about my platform."

Clearly, you'd not use the word platform if you are in a pageant that doesn't have one. Wanting to do a good job as the titleholder is enough. Whatever is right for *you* to say is what you should say (as long as it has more Sleuth Factor than Bungle Factor).

And indirect request is similar but has more of an "if" feeling to it. For instance, if a question you get seems to call for it you might start your responses with something like "If I am chosen for the title, I'll _____ ." And then continue on with your response. Or it may be more appropriate, depending on the question, to work a phrase like that into the middle or end of a response.

Sometimes you start out saying something indirectly and it turns into something more direct. Sometimes just the reverse happens. Don't fret about if it is one or the other—just do what works for you. Start practicing asking for the job in different ways when it feels right in your answer and you'll feel more comfortable when the time comes.

One last thought on this: Don't overdo it!

Usually asking for the job once during the interview is enough— Maybe more than once if it is a longer interview or if the response *really* calls for it. But I wouldn't do it more than once or twice and never force it or it'll seem like you are trying too hard. If you force it or do it too much it will show that you don't know when "enough is enough" or recognize what a sensitive balance is or, perhaps, are overly ambitious. A little ambition is a good thing, too much comes off as un-Queenly.

So you can Sleuth in "asking for the job" anywhere in the interview (including in the Opening Statement) but I mention it here in the Chapter on "Ending the Interview" because if you haven't said something that directly indicates you want this job, do aim to include it at the end somehow.

Be Polite – Say "Thank You"

Whether you are invited to give a closing statement, add anything to wrap up of your own accord, or the interview is simply ended because the time runs out, it is polite to thank the judges. Do thank them, even if it is "just" the two words "Thank you" as you rise to leave with a warm smile, and making eye contact, and nod of your head to the judge (or panel) when you are called out of the room.

After the Interview

Woo hoo! Your personal interview is done. You did it! Now what? You smile and get back to it. Here are a few things to keep in mind as you do.

Reflect But Don't Overanalyze

After the interview, you might be tempted to over-analyze what just happened. This is normal for most people and certainly is something that achievers, over-achievers, and perfectionists are inclined to do. (And a fair amount of pageant contestants might describe themselves in one of those terms.)

A little reflection on how it went is good and healthy but try to avoid *over* analyzing. In the excitement of a pageant, over-analyzing something might start you worrying you didn't do well enough, etc. and tarnish your attitude or performance in other areas of the pageant. We don't want that.

I recommend that, *if* you can, you go up to your room to collect yourself before returning to rehearsal and write down a few things. Even 5 minutes of "me time" can bring nice closure to your interview experience whether you are happy, sad, or neutral; whether you are still nervous or completely excited about what comes next.

If you can go to your room for a couple minutes, just jot down what questions you can remember being asked. The answers too, if you have time. Write a few words about how you felt the interview went. Allow yourself a little reflection, sure, but keep it short for right now.

And be sure to end on something positive—something you did right, about the laughter you shared with the judges, how great you looked, something good! Congratulate yourself for doing it! If time is short, just get a few questions down and maybe a word or two of what you said to jog your memory for later.

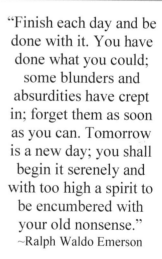

If you don't have time to go to your room, maybe sit in the lobby for a moment and just breathe a few calming breaths and let it all sink in. You can reflect through writing a little more later that night, so don't worry. Do reflect just a bit but, for now, you will want to focus more on what comes next at the pageant.

When you get home from the pageant you can go over your interview experience in more detail alone or with a pageant friend or coach, but don't do it at the pageant. Stay focused on what comes next, shining wherever you can—especially in on-stage interview.

"Finish each day and be done with it. You have done what you could; some blunders and absurdities have crept in; forget them as soon as you can. Tomorrow is a new day; you shall begin it serenely and with too high a spirit to be encumbered with your old nonsense."
~Ralph Waldo Emerson

Don't Talk to Others About It

It may be tempting but resist talking about how your interview went or what questions you were asked, etc., with the other contestants.

You certainly can wish someone success on their interview without telling them how yours went, giving them hints, or telling them to watch out for certain questions or judges. Let them have their own experience and allow it to be a level playing field.

While we hope for a friendly pageant experience where you make great friends, remember that it *is* still a competition so practice together at home, if you want, but once you are at the pageant, take care of you.

Be a "good sport" and aim to be friendly and supportive with everyone—*never* do anything to undermine or hurt another contestant. But you don't have to give them interview questions either.

If someone directly asks you, you can say something conversational without going into detail. You might say, "The time just flew by" or "Everybody seemed really nice." Those are fine things to say. You can even say "I think I did okay! And I hope you do too…have fun!

Don't say "Well, if you ask me the time keeper is rude when she cuts you off" or "I struggled with a question on ____." That's too much information. Remember the other person may be asking to be polite. And you don't want to say anything that will pull down her mood or make her worry.

You may be tempted to hang around if the schedule allows, and listen to what other contestants are saying about their interviews. (They didn't read this book or they wouldn't be talking about their experience.) If this is *before* your interview and you are just standing there waiting, you may not be able to easily escape this.

And, on the positive side, maybe you'd pick up an interesting clue to what sorts of things the judges are asking. But you may be better off focusing on yourself and what you'd like the judges to know about you so you can, Sleuth-like, work that information into the interview regardless of what questions you are asked.

By all means, though, don't hang around *after* your interview to compare notes with others. Avoid being gossipy or talking about your fears. If you are stopped or linger after your interview, be polite and say supportive things but don't get into details. If you want to "bond" over this with others, save it until the personal interviews are done. Remember, right after the interview is a good time to take a few minutes for yourself, if you can, or return to whatever task the pageant has scheduled for you.

"I wanted a perfect ending. Now I've learned, the hard way, that some poems don't rhyme, and some stories don't have a clear beginning, middle, and end. Life is about not knowing, having to change, taking the moment and making the best of it, without knowing what's going to happen next. Delicious Ambiguity."
~Gilda Radner

Review

Woo hoo! We've gone through your whole personal interview day! (And more, because we even looked at what to do at home before you came.) Take a few minutes to review this book below (where I'll say things in a slightly different way to help them sink in even more deeply) and do the exercises before we move on to the next book.

- ***Mistakes happen.***
  A good titleholder will know how to take lemons and make lemonade, roll with it, take it in stride or whatever phrase you like that shows you can handle yourself and are resilient.

- *Closing statements may not be required.*

  If a judge offers you the opportunity to wrap things up (or you create the opportunity) be ready to share a key point about yourself or ask for the job.

- *Asking for the job is appropriate if it is done appropriately.*

  And, obviously, you aren't asking in a way that demands an immediate answer. You are just letting them know you are serious and enthusiastic about this opportunity. We covered three ways to do this (with some examples here but there are more scattered throughout the book).

- *Depending on the size of the pageant and the system, it can be a lot of work and time to be a judge.*

  Contestants should be appreciative that we are all in this together and the judges are an important part. As such, it is good manners to thank the judges as the interview wraps up. Queens have manners and know when to use them. (Even if it wasn't much work for the judges it is *still* appropriate and necessary to say "thank you.")

- *After the interview, it's good to check in with yourself on how you did but always focus on the positive.*

  Make a note or two but save serious analysis for later. Reflect enough to help you if you get an on-stage question but that's it. Take a few minutes to yourself and then get back to the other fun and work of the pageant.

- ***Resist the urge to talk to the other contestants about your interview.***

  If you feel you really want to discuss, wait until after everyone has gone through the personal interview. But it is still better not to do it. You can talk about it as much as you'd like to friends, family, and coaches when you get home.

Exercise 13.1: Practice Rolling With It

Even in your preparation at home—when you are practicing out loud alone, taping it, or with a helper—practice having a good sense of humor about mistakes and interruptions. If you get angry with your little brother for mocking or mimicking you, making noise or whatever, see if you can be patient and Queenly about it instead. Pretend it is practice for staying serene if you ever have to interview in a less than optimal situation.

In the different areas of your life, watch how people handle mistakes and mishaps. Notice how you handle them too. Model yourself after the good examples. If you learn to bounce back quickly with all sorts of disappointments and surprises in your life, you'll be very well prepared to handle it in an interview setting.

Exercise 13.2: Prepare for a Closing Opportunity

Think about all you've done and how great you are. Review your pageant paperwork for details of what you included. And think about your goals and dreams. Put together a short list of "Talking Points" which is like a list of "bullet points" with a word or phrase you'd like to be sure your audience (the judges) hears before the interview is over.

As the interview progresses, you'll work those into your responses where you can but if by the end you've not gotten to do so with something important then *that* point is potentially a great candidate for you to use in a closing statement.

Again, pageants rarely require a closing statement (like they might with an opening statement) but you'd be wise to be prepared with content for one in case a judge offers you the opportunity to close the interview. You can't *pre*-prepare these in the way you can with opening statements because you'll need to adjust your closing statement to fit what was said (or not said) in the interview itself. So if you have those bulleted Talking Points in mind, you'll be ready to pick one of those to wrap up the interview, if given that opportunity.

Exercise 13.3: Practice Asking For the Job/Title

As you prepare and practice questions at home, be sure to try your hand at "asking for the job" in direct and indirect ways. It won't work with every question but start noticing where it would be natural to add in a comment that shows that you do want the title. Try the different ways described in the chapter and see what works for your style.

Exercise 13.4: Prepare to Reflect

Imagine you've just completed your personal interview. You are leaving the room and you are excited. Your head is also whirling with what was asked and what you said. What would want to remind yourself of just then? What sort of questions would you have for yourself?

Whatever it is that you know are your strengths and weaknesses, make up a little checklist and take it with you to the pageant so you can jot some notes to yourself afterward. Perhaps you'd have on your list: Did I smile? Did I use my voice well? Did I stay on target or did I ramble? What sorts of questions did they ask? Did I do well at each type? What do I need to work on? What did I do really well?

I encourage a little immediate post-interview reflection if you have time. (Later that night if you don't. And more serious reflection when you get home). But your head may be so full of excitement that you can't think about what to reflect on! Simply jotting down a few of the questions you were asked is a good place to start but having a checklist to help you remember what to reflect on is helpful too.

"Anyone who stops learning is old, whether at twenty or eighty. Anyone who keeps learning stays young. The greatest thing in life is to keep your mind young."
~Henry Ford

The final 6 at my national pageant. There were only supposed to be 5, but there was a tie! I am on the right.

a pageant is just the beginning...

PAGEANT
ℐnterviewing
SUCCESS

Optimize
On-Stage Questions

Dr. Stephanie Raye, PhD
Former Miss American Petite

Book 14
Optimize On-Stage Questions
Table of Contents

Pageant Interviewing Success: Optimize On-Stage Questions

We've covered a lot of ground. We've walked through how to prepare before coming to the pageant all the way through the personal interview experience from the night before to walking out the door. But what about on-stage interview?

Most of what we've talked about thus far will also apply to doing well for your on-stage questions but being on a stage does have a different feel to it. Let's delve into some specifics for this to help you be better prepared for this special occasion of you about to win the crown! Along the way, we'll cover a few more examples that would apply on or off-stage.

Your Time to Shine—Grace Under Pressure

Handling on-stage questions, introductions, and conversations are *key* to winning the crown. Doing a good job with whatever is handed to you shows the judges you have the skill to think on your feet. If you can do it there, you can do it anywhere—like in the public appearances or media interviews a Queen will have.

Yes, you showed your ability to think on your feet in the personal interview but it isn't quite the same. We use the phrase "think on your feet" figuratively in most cases to mean "think fast and well" because you are usually (not always!) sitting down in personal interview.

In on-stage interview you need to think on your feet while you are standing in your heels in front of possibly thousands of people or an even bigger televised audience. (The exception would be important pageant systems like Ms. Wheelchair America and Ms. Wheelchair USA where accomplished, beautiful women who happen to use wheelchairs compete and do a fabulous job representing their titles.) Whether you are literally on your feet or not, being "on-stage" can feel different than being in personal interview. For some it is easier, but for most it adds a little bit more pressure.

If you've done well enough to make it to the on-stage interview questions (usually semi-finals or finals), then how you handle this can help you seal the deal. You may have "just made it" into the finals (perhaps scoring lower than anyone else) but if you are on-target, confident, and charming with your on-stage response you could leap frog over the early "favorites."

That's true especially if your pageant cleans the slate between rounds—meaning that scores start fresh and if you got a lower score earlier on it won't pull down your score in a later rounds. (At the time I wrote this, for instance, the United States system was doing that. But every pageant and system may change how they score so just check for what's current in the system *you* are competing in.)

The USA, America, United States, International systems, etc. may or may not clean the slate so check the website or with the Director so you know this and how much each category is worth. That said, don't over-worry about it. As a Pageant Sleuth you'll be fine either way!)

Question and Answer Content— Optimizing the Response

As we've discussed, most pageants have personal interview, either panel-style or one-on-one with judges. Most also have an on-stage public speaking aspect for which you'll want to be prepared. Sometimes it is as simple as introducing yourself to the audience, other times it is questions from the judges or the Master of Ceremonies (MC or emcee) usually at the semi-finalist and/or finalist stage of the contest.

For instance, in my pageant system, all contestants introduced themselves as part of the opening number. Then, later, the semi-finalists were each asked a question from their bio, and the finalists were asked a "what if" kind of questions like:

- "If you could meet any famous person, dead or alive, who would it be and why?"
- "If you were crowned Miss American Petite, what would you like to accomplish during your reign year?"
- "If you could live your life in another woman's shoes, who would it be and why?"
- "If you could enter a time capsule to go forward or backward in time, what period would you visit and why?"
- "If you had the opportunity to be an ambassador to another country, which country would it be and why?"
- "If you had a million dollars to give to any charity, who would you give it to and why?"

Questions like these are broad and a contestant can *Sleuth* them with a little thought or *Bungle* them easily if she isn't paying attention. Paying attention can be a little more challenging in front of an audience.

Have you noticed how often, across pageant systems, a contestant appears to have *not* been listening because she doesn't really answer the question? Whether she was nervous, just didn't listen, or tried to avoid the question (but in a non-Sleuth way), it doesn't appear to be her best work.

Have faith, you can do better! You can stay focused and perform well under the pressure of being on stage. In fact, with a little practice and a positive attitude, you may find being on stage energizes you and brings out your best.

So let's look at some Sleuthing with just one of the on-stage questions above to see what opportunities are there to grasp or lose. I wish we had the time and space to do them all since they are so fun to look at and we can learn so much from each example. But we can't.

That's okay, you'll get the idea from careful consideration of one. We'll keep building your Sleuthing skill and start to tie into considerations about the on-stage part of the pageant and how that relates to interview and what you put on your application materials.

One of the main differences between personal interview and on-stage interview is that it isn't just you and judge(s) any more. You now want to consider how the audience will react and you have an emcee in the mix. And, remember, you parade in your gown and fitness-wear while the emcee will tell the audience information about you from your materials. (Another reason to think them through with care.)

Example

Emcee

"If you could meet any famous person, dead or alive, who would it be and why?"

If you were to get a question like this, consider choosing someone that relates to your platform or your passion. Imagine if a contestant said this:

Contestant

"I think it would have to be Jerry Lewis. I just appreciate everything he does for Muscular Dystrophy. And he is a wonderful person. He gives so much of his time and I would love to meet him. I've always said I'd like to sing on one of his telethons, someday maybe."

There is nothing "wrong" with this answer as it answers what was asked. It also shows her appreciation for charity and her desire to sing. But it isn't a particularly *winning* answer either.

True, she didn't trip over her words or awkwardly avoid the question so she did not seriously bungle. But neither did she Sleuth so, in the end, it was a mild Bungle because she could've power-packed her answer a bit more. Here are a few things she could have pulled to mind in the pause before she answered.

Imagine if during one of her walks (in her gown or swimsuit), the emcee had told us that this particular contestant was passionate about giving kids opportunities. Besides the audience and judges, the contestant heard it too. So even if she forgot that she put it on in her application paperwork, it should have been fresh in her mind.

If that were the case, it would have been good if she'd made a connection between her choice (Jerry Lewis) and how that *relates* to her passion, after all, the judges heard *many* intros and tidbits of information, so they may have forgotten this detail about her. Had she made the connection it would help "connect the dots" for them as Jerry Lewis' work has been great for kids.

Something like this perhaps:

Contestant

"I'd choose Jerry Lewis. I just appreciate everything he does for the Muscular Dystrophy. He gives so much of his time and I would love to meet him as we share a passion for helping people, especially children. I love to give kids opportunities through my work and he does the same—so much good comes from his telethons! I could learn a lot from him and we could swap some good stories."

This simple change would have made her choice seem more thoughtful instead of perhaps leaving the judges with the memory that she chose Jerry Lewis because she'd like to sing on television. So while she made a good, thoughtful choice she could have made the connection clearer.

Taking it a step farther…If you are asked a question like this, a more advanced Sleuthing awareness might lead you to choose a woman. I'm not saying that you should avoid choosing men. Men are great! But I *am* saying to be thoughtful about your choice. And, where possible, see if choosing a woman could works equally as well for you. Why?

Some people in the outside world think pageants are for girls that are more interested in beauty than brains. We (the pageant world) know better. *Many* pageants have achievement or scholarship aspects to them—but it can take others awhile to let go of their biases. When a pageant girl focuses on women that are known for more than their beauty it helps break the perception and build awareness about women's achievements.

Choosing a man or a woman won't make or break your chances. I'm just taking this opportunity to illustrate that had this contestant chosen a woman who'd contributed to society in a meaningful way, she'd have shown she's appreciative of such contributions. She'd remind people that women everywhere are more than their physical beauty. If she could choose a woman who also relates to her passion, even better!

So again, in the example above, she didn't seriously bungle her response, but she *did* let some opportunities slide. A true Bungler response would have been, for instance, to choose someone who was *not* famous. Let's take a look:

Example

Emcee
"If you could meet any famous person, dead or alive, who would it be and why?"

Bungler
"I'd choose my grandmother because I never got to meet her and she's famous in my family."

As *sweet* and cute as it is to say, it really doesn't answer the question and leaves a *lot* of potential on the table. It feels like the contestant might be avoiding (but not in a Sleuth-like way) the "famous" part of the question, perhaps because she just never thought it through or because it is otherwise "too hard" for her.

Or worse, it could make her seem like she's intentionally trying to pull on the heartstrings in a way that could come off to some judges as *smuggling* in emotion in a situation where it wasn't occurring naturally.

If it is true in your heart that you'd want to meet your grandmother (I suspect most of us would) then *find* a way to *Sleuth*; find an honest way to connect what you want to share to the actual question you were asked. In this case you'd be tying into in the "famous person" part of the question. For instance:

Emcee

"If you could meet any famous person, dead or alive, who would it be and why?"

Contestant

"A famous person...I'd choose to meet Madame Curie who was the first person to win *two* Nobel prizes. She also directed the world's first studies into how radiation might cure cancer. What courage and determination it must've taken to be such a pioneering woman! And I'd like to thank her for the difference her work has made because even though radiation didn't cure my grandmother it did give her a few more years of a good life. Unfortunately, I was too young to remember her so if I were to choose someone who *wasn't* famous, it'd be grandma."

So *if* you want to bring a family member in—whether or not tugging on the heart strings is your motivation—you want to do it in a way that still *answers* the actual question you were given. And an answer like this also shows you are smart (a touch of health science and world culture shows here), thoughtful, sensitive to women's issues, and are gracious, grateful, and caring. All things we want a Queen to be.

Note: No matter *who* you choose, it'd help if you knew some more things about that person—that's part of *preparation*. This is important because if this question comes up in personal interview (rather than on stage), the judges may ask you more about it as they have time to follow-up. Also, if you win, the media or people at your appearances may ask about who you admire or who you consider to be a role model.

Know Your Role Models

Let's spend a little more time on this to help you be prepared and optimize your responses. We'll use this as an example that everyone could benefit from but pay *special* attention to it if you are actually in a pageant that asked this question on the paperwork.

Different versions of the "What famous person, alive or dead would you like to meet?" question include:

- "Who would you most like to meet?"
- "Who do you most admire?"
- "Who do you consider a role model?"

You should know some basic information about anything you put in your paperwork or decide to mention in an answer to a question. You don't have to memorize it all but do look up a few things and try to remember one or two interesting facts that are meaningful to you. Look up items like those in the accompanying box on the topic called "Basics to Know About Your Role Model."

Madame Curie: what a great woman from the not-too-distant history, eh? Her work *still* has impact. And she was an inspiration to *many*, including her daughters—one of which went on to earn her own Nobel Prize. (Winning one of those is *way* harder than winning most anything else so we must respect and honor their achievements).

And Madame Curie was generally generous. For example, she intentionally did *not* patent her special radiation process using radium so that the whole scientific community could easily use it and study it. She showed she was not greedy with that choice and may have foregone some great profits there, but she saw a bigger picture than just how much money might line her pockets.

No matter how fine a person your "famous" "most admired" "role model" may be, remember that no one is perfect. Especially when someone is famous, the media, historians, or their critics will look for where they aren't perfect. So know what your role model may have struggled with as well.

BASICS TO KNOW ABOUT YOUR ROLE MODELS
Information and Example (with Madame Marie Curie)

When s/he lived?

- 1867- 1934

Origin and heritage?

- Born in Poland, much of life in France

Famous for what?

- Winning two Nobel Prizes – 1st to do that too!
- She was the first—male or female
- One for physics, another for chemistry

What difference did s/he make?

- Started work with radiation, discovered two elements – "radium" (and "polonium" too)

Anything else?

- *First* woman whose remains were allowed to be laid to rest in a very special place where previously only men were honored (the Panthéon in Paris). Her remains were moved there in 1995.

Why do *you* like him or her?

- Courage and determination it must've taken to be such a pioneering woman in that time and in those fields

How might it relate to your platform or passion?

- (You could feel this way even if you aren't required to have a platform or do not choose one that is cancer related.)
- I care deeply about health and wellness, especially around the prevention, treatment, and cure of cancer. Several in my family have suffered from it, as have millions of others, so I appreciate that Madame Curie's was the first to direct studies on radiation and cancer.
- I'm passionate about it in my own way as I demonstrated through walking over 60 miles in just 3 days to raise money for breast cancer awareness and research. Training for that—and then doing it!—took a lot of courage and determination.

You don't have to bring up their negative side, (I'd recommend you *don't*) but *if* someone else does you can put it back into perspective and keep the focus positive. How? You can nod and give a concerned look tempered by a small knowing smile and say something like (depending on the situation):

"I know _____ is reported to have had a problem with _____ . If that is true, I think it is even more remarkable that she accomplished as much as she did."

"It is even more inspiring that they overcame that."

"It's unfortunate things took a downturn for him but I'm still grateful for what he did when things were at their best."

"Thank goodness we can forgive mistakes as it certainly seems more important to focus on the fine accomplishments rather than the mistakes."

In *your* pageant they may, as does the Mrs. (and Teen and Miss) International Pageants, say "no political or religious questions allowed unless it pertains to the platform." (At least they said that at the time I wrote this.) So if your pageant says something like that you'll know to focus on knowing a lot about your platform—rather than a bio question or "what if" question—for your on-stage interview. But even then you never know what angle the question will take. Aim to be prepared.

If you feel certain the questions you get will focus on your platform, then know something about the key players (current and historical) around your platform.

"Tell me whom you love and I will tell you who you are."
~Houssaye

Delivery Style and Time

No matter what your on-stage question is, keep your answer on-target (answer the question) and deliver it with natural ease and friendly authenticity—characteristics you *can* display under pressure if you:

- Practice out loud in advance, and-
- Remember that these are *nice* people-
- And you're "just talking"

To keep it conversational, you do *not* want to ramble on. *Especially* on stage, don't ramble. Keep your answers relatively short and always to the point. Why? Because, the judges may be (usually are!) looking to see:

- How you'd handle questions from the media
- If you are sensitive to situations where time is an issue
- How well you "think on your feet"
- If you can stay within time limits

Let's discuss a bit more why the judges would be watching for these things. Part of what a titleholder might do is to interact with the *media*. Both audiences tend to prefer responses that answer what was asked in a tidy "sound bite" that they can use in their television or radio show or written article.

Also, remember that the pageant is a live production—another media situation, especially if it is televised—so the pace of the show needs to keep moving. You shouldn't over-worry about this but do be sensitive to the situations in which you find yourself.

Being sensitive to situations where time is an issue relates not just to the media but also to the fact that a Queen's day can be pretty busy. If there is a Question & Answer session after an appearance, you need to be able to answer many of the questions (so hopefully no one will feel left out).

That usually isn't too tough but situations vary. You may have helpers and "handlers" (people that coordinate your schedule at or between events) politely pressuring you that there is not much time to get to your next appearance and/or the site needs the room for the next event. (There are ways to gracefully cut short a Q & A session but they are outside the scope of this book. I'll aim to help with this in my blog or on the website in a different publication. Remind me if I forget.)

How does all this relate to thinking on your feet? Besides being aware of time demands, most everyone—the judges, the audience, the media—wants you to be able to deliver a solid response to the question that preferably won't bother anyone (or at least too many people) in the audience and reflects well on you and the crown.

An on-target answer is important because it can be a challenge for a listener (even a professional one, like a judge or reporter) to find the heart of the answer if it is couched in too much stuff—assuming a *real* answer is even there.

For instance, let's examine Sarah Palin for a moment. She's done wonderful things including governing the largest state in the Union (Alaska), and running for national office on a presidential ticket. This former beauty queen, as articulate and beautiful as she is, was often constructively criticized for rambling responses that didn't "nail" the answer head on. As great as she did on many media questions, folks often will remember or talk about her responses that were either off-target in some way or maybe had good content in there but that ran on too long or in too many directions. No one wants to work too hard to sort out the answer from the non-answer stuff.

So answer the question! You don't want to deliver clipped responses that make it seem like you are in a hurry. But don't do too much more than answer the question unless you are being a *Sleuth* and working something important and relevant into your reply.

Whatever you do, on-stage at least, try to keep it to around 30 seconds—which goes by *faster* than you think.

This is important because some pageants will specify a time limit for your on-stage responses. *Know* the rules for *your* pageant. *If* they have a time limit, obviously you should aim to respect it. It may be that it is "no big deal" if you go over a little or you could be penalized.

For instance, the well regarded Teen, Miss, and Mrs. International Pageants have an on-stage question where the time limit is 30 seconds. At this writing, their rules are that you lose a point off your score for each second you go over. They're very up front about this and in their pageant you *know* the question will have something to do with your platform.

So if you're in a pageant that does this, don't worry. Have faith that with some thoughtful preparation you can know a few key statistics, a *brief* anecdote, a couple key names and goals. (Make your "Talking Points" list.) Then depending on what question you get, you'll be able to comfortably put together a few bits of your information to *answer the question* within the time limit.

You might think that memorizing an answer would help. But, as we discussed earlier, it may be wise to avoid word-for-word memorizations. Unless you practice to make it sound natural (like an actress) memorized answers can too easily sound canned and *artificial*. For some, memorized answers work and relieve their stress. But, for many memorized answers can increase stress levels because the person may feel pressure to "perfectly" deliver the prepared answer.

You don't need anything adding to your nervousness in a situation where the "at ease" relaxed person tends to shine more. And even if you are such a great speaker or actress that no one can tell that you memorized it, it is still taking a risk because you might be so tempted to deliver what you have prepared that you may fail to answer the question you are *actually* asked.

You may try to force-fit your prepared answer in and wind up bungling. I don't recommend you risk it but you will know, with practice, if you can slice up a memorized answer to work in response to many questions.

In any event, you already *know* you can prepare well and try different responses to a good variety of practice questions to sound as good or *better* than what you may think a *memorized* answer sounds like. You can memorize facts, statistics, a little story or two, but consider them "bullet points" that you then mix and match to fit the question.

So we just went into detail around one example of an on-stage question. There are many other questions in the book series. In the end, the kinds of questions you get may not be *that* different than the ones you might get in personal interview. But on-stage you have just that one question to make a strong impression—your interview score for that semi-final or final round depends on one question.

So while much of your interview preparation will overlap, keep in mind that on-stage interview does have some unique elements to it and prepare and practice accordingly.

Eye Contact

We covered eye contact in detail in *Book 7: Making a Strong First Impression* but let's review and shift it a bit for the on-stage part of the pageant.

When you approach the emcee and take your position, smile and make eye contact with him or her (I'm going to use "him" from here forward for easier reading). Don't allow your nerves, the lights, the audience, the judges or the audience lead you to forget you've got a living, breathing person right in front of you who deserves your attention. So nod and smile at him, acknowledge him, and listen to what he says.

If the emcee is asking you the question keep your eyes on him, and keep a pleasant expression on your face, until he is done. Pay attention, and perhaps nod once or twice as you listen (especially if it is a long question). Resist the urge to look elsewhere—like the floor or ceiling—and resist rolling your eyes as you think or listen. Think of it as if you are in a conversation with *him*.

When the question is done, pause for a second to think and begin your answer. You might start with your eyes on the emcee briefly but then move to take in the panel of judges and the broader audience. Especially if the stage lighting lets you see the judges, be sure to "talk to" one or two of them or "scan" slowly across them as you answer. Review the section on eye contact earlier in the book and practice. You won't need to over-think this if you practice just a little.

If the judges are asking the question, they'll usually bring up the lights so you can see them. Look at the judge who is speaking to you until the question is fully asked. Then start your answer looking at that judge but then feel free to take in the emcee, the other judges, and the audience during your reply. Let it happen naturally. Don't stare the whole time at the emcee or judge who asked the question.

You might be wondering, how to "take in" an audience that is large or that you can't see because the stage lights are so bright all you can see is a great black hole out there.

If you can see the audience, just let your eyes land on a friendly face or two at different points in the room. Don't actively look for your family or friends as that will look awkward and take too much time. Just move your eyes over to one area of the audience and talk to a random person if you can see them.

Even if the person you happen to look at isn't smiling, just talk to them like you've known them forever. But just for a couple seconds, then move your eyes over to the other side and "talk to" someone there. Pretending to talk to someone you know tends to relax a speaker (you!), it animates your face and allows your head to move more naturally than if you just rotate it back and forth.

If you cannot see the audience, make believe you can and choose a distant area in the darkness to talk to briefly, bringing your eyes back to the judges or the emcee—to the people you *can* see!—for most of the time and to wrap up your response.

Smiling Some More

And *smile*. Smile while you walk to your position. Smile as you listen to the question and, yes, you can keep something like a smiling face while you speak. Smile more than you think you need to and that'll be just about right!

At home, practice looking in a mirror and smiling while you talk. It's easier than you think but can take a little practice. Try speaking while looking unhappy, bored, or neutral and see what your face looks like. Then try speaking with a smile on your face—let your eyes and face come alive. You can feel the difference and people can *see* the difference.

So once on stage, look happy and smile. Some facial variety is okay—but keep your smile (or close to it) on. (Review *Book 7: Making a Strong First Impression* for more on smiling.)

Let's be clear, I'm not suggesting you be a ventriloquist (don't try to talk without moving your lips just to keep your full smile on!). Don't try to talk *behind* a smile. You are simply speaking *with* a smile that enlivens your voice.

What If Your Lips Stick to Your Teeth?

What?! If you are new to pageants, you may never have smiled so much in your life. When you do, you might find that your lips stick to your teeth a little bit when you least expect it. Hard to believe when your smile sort of keeps your lips up off your teeth but it can happen. You don't have to lose sleep over this, just be aware of it so if it happens you'll not be surprised or frustrated.

You might feel an irresistible urge to run your tongue over your teeth. Try to avoid that if you can until your back is to the audience. Even then, it is harder to know when "no one is looking" because if the pageant is taped or televised, there will sometimes be a camera taping you as you come back from the catwalk too.

Try to avoid doing it but don't worry about it if you accidentally do it. It isn't the *end* if you are seen doing that—after all, people are human and there is so much going on it will likely be forgotten quickly enough. But do avoid doing it when you are the center of attention—like right during your on-stage interview question.

You may want to moisten your teeth quickly just a bit when the contestant in front of you is completing her response or her walk. While everyone is clapping for her, they probably won't notice your quick facial change to moisten your teeth.

Another "trick" is to smear just a bit of Vaseline on your teeth so your lips will be less likely to stick. *Not* too much as you don't want it to show. Petroleum jelly is pretty bland. It doesn't taste or smell good but it isn't bad either. Use your head to decide if using tricks like this feel right for you. (Like don't use it if you have an allergy to it!) All I can say is it worked fairly well for me and a number of others.

If you do decide to use it, you'd naturally try it at home first and check your look in a mirror. It's clear and shouldn't show (you don't need much) but in this day and age, it might not hurt to check yourself on a High Definition camera for your "close-up" to be sure you're okay. If you are in a state or national pageant that is televised you may find yourself under brighter lights than you ever have been in before. (More things show.) Whether the Vaseline trick works for you may depend on the shape of your own smile—how your lips relate to your teeth, etc.

Whatever the case, don't stress over it. As I said, I'm just letting you know so it won't catch you off guard if it happens to you (and so perhaps you can prevent it).

"In the fields of observation chance favors only the prepared mind."
~Louis Pasteur

Other Stage Considerations

Lighting and Make-Up

We discussed make-up before and the importance of practicing with your products and getting professional advice, if need be. Under bright lights, you'll likely want to adjust your make-up. Make-up for stage is usually a little bit "heavier" so the lights don't wash your coloring out too much and your face still shows up at a larger distance.

At least give a little more attention to defining your eyes (including eyebrows) and lips. Make-up styles change so stay current. And keep in mind that the quality and color of your skin will factor in. And, if that's not enough to keep in mind, sometimes the lights will make colors look different.

In the end, stay aware. Notice the lights and how it works on your and others' faces during rehearsal, if your pageant has one. Practice if you can. If it is a large, prominent, or national pageant, consider getting professional advice. *If* it is televised, chances are there'll be plenty of advice to be had.

If not, and if you are in it to win, increase your attention to stage make-up as you get to higher levels in the pageant. Local preliminary pageants may not have bright lights of a different quality than you are used to, but as you climb in the ranks it is more likely.

Just watch out that you don't wind up looking like a clown. In those times between pageant segments where you're back stage, try to keep your hands off your make-up. If your make-up artist (if your pageant allows it) or you applied it well at the beginning of the night, you shouldn't need anything but maybe the faintest touch-up as the night wears on.

Don't let your nerves find you continuing to apply layers of blush or whatever. I know in my pageant several of us kept putting on a little more blush on, as if the people in the *very* back of the auditorium needed to see our cheekbones. It is better to do your stage make-up for the judges or the camera, not the back row. (I think some of us overdid it!)

Body make-up is yet another thing to keep in mind. Bright lights will show more of everything. So if you have scars, tattoos, birthmarks, etc. that you want to cover, be sure you get a quality body make-up that works with *your* skin tone and blend, blend, blend. Make-up can also be used to add contouring.

For more information on body make-up, see a cosmetics expert or search the internet. New products are coming out all the time, but an effective one that has been out there a long time is Dermablend so look for their website as it is a good place to start.

Lighting and Lint, Nipples, Bra Straps and Gaps

Keeping an eye out for wardrobe details are important in the personal interview because you are up close to the judges. On stage the same details matter, even at a distance, as stronger lighting shows more.

So, as we discussed in *Book 5: Optimize Your Outfit*, keep an eye out for stray threads and lint. Consider using nipple shields so there are no, shall we say, distractions from your pretty face and overall look. And be sure that your gown does not gap and no bra straps slide out when you walk, etc.

Clearly, you will have chosen your gown well and have it fitted properly. It's best if you are at your ideal weight a month or so in advance so you have time to adjust your wardrobe. But, still, weight changes can happen during pageant week (if you are at a larger pageant), so be prepared with "fashion tape" to help be sure your gown performs as well as you do.

Even a perfectly fitting gown may be more "secure" if you use a little fashion tape. Practice with it at home, as always, and keep some in your pageant kit. You don't want anything distracting the judges, audience, or camera from *you* and your interview answers so make sure your wardrobe is working *for* you, not against you.

There are many useful places to find quality bras, nipple covers, fashion/apparel tape, and products to avoid pesky panty lines. Some products you'll find in physical stores and with an internet search on certain key words you'll find old and new options.

Microphones

Why am I spending time on this? Remember, this book series is for all sorts of pageant contestants. Some of you are no doubt quite experienced, but for some contestants the on-stage interview may be the first time they've used a microphone. If that's you, don't worry, as it doesn't have to be something to be nervous about. Even if it isn't the first time, here are a few things to remember.

Who Should Hold It?

There are pros and cons to holding your own microphone (mic) or letting someone else hold it. If you hold it yourself, you can be more confident it will follow your mouth if you turn your head while speaking.

But if you tend to gesture or move your head much, you might accidentally move it away from yourself unless you train yourself to keep the hand with the microphone "linked" to move with your head. I recommend against too much gesturing in a pageant setting (we don't need arms wind-milling around) but a little gesturing is natural (we don't want people standing like robots).

You'll usually keep your gestures between your shoulder and hip level (no big reaches above your head or dipping low) and not too much wider than the width of your elbows if your hands were on your hips. Natural gesturing shows you are comfortable but you do want to keep the attention on your face, so don't go overboard with gestures.

Freedom is in how you define it—do you feel more "free" with the mic in hand so you are "in control" or with it out of your hand so you don't have to worry about it? If you are facing a stationary microphone, you have no choice. If you are working with an experienced emcee, it's probably best to let him or her hold it for you. Still, if it is up to you then the tips in this section will help you decide.

Be confident that in time you'll be comfortable with any sort of microphone and situation so you will be able to adjust with ease.

If you are nervous enough that you think your hands will shake, then don't reach for the microphone from the emcee. Most emcees are experienced and will notice that you do not reach for the mic and honor your choice. And if they are experienced, they'll usually hold it for you just right.

Observe

Pay attention to what happens in rehearsal (if there is one—some preliminary and local pageants won't have rehearsals). If you do get to rehearse, just take note of how you feel if you get to "practice" with the mic. Or observe the emcee or microphone situation. Some emcees will *not* want to release the mic, others will expect you to take it. And sometimes it will be a microphone stand—not a person—holding the microphone.

Practice

In addition to observing, a little practice will go a long way to making you feel comfortable. Practice at home with handling a pretend microphone if you need to (my friends and I used a wooden spoon when we were little). If you want to pretend you are practicing with a microphone in a stand, just use your creativity to create a substitute.

That said, it seems that more and more people have karaoke machines at home as there are more affordable ones than they used to be (or you could check Craig's List, Ebay, etc., for used or discounted ones).

Another option is to ask around, you may have a friend or family member with one that you didn't know about. Someone at school or church may have one. (And, if you are old enough, you may find a "karaoke night" somewhere). So *if* you are worried about it or just want to feel *more* confident, find a way to practice a little with a microphone.

Where to Position the Microphone

The simple answer is to have the microphone close enough that people can hear you, preferably without blocking your pretty face.

If the emcee holds the mic, he will usually know where to hold it in terms of not blocking your face. It usually needs to be near your mouth but you do *not* need to "eat" or "swallow" the microphone. Below your lips, a couple inches in front of and below your chin usually works.

If the sound system is decent then having it block your mouth or chin should be unnecessary. And in certain high-end situations, a stationary mic is so sensitive that it may be placed much lower than you'd expect. Just pay attention…if the mic is very low and working fine for everyone else, then it will work fine for you too (assuming you don't whisper!).

In many situations, however, it will be the emcee holding it. In the unlikely event he is holding it too close or too far, you can *move* yourself, just a tiny step forward or backward so it is the right distance for you. Just as if you were adjusting yourself to speak into a microphone stand.

Some would say that instead of moving yourself, you can gently and professionally guide the emcee's wrist to move the mic closer or farther away. If you do that, notice that I said his "*wrist*" because if you touch the *mic*, he'll likely think you are trying to take it and release it to you. But if that feels awkward or like it will draw too much attention, just move yourself.

As I alluded to a moment ago, sometimes the microphone for on-stage interview will be in a stand rather than in an emcee's hand. This is also true if you are in a personal interview setting that is meant to imitate a pressroom setting.

Whatever the case, if the mic is not adjusted for your height, fix it. It is usually best to adjust a mic using two hands, if possible; one to hold on to the stand near the top and the other to actually move the mic holder up or down on its pivot. (Or, rarely, if it is a floor microphone, you *might* need to put one hand near the top of the stand, and one down adjusting the ring in the middle to lower or raise the stand.) Sometimes there will be someone to adjust it for you.

It is usually *not* wise to just grab the head of the microphone and push up or down. Touching the "live" part of the mic makes noise and may not be effective for adjustments because the plastic or metal ring that actually is in contact with the mic may be too loose or too tight. Keep control by using two hands if at all possible.

No one will fault you for adjusting the mic, especially if you do it in a calm, professional way. This is *your* time on stage and you want to look your best so:

- ***Don't lean down to a microphone.***
  You don't want to risk slouching and we don't want to see the top of your head.

- ***If you** must **lean, do it from the hips, not the waist, shoulders, or neck.***

  You don't want to ruin the visual line of your dress or, worse, have your dress gap or your breasts or undergarments show.

- ***Don't crane your neck up to reach a microphone.***

  We don't need to see up your nose. If you will be tilting your head up even a little, be extra sure your make-up from your face down over your jawline to your neck is well blended. (You'd do that anyway, right?)

- ***Don't shout into a mic.***

  Speak with calm excitement. If you tend to have a loud voice or increase your volume when you are excited or nervous be careful you don't sound *really* loud in a mic. You may need to step back just a bit or watch your volume level.

- ***Don't whisper into it.***

  Speak in a normal volume. If "normal" for you is too soft (if people ask you to speak up very often), then step it up a notch.

All the advice in the world won't help as much as you paying *attention* to what you hear and see at the pageant venue. Notice how easy or hard the mic stand is to adjust. Notice how the emcee handles the mic. That will help you know how to adjust to the situation.

Mind Your "P" and "B" Sounds

Keep an eye (okay, an ear!) on words with the letters "p" or "b" in them. Sometimes the way we use our lips when we say "p" and "b" sounds can make the letters "pop" or sound louder than you'd expect.

Turning your head *slightly* and *momentarily* away from the mic on those popping letters can go a long way to correcting the problem. Just start noticing it in your conversations leading up to the pageant and you'll increase your awareness on softening this.

Remember, this section is about microphones during interviews. If your pageant has a category for talent, be sure to practice using mics appropriate for your talent. Lavaliere mics versus hand mics versus headset mics all have their pros and cons.

Your Body and Mind Need Fuel

You can't run on an empty tank. Just like you can't give from an empty cup. You must take care of yourself first before you can do just about anything (or at least before you can do it well). We mentioned a little about the importance of good nutrition earlier in the book series in what you can do to get ready for the pageant. Now you are there and on stage!

Take care of yourself during the (potentially) long hours of the pageant competition night(s). Actually, you want to keep good care of yourself all the time leading up to the pageant and during the several days of rehearsals and appearances that can occur at the higher level pageants.

But once the actual pressure is on—the big night is here!—make sure you've had good nutrition and are drinking enough water. It can be tempting not to drink because you don't want to mess up your lipstick or accidentally spill on your dress but you *must* stay hydrated that night to be at your best. (Use a straw if you must.)

And make sure you have a handful of raw nuts, or the like, to nibble on every hour or two if you need to stabilize your blood sugar. Choose something that is not greasy, won't stick in your teeth, etc.

I speak from experience. I remember at my national pageant, I'd thought I'd done pretty well with all that and I *still* started to feel a bit weak and dizzy. Clearly, I could have done better and clearly I should have had a protein bar or something in my kit. You spend more energy than you expect during pageant week and especially on the big night(s).

If it hadn't been for Miss Maryland, I don't know what I'd have done. We were waiting for what felt like a very long time during the entertainment before they announced the semi-finalists.

I mentioned how I was feeling tired and woozy and she very kindly fed me! I think it was a Snickers bar—thank goodness for the nuts in the candy bar. It wasn't health food, I know, but a few bites were all I needed. I learned my lesson.

With a little protein and sugar to re-fuel me a bit, I was feeling more like myself and I aced the semi-final on-stage question, then the finalist level questions as well. As you know, I won. I'd like to think I would have won even without Miss Maryland's kindness, but who knows? I'll always be grateful for her kindness.

Without the extra calories she gave me, I may have faltered in my steps or—focusing back on the interview—my mind may have wandered causing me to lose concentration on what the judges were asking. Or I could have stumbled trying to get my thoughts together for my response or on getting the words out of my mouth. None of that would have been good. In a tight race, a point can make a difference in who wins the crown.

Seriously, to optimize your interview performance *eat* enough (good) food *often* enough to support your brain and body. Know yourself well enough to know what that is and be prepared with food in case you don't have a Miss Maryland treating you with kindness. (Some productions will have food available but you should be sure you have what *you* need with *you*, especially if you have food allergies, etc.). And, again, drink enough *water*.

Hurry Up and Wait

What's interesting about pageants is that once the opening performance number is over, there can be a lot of "hurry up and wait" time. You'll rush to change into your next garment, fix up a little, then wait. Sometimes back stage, sometimes on-stage. You've worked for a long time to get to this event and it will miraculously fly by and drag out at the same time!

Depending on how many contestants there are, the wait can be short or long. Imagine waiting for possibly dozens of women to walk out and do whatever the pageant requires, taking their turns in their fitness attire, gown, etc.

So then you wait for the announcement of the semi-finalists during which time there may be entertainment. Or the emcee introduces the judges and goes over the prize package while the calculating is going on. If you don't make it into the semi-finals, the tension disappears and new emotions arise, but you'll make it, right!?

Yes, you've made it to the semi-finals. Then you wait for, say, 15 women (again, it will depend on your pageant how many are in semi-semi-finals and finals) to each take their turn at the next level of competition. And you wait while the finalists are announced. You'll make that cut too, right? So you wait some more.

All the time you are waiting—whether backstage or on stage—you might feel "stage fright" or you might feel calm and be a great example of "stage presence." I suppose you could feel a little of both. We'll talk about both, and aim for a larger great stage presence.

But before we move on two more quick recommendations:

- *Avoid "comparing notes" between semi-finals and finals.*

  If you are fortunate enough to be selected for these levels, don't spend the minutes worrying about what you did right or wrong, or commenting on others. Try to enjoy the moment while you gently stay focused on what comes next. There's time after the pageant to analyze how you did. Now's the time to *be* your best (that's what you prepared for) and have a nice time. No criticizing yourself or others. No worrying too much about anything. Just enjoy the moment.

- ***Don't get so distracted in last minute primping that you have to rush to line up.***

  Stay aware of what's going on. You look great. Take some even, slow breaths rather than apply any more make-up or the like. If you are rushed and nervous you are just likely to mess something up that was already fine, than you are to improve something that was fine already.

Stage Fright

The focus of this book series is on interview and as on-stage interview is a form of public speaking, it is no wonder it makes folks feel a little nervous because:

- Speaking in front of groups (even small ones) is something many people fear more than anything else.
- It could be one of the first times (or few times) you are on stage, which is usually a larger group.
- You've done it before—maybe even done very well!—but it isn't typically something we do every day so it is still "unfamiliar."

Earlier in the series we talked about a few ways to keep a positive, calm attitude while you wait for the personal interview but what about while you wait for on-stage interview?

Stage fright is just another way of saying feeling nervous around "performance." It's a kind of temporary anxiety. Notice I used the word temporary—it doesn't have to be with you for long when you feel it. In fact, it often disappears once you are out there doing what you came to do! And remember that it won't kill you—so that's a relief!

Not everyone feels super-fearful of being on stage or speaking in public but many, many do as "public speaking" is always around the top of lists of what people fear most. Your on-stage interview is a version of public speaking.

Some symptoms of stage fright include:

- Sweaty, cold, or shaky hands
- Shaky knees
- Tight throat or dry mouth
- Facial tics or trembling lips
- Nausea (queasy, sick to your stomach)
- Increased pulse rate (heart may feel like it is pounding)
- Feeling strange or weird before or just as you get started on stage

So if you feel those things, relax! You're perfectly "normal" and you are not alone. Don't be too hard on yourself if you feel a little (or a lot) of fear. With intention, practice, and experience you'll feel less of it and can use it to your advantage to shine.

Remember "Pageant to PhD" is all about being aware of how what you are doing now in the pageant will help you later in life. So know in your heart that learning to reduce and deal with stage fright will really help you in all sorts of interviews, work presentations, and performances throughout your life.

Handling Stage Fright

Just as we discussed in handling fear while waiting for your personal interview, there are things you can do to help with stage fright on the big night of the pageant.

You can certainly still take some *subtle* deep breaths, and you can think positively and imagine your success but you also have to *pay attention* if you are standing on stage! If you are waiting back stage, you have more freedom to stretch a bit, maybe yawn to relax your face and throat but you can't do that on stage.

While I will offer you additional assistance with nervousness, relaxation, and confidence on my website, let me offer some options here as well. Experiment and find what helps you. Just use your head about whether they are appropriate to use *before* you are on stage versus *while* you are on stage:

- Take deep breaths or focus on a pattern of calm, steady breaths.
- Imagine each breath stabilizing where you are shaking or relaxing where you are tight.
- Feel your feet on the ground—get "grounded."
- Yawn once or twice to relax your face and throat.
- Walk around gently and slowly to calm yourself.
- Lean on something to rest (if sitting will mess up your outfit).
- Distract yourself by chatting with another friendly contestant back stage (keep it light and positive).
- *Smile* and mean it. Make it about making *them* feel comfortable instead of you feeling comfortable.
- Pretend you are there with a group of friends.
- See yourself succeeding.
- See the result you want to create (rather than your fear).

- Take it one step at a time, don't get too far ahead of yourself.
- Imagine the judges and audience happy to see you, happy with who you are.
- Tell yourself you've overcome more than this: that this is easy!
- Play the role of being comfortable with the situation (like a Queen).
- Focus on how really good you are.

A quick note on the advice to "focus on how really good you are." Remember that you *are* great. A number of people feel fright because they are worried about feeling judged, about failing, about doing "good enough," and other things that make a mountain out of a molehill. Yes, you want to do well, of course. But don't worry about it. Focus on loving and accepting yourself and drop the doubt. The time for doubt is behind you now.

Stage Fright and Preparation

Your preparation will help you feel less fright. If you follow the advice in this book, you'll probably feel pretty good about your readiness for interview and on-stage questions. And hopefully you'll feel healthy and beautiful on the inside—just as you know your outside appearance is also healthy and beautiful.

And in regard to *any* part of the pageant, small or large, you'll have paid attention (right?) in rehearsal and practiced in your mind so that will relieve some fright. No matter the size of the pageant, with or without rehearsals, you'll pay attention, listen to the pageant staff with care and gently observe what's going on around you so nothing will catch you off guard. Just trust in yourself and know that it will work out fine.

Remember that while we have talked "seriously" about pageant preparation, it doesn't mean that your time readying for and being at the pageant can't be fun. It *should* be *fun* or an important part of the experience is lost. Allow yourself to have fun.

So have fun! If you look like you are having a good time, you will be more confident. Pretend if you have to because, before you know it, you'll have talked yourself into saying "I can do this. This is fun!"

"You gain strength, courage, and confidence by every experience in which you really stop to look fear in the face. You must do the thing which you think you cannot do."
~Eleanor Roosevelt

Make whatever fear you have left your friend. Whatever fear you have left is something you can control and let it sharpen your senses and put a spring in

your step. Let it motivate you to be more conscious of your posture, your expression, and your breathing. In the end, a little healthy fear might help you be at your best.

Stage Presence

Yes, we may have to deal with some stage fright but where the focus should be is on our "stage presence." Being present is being so "in the now" that all those worries about if you prepared enough are gone. You are just there, enjoying the moment and being fabulous.

Having stage presence means showing some charisma and energy in how you move, smile, and in who you are. It is not about the gown or the swimsuit. The only thing it has to do with is that *you* feel great in whatever you have on. If you were once worried your wardrobe wasn't "perfect" then the time for that worry is behind you now. You are *in it* and you want to show you feel *great* in it.

Again, it is less about the clothes and more about how you *feel* in what you have on and what you non-verbally communicate while you are out there. Unless your outfit is a true disaster, your attitude can go a long way to over-coming little things. No "problem" with the gown or other attire is going to hold you back from shining. If something weird happens, shine in spite of it!

Once the time comes to be out there, it is about the confidence you have, the feeling you project when on stage. Believe—tell yourself—that the stage is *yours* so you are excited but comfortable. Believing it is yours will help you portray enjoyment and confidence. Act like a hostess who is entertaining her guests, or like a Queen making an appearance for those who love her.

Related to that then, if believing the stage is yours doesn't feel natural at first, then *pretend*. If you are nervous, then play the *role* of someone who is not. Most of us played dress-up or some form of "make believe" in our minds or in our lives with our friends or alone in the mirror. We are usually pretty confident waltzing around our house so make the stage your living room and *act* confident. Faster than you think you'll *be* confident. Over time, it will be second nature and won't be an act anymore.

Review

We're almost done! Let's review before we go on to the final book.

While it may not feel like an "interview" compared to the personal interview that will last longer, the on-stage question is a form of interview and public speaking that can make all the difference in whether or not you take the crown.

Much of what we covered in the rest of the book series also applies on stage but there are a few additional considerations.

- Considering the emcee, the audience, and the other contestants broadens who will be hearing and reacting to your answers. Yes, the judges may be the only ones officially scoring you but be sensitive to who might be in your broader audience.

- Keeping your answer to around 30 seconds in length is important. If your pageant doesn't impose a limit, you can go over that if doing so really "adds" to your response. But if your pageant suggests you stay within 30 seconds (or penalizes you if you don't) then learn to start and finish in that time frame.

- Bright stage lighting can make colors change, other colors "wash out," and all sorts of little things show. Take care with the details with make-up, posture, and wardrobe.

- Eye contact and smiling still matter on stage.

- Microphones can be tricky but usually aren't a problem if you pay attention. Watch your body posture with stationary mics and watch your gestures and head movements with hand-held mics. Watch your volume if you tend to have a very soft or very loud voice; otherwise, speak normally.

- Focus on having a good time and a confident stage presence. Let stage fright leave you. We went over some ideas to help with that.

Exercise 14.1: Research Your Role Models

Whether it is someone you admire or it is, even more important, a role model, look into them in more detail. Look at the example in the book and identify a few interesting things about the person that may come in handy to know.

Also consider if there are other people you admire. Maybe there is something in the world you appreciate and you've never stopped to look up who discovered or invented it or made it possible for us. Even if the person you have in mind is a family member, still look into them too. You might not be able to easily find information on the web about them (as you would a scientist, literary figure, or celebrity) but you can ask that person directly or ask other family members. You might learn something really amazing!

Exercise 14.2: Practice Your Timing

Even if your pageant doesn't have a 30 second time limit for on-stage responses, practice it anyway. Start with the short list of on-stage questions the finalists were asked in my pageant in this book. Then go through the other questions in this book and all the other practice questions you might have—like the ones I'll post on a blog or the like (see my website for current delivery methods)—and answer them in 30 seconds or less. Clearly you'll need a watch with a second hand or some other sort of timer.

Another way to do this is to tape yourself answering several questions without timing yourself and when you listen to or watch the tape, time the responses then.

Either way, start training yourself to notice what is too long. But *do* make use of the time you have. Remember to be a Sleuth and use all the good information you can about building solid content and sharing what will help you stand out or impress the judges that you are the right person for the title. Imagine you are responding to the media in a press conference. Try your hand at the Reporter Technique or the S.T.A.R. technique—see if you can get good at both getting to the point and including a bit of interesting information in a short period of time.

Exercise 14.3: Work on Your Talking Points and Bullet List

We've introduced this idea before—that you have a list of bulleted phrases about which you are ready to talk or key points you'd like to make if given the opportunity. Time to pull that out and re-visit it and see if you can talk about each one in 30 seconds. Then see what you'd say if all you had was 15 seconds per item. Then 10 seconds.

Then 5. Seriously. Try it. As the time gets shorter you don't talk faster! You make choices about what's more important to say.

Then you'll be better able to focus on one or mix-and-match parts of several to answer questions. This is especially important if you are in a platform sort of pageant and they time your responses. Make and practice with a list that is about you and a separate one for your platform.

Exercise 14.4: Practice Smiling Some More

If you did the smile exercise from *Book 7: Making a Strong First Impression* you may have noticed already if your lips tend to stick to your teeth when you smile for longer periods of time. If you haven't noticed yet, start paying attention to it.

As you prepare for the pageant, smile all the way to work, school, or wherever. Take note of when your lips start to stick (*if* they do). Remember, if you get to be a finalist in a large pageant, you could be smiling quite a bit for several hours in a row. So pick a couple days where you can smile a long time, off and on, for a couple hours and see how your lips do.

Yes, you'll have time off-stage where you can get a drink of water and moisten your mouth but if you make it to the finals you may have a stretch of time where you are on stage consistently. See if you can mimic the conditions a couple times and you'll get a sense of if this is something you need to think about.

If it is, try Vaseline and see if helps. (Some report that Vaseline also keeps lipstick from transferring to your teeth.) Practice before you decide if this works well for you or not. Learn how much you need, check your look in the mirror, in different light, and see if anyone notices it if you walk around with Vaseline on your teeth. (You might try a few HD photos too.) New tips and products are coming out all the time. If one tip doesn't work for you, don't worry, you'll figure out your own personal solution.

Exercise 14.5: Practice With a Microphone

If you have little or no experience with a microphone, find a karaoke machine that comes with a mic to buy or borrow (see the book for ideas from whom to borrow). Every microphone is different but at least get used to having one in your hand, play with the distance from your mouth, and see if your "p" and "b" sounds are noticeable. If you can get a hold of or approximate using a microphone stand, play with that too. Do so in front of a mirror and notice how one can mess up their posture or the line of their gown if they aren't careful when leaning down or reaching up to a mic.

Again, the microphone at the pageant is going to be different (and probably better or more sensitive) but a little practice will still make you a bit more comfortable. If you can practice with more than one or actually get into a room or space with a real mic and speaker system, all the better.

Exercise 14.6: Build Your Public Speaking Skills

Consider taking a class in public speaking or signing up for Toastmasters. If you've had to do any appearances (or will be starting soon), you know that these skills will help you with more than the pageant interview or the on-stage question. The same goes with job and school presentations, etc. These skills will help no matter what. And getting a little experience will help reduce stage fright too.

"You're not obligated to win. You're obligated to keep trying to do the best you can every day."
~Marian Wright Edelman

---

a pageant is just the beginning…

PAGEANT
ℐnterviewing
SUCCESS

Post-Performance Review

Dr. Stephanie Raye, PhD
Former Miss American Petite

Book 15
Post-Performance Review
Table of Contents

Pageant Interviewing Success: Post-Performance Review

Finally! The moment has arrived. The emcee has announced the semi-finalists, the finalists, and now the titleholder will be named. A lot of emotions can come up if you do not make it to whatever level you hoped. A lot of emotions can come even if you do! Let's talk a bit about emotions and a few other topics—like post-pageant assessment—related to handling the post-pageant game well.

"If one dream should fall and break into a thousand pieces, never be afraid to pick one of those pieces up and begin again."
~Flavia Weedn

Emotions

If You Didn't Win the Title

If you entered to place or win, and know you actually did your personal best to secure the title, you could be very disappointed if you didn't win. You might also feel sad or angry. You might feel confused. You could feel apathetic—indifferent—or at least tell yourself that you don't care.

Sometimes a first or second runner-up, might feel especially like it "just isn't fair" forgetting that all the contestants were subjected to the same tasks and scrutiny. She might think "I know I'm the prettiest" forgetting that it isn't all about beauty not to mention that beauty is in the eye of the beholder. Just remember that you are *still* beautiful, successful, and talented whether or not you won or placed. As cliché as it sounds, it is true that you are still a winner even if you don't leave with the title.

Having "negative" initial reactions like this are human. But holding on to them for too long or saying out loud everything you think and feel is not recommended. If you have big reactions or emotions, acknowledge them but then let them go. You can talk with a trusted friend or coach when you get home.

Put another way, you don't have to deny what you feel or pretend you don't feel anything but you don't have to amplify it by focusing on it. Neither do you have to share it with all the other contestants unless you do so in a supportive way. You don't have to be silent, but if you want to talk, do keep it more neutral to upbeat.

Maybe you share with someone you made friends with that you'd hoped to do better. Or you listen as they say that. Then say something encouraging that helps make things feel a little better by focusing on what you did right, what you learned, and/or what you want to accomplish next time. Do these things without being negative about the person who did win (or the other runners-up).

The idea is to be Queenly even if you didn't win. Congratulate the winner and the contestants who placed (were named as runners-up). Say thank you to any pageant staff or judges you encounter. As you pack up your stuff back stage, it's okay to keep to yourself if you need to but don't be sullen or pouty.

And while the temptation is natural to think only about ourselves (since we are all too aware of how we feel inside!), if you can muster it take your mind off yourself and intentionally be supportive of others as you pack up to go. The fastest way to get over feeling sad is to focus on someone other than yourself. Help others, encourage folks to try again next year, or just be generally friendly.

> "Not everyone can win the crown, but everyone can win a positive attitude."
> ~Dr. Stephanie Raye

In the end, remember what I always say: "A pageant is just the beginning." Whether or not you win the title, you took a risk, learned some skills, and helped yourself to be even better for whatever the next step in life is for you.

Reactions of the New Titleholder

If you won, *wow*! Every person has their own reactions but, if you are like me, you'll feel excited, half-surprised (everyone else is so talented too!), and *very* tired as you come down from the tons of activity and excitement of the event. Depending on your pageant, your appearances could start the very next morning (or that night!).

You may be so tired that you sleep heavily. Or the opposite could happen—despite how tired you are you might not sleep well that first night because you are so excited about the new chapter of your life that has just begun. All that hard work, now things could change. There may be some things you have to leave behind for a while to make space for what comes next. And it all came to a climax on the stage that night! Now it is sinking in. It could be very late before you get to bed because of photos or get-togethers after the pageant, and then you might have to get up super early for still more photos, etc. It's all good.

You will likely feel very happy. At the same time, you might temporarily feel a little fearful, perhaps, as you step into the new role. Your brain may be spinning with what sort of appearance opportunities you'll be given and others you'll create on your own. And yet you may also feel sad for your friends who didn't win or place.

You may find yourself practicing your diplomacy skills right out of the gate as, unfortunately, you might find some contestants aren't happy for you and show it. It isn't necessarily because they are "sore losers" (though they might be!). It could be because they aren't yet skilled in coping positively with disappointment. Previously friendly contestants might avoid eye contact with you, say something negative to you directly, or you might overhear them saying something "sour grapes" about the title, pageant, or you.

You'll have to use your head about whether to respond or ignore certain things. Just remember to be gracious, whatever you do. Being arrogant, snobby, or critical of others is not Queenly. (Even if they start it!) The key to remember is that *their* reaction really has nothing to do with *you*. They are just dealing with their own emotions so don't take anything personally. Be understanding and forgiving in your own thoughts even if it isn't the time or place to try to express those thoughts to someone who isn't wanting to hear them.

One more thing: You've just won a great honor but, remember, don't turn into a prima donna just because you did. No one would be happy to see that. That'd be a Smuggler thing to do if you were nice all along the way and then turned into a "spoiled brat" after winning the title. Ick! That's not likeable.

You don't need to be everyone's Best Friend but the public and the pageant want likeable Queens. And, in addition to your duties as the new titleholder, you may also now be preparing for the next higher level pageant. So do your best to be your *best* self all along the way.

On that same note, remember that once you are "free" from the big push to win the title, you are now in some version of the spotlight. So, if you are of legal age and if it is your style to think you can (or least shout) "party" to celebrate or otherwise "let loose" at any time during your reign, it'd be wise to remember the glare of that spotlight.

Just as we discussed in controlling your image (especially in terms of what winds up on the web) as a contestant, it is even *more* important to do so as the titleholder. It matters so much that some pageants have chaperones for their Queens.

So be happy and have fun but remember you are "on the job" now. Review your pageants rules and contract about what they expect in terms of conduct and comply with it. Always err on the side of being regal. You can be charming and relax—you can largely be yourself—but "losing control," being loud, rude, obnoxious, difficult, or using illegal (or even misuse of legal) substances is not Queenly and won't reflect well on you, your title, or your pageant.

I know. You would never do those negative things but I have to mention them because you will see, from time to time, a negative news item about a titleholder so some folks may not have the good sense that you do (or they had a moment of weakness or some misunderstanding happened).

And what do these cautionary reminders have to do with pageant interview success? Why else did I include them here? Because you just won a title and will likely be competing for the next level of title soon (unless you just won the top level!) so whatever you do could become fodder for the next pageant interview.

And if you did just win the top level of your pageant, then congratulations! Still, you must remember that "a pageant is just the beginning." Beyond being sensitive to how your choices reflect positively or negatively on your title, consider yourself as building experience for your next opportunity (in whatever you want to do) and you never know who is going to offer it you. So be your best you and more doors are likely to open for you.

Reactions of the Former Titleholder

Lady, you probably just had a big year! Take a deep breath and pat yourself on the back. You made it. You can wish the new Queen much success and sit back and reflect in a way that you may not have had a chance to do for a while.

Okay, it's true, depending on what level of title you just passed to the next Queen, what pageant system you were in, and your own ambition, etc., you may not have had *that* busy of a year. It's hard to say as some local and preliminary titleholders are kept (or keep themselves) as busy with many appearances as a state or national winner.

Chances are if you were, for example, a Miss State America you were pretty busy. Miss Arizona-America 2009, Erin Nurss, made over 230 appearances during her reign doing, among other things, a lot of speaking for her platform "Be Fit, Fueled and Fabulous." Arizona is a big state (it's the 6th largest) so she had to do some traveling for that goal of promoting health habits and wellness in youth. "It makes for long days and a quick year," she said.

If you were a national winner in any system—especially a large, long-standing system like Miss America or Miss USA—you were likely pretty busy as well. But whatever your title, and even if your pageant doesn't coordinate a lot of appearances for you, you may have showed great initiative in booking your own appearances to make the most of your title.

Whatever the case, your year is complete and you may feel a number of things. You may feel grateful but relieved to be done—happy to pass the crown and sash on to the next winner. (Well, actually, you get to keep them but you know what I mean.) Or you may feel sad, like you'll miss the hustle and bustle of your reign and be thinking of what other pageant you can enter, and maybe win, so you can continue on similar path. You may feel some of both.

It may feel weird at the pageant where everyone notices you and is interested in *you* until the crowning and then all the attention shifts to someone else. That may take you by surprise. It can be hard to not be the center of attention any more if you are the sort that likes it! If you aren't, you may be fine with this.

Whatever you feel, remember that as a "former" Miss _____ you're always going to be special in that relatively few people have done what you have. Even with the increasing number of pageants out there, the number of people that win titles is still proportionally *very* small considered to the number of people on the planet. In other words, there are billions of people on Earth and only a tiny, tiny fraction will have won a state, national, or international pageant title. Take joy in what you accomplished and remember that the pageant helped prepare you for whatever comes next. And what that is, is largely up to you.

You may decide to stay around the world of pageantry. You might compete again or work with pageants as a Director or any number of opportunities. Or you may move on to focus on whatever else is going on in your life, taking your pageant experience and skills with you to give you a different sort of edge than most people will have.

Thank You Notes

As we talked about in *Book 13: Ending with Grace and Ease*, be sure to thank the judges as your personal interview ends. That's all you can do right then. But then after the big pageant night, you might be able to locate some of the judges as the room is clearing and thank them again if you want to.

And, certainly, if you win or place you should try to make eye contact with the judges and say or mouth the words "thank you" to the judging panel as (or right after!) the announcements are made. And perhaps you will see them when you are doing post-pageant photos. (Often there are pictures of the new titleholder with the previous titleholder, with first-runner up, etc.)

Whether or not you win or place, it is good manners to send a thank you note to the judges, Pageant Director, and possibly other pageant staff, after the pageant. If you have a program book that lists the judges you may be able to figure out where to send them from that. And some websites of larger pageants will mention who the judges were for a particular event. Or the Pageant Director may see fit to provide addresses and such, if you ask.

Obviously I'm suggesting here that you write an "old-fashioned" handwritten note on real paper. Imagine that! Now that email is so popular, a hand-written note makes all the more of a positive and unique impression. But, if you can't get the addresses, then an email is better than nothing. Just be sure you use proper capitalization, grammar, complete sentences, etc. Avoid Instant Messaging or Text

Messaging type approaches for this sort of professional communication. If it must be electronic an email or nice e-card would be the better choice—but aim for real paper if you can manage it.

If you hit block walls in your attempt to do this (with "real" addresses or email addresses) in your particular pageant then so be it, but at least try! It is a nice gesture to drop a brief, professional thank you note to people after the pageant. It is unlikely anyone will think *less* of you if you don't, but people will likely think *more* of you if you do as such gracious courtesies are becoming less frequent.

You may think "Why should I bother? It's over!" but, as you've heard me say before "A pageant is just the beginning." Taking 10 minutes to write a few thank you notes is a good practice to have no matter what comes next in your life, whether that includes more pageants or not. And, perhaps, your kindness may be remembered in the future. It may open doors or who knows what else.

Whether you win or lose, say something to the effect of "Thank you for taking the time to judge in the recent _____ pageant. It was a great experience and the judges play a big part in making it all possible."

> "Appreciation can make a day, even change a life. Your willingness to put it into words is all that is necessary."
> ~Margaret Cousins

Whatever works for your style but do not get too personal. If you shared a big laugh in the interview or something else really sticks out in your mind, you can mention it to help them remember who you are or show appreciation for something they said or did. But, whatever you include, do aim to keep it relatively brief. Also, don't ask for anything. This is to express gratitude, not to make requests or otherwise keep in touch.

Speaking of Mail

I got mail from strangers after winning both the state and national pageant. Back then, email wasn't the primary form of communication so these came to a physical address. I had a Post Office Box for privacy and I'd recommend that may be a good idea for any lovely woman out there.

Fortunately, I didn't ever get creepy mail. It was usually someone noticed an article in the paper and dropped a quick line of "congratulations" to me. Very nice. Many people in the community, especially professionals who may see a pageant connection, may drop a line. That can be good networking for you (they could sponsor you) and for them (you could do appearances or endorsements for them).

Anyway, don't be surprised if people start communicating with you from "out of the blue." Depending on your pageant, there'll be a way for folks to reach out to you through the pageant. For instance, they'll have a way for people to request appearances. They may ask you (or you may decide to on your own) to keep a blog or other sort of way of communicating with your social network.

So people may contact you that way. Still some may seek or find your personal email address and, as in all cases, you want to be a polite Queen and assume the best of everyone. (But if anything is inappropriate feel free to *ignore it*!! And report it if necessary or wise.)

While web communication is more common these days, traditional mail or phone calls may occur too. It's all good. Not everything will require a reply so don't feel like you must write back but use your head about that and err on the side of kindness. (Like if a little girl writes and it doesn't seem to ask for or require a reply, it still may be a good thing to do!)

Post-Pageant Review: External

Celebrate!! You finished the pageant! Whether or not you won or placed, you still are a winner for putting yourself out there in way most people do not. You took a personal growth risk and deserve congratulations!! You want to focus on what you did right and enjoy the experience for a while. You want to relax a bit from the busy pageant competitions. Catch up on your sleep. Rest up.

So not right away—but don't wait too long either!—review how you did in the pageant. To get the most of the experience, you must do this even if you did great (even if you won). Whether you are a first-timer or have been in pageants before, you'll get most bang for the buck out of your pageant dollar if you finish out the experience with a good post-pageant review. Not that night, maybe not the next couple days, but *do it*. (Like within a week or so. Then do it again if/when you get your scores.)

Even if this was your last pageant, doing a post-pageant review is good for personal growth. But if you will compete again to win the title—or you *won* the title and want to improve your chances at winning at the next level—you definitely want to do this. It doesn't have to take a lot of time or energy but it can garner good insights for you.

"We don't learn from experience. We learn from reflecting on experience."
~Dr. Stephanie Raye

How do you do a post-pageant review? There are probably as many ways as there are people, but here are a few potential ways...

Scores

Some pageants give you feedback on how you did—like in the form of your scores—which help you know where you could stand to improve. Some don't. As mentioned earlier, it's great if a pageant does. *If* they don't it doesn't mean they are a "bad" pageant but it is a missing piece of information for you.

If getting scores is super-important to you, ask the pageant about it before you apply to it so you know up front that you will, or will not, get them. That way you can decide whether or not to participate, or at least you will not be unhappy to find out later that you don't get your scores. It isn't the "end of the world" but they are nice.

Some pageants are well-oiled machines and your scores will be given to you automatically—hopefully that would occur within a month or two after the pageant while the experience is still fresh enough in your head for the feedback to be of most value.

Other pageants may give you scores *if* you ask (rather than it being automatic). If that's the case, then ask. It never hurts to ask. And if enough pageant contestants ask nicely, perhaps the pageants that don't provide scores (or some other form of feedback) will consider beginning to provide them.

Ask the Director

If your pageant doesn't give scores, you can still talk to the pageant director for any general comments or feedback they can give you to help you prepare for next time. You'd have to use your good sense to know when is a good time to do that. It might be possible that you could ask right after the pageant but you also might want to wait a day or two. Don't wait *too* long as memories will fade.

But you don't want to interrupt the Director if he or she is in the middle of something at the end of pageant night. That said, they won't be glued to the new Queen the whole time (she'll be pretty popular that night) so if you see an opportunity, feel free to approach him or her. And if you are worried (or you get signals) that now isn't a good time you can always say "I realize this may not be a good time but could I call you in a day or so to touch base briefly? It might help me decide how to approach the next pageant, if I enter."

Remember, while many Directors may be in pageants for their passion for pageants or the love of community service, being a Director is also (usually) a *business* for them. A Director should be willing to at least give you some broad strokes of feedback, if they can. Realize that they may have been busy handling something while you were in the spotlight, or whatever, so they also may *not* be able to. So you should handle it gracefully if they do not. Don't be demanding or act with a sense of entitlement.

> "Far away there in the sunshine are my highest aspirations. I may not reach them, but I can look up and see their beauty, believe in them, and try to follow where they lead."
> ~Louisa May Alcott

Watch the Video

First, not all pageants are videotaped. But if yours was…

Watching the video can be tough to do. It's like hearing your voice on an answering machine and saying "What!? Is that what I sound like? Is that me?!" Watching and hearing yourself in living color is like that multiplied by 100. At least until you get used to it. And in these days of You-Tube and many people having video cameras (even on their phones), you may be quite accustomed to seeing yourself in video.

Either way, it is worth doing so you can see yourself in action. Watch it with notebook in hand and pretend you are a judge. Look at each contestant's stronger and weaker points. Write them down. In on-stage interview, listen to what they said, how they said it, and look at their face and body language. Stop the tape if you need to and see how you would have answered their question. Do you think you could do better?

If you do this—if you take a judge's approach—you'll be helping yourself look at the event (and yourself) objectively rather than subjectively. You'll be in a more analytical state of mind so by the time it is *you* walking across the stage, you'll be in "judge" mode instead of feeling a range of other emotions you may be inclined to feel when watching yourself.

If you happen to be the first contestant on the video in the semi-finals or finals you might consider fast-forwarding over yourself until you've have played judge with the others. That's your call on whether or not you want to do that but certainly if you are the first, be sure to *re*-review your own performance again after having judged the others.

Again, not all pageants will be videotaped. Some will put videos (at least clips) online. If yours is taped and buying the tape doesn't fit in your budget, see if you can borrow it from a friend who did get it, or share the cost with a couple other pageant contestants.

Depending on the size, level, and video services contracted, your DVD may contain the preliminary night competitions. That is, some pageants have enough contestants that they alternate groups competing in different categories on different nights so the nights aren't so long. Then the final night is focused on the semi-finalists, finalists, and crowning.

If you can see the preliminaries, that's great because you will be better able to see why some made the cut to semi-finals and some didn't. At least you can with the parts you can see. (For instance, you probably won't get to see personal interview footage which, as we know, can impact scores!)

Ask Others

Whether or not you get scores or your Director gives you feedback or not, you can ask a couple *trusted* others who were there and/or understand the pageant you were in (and can maybe see the video). I say "trusted" others because you want to ask someone who cares about you but will also be able to be honest with you.

You don't want to ask someone who won't be objective about what they say. While just getting compliments is nice (and worthwhile!) you want more than that right now. It won't be as valuable to ask someone who only says nice things and blankets you with praise.

Your parents, for instance, *might* be able to tell you how you performed differently on-stage than the other girls but they may also be unable to see your "flaws." Or, conversely, they may be *too* critical and not see what you do well. You don't want to ask just anyone. Or, at least ask more than one person to balance out any one person's tendency to be over-flattering or over-critical.

Ideally, you want to ask someone who has a good eye and will give you a fair, even-eyed assessment of your strengths and areas that need improvement. Remember you'll likely have *both*. Too often, we focus on what we do less well—and that makes sense as we want to improve—but remember to take pride in what you do well too!

Use your stronger areas—the places where you have success—as a model for how to improve in the other areas. Yes, each judging category has its own way to prepare to be your best. But just remember that if you've excelled in any area that since you *did* do what you needed to there, you are strong enough and smart enough to do what you need to in the areas you are weaker.

On Taking Criticism: Constructive vs. Destructive

A Queen, and any potential titleholder, needs to be willing to ask for advice and be willing to *take* advice. Maybe she doesn't need to take every single piece of advice (not *all* advice is good), but she does need to be willing to see herself and others objectively enough to know what to take and what to leave. That can come easily or that can take practice but, either way, you don't have to do it alone. That's why you do a post-pageant review.

As you'd guess, if you are asking for scores and feedback from others you are opening yourself up for criticism. I've mentioned already that you intentionally want to choose folks who are willing to tell you the downsides to your performance as well as the upsides. Balance is good.

What we are looking for here, and what you want to ask people for, is "constructive criticism." Folks can be critical without having your best interest at heart or offering any ideas on how to improve. That's not so constructive.

That said, *you* play a role in whether *any* criticism turns out to be constructive or not. Your attitude and openness will predict whether you can find a nugget of potential wisdom in anything you are told. The word "constructive" generally means to build up, as opposed to "destructive" which is to tear down.

Even if someone is destructively critical, *you* can choose to let it roll off of you (like water off a duck's back) or whether to consider if there is *any* truth to what they said (sometimes there might be). If you see yourself as the main carpenter (or architect or seamstress, whatever works for you!) of your life, you can help ensure that you turn most any experience into something constructive.

Similarly, you don't want to sabotage your constructive criticizers by asking for their input and then getting overly sensitive about everything they say. Your helpers may be picture perfect in how they are helping you with feedback but if you have a defensive or sulky attitude *you* are the one who turned something constructive into something destructive.

I emphasize the role of personal responsibility here because if you are going to make it in pageants—or the world—you'll find it goes better for you if you are "resilient" and bounce back from small and big hurts faster rather than slower. Not taking everything too personally helps you bounce back more quickly.

I also emphasize this because, as you've heard me say, pageants are essentially an elaborate job interview. That's true, but it is probably the most highly personal sort of interview you'll ever have because few job interviews include a fitness/swimsuit component (don't fool yourself, though, employers notice fitness levels) and all the other little things about pageants that make it seem extra personal.

You have really put yourself out there in a courageous, personal yet public way and yet, paradoxically, what happens in the end isn't personal at all. In pageants the "judging" aspect is made clearer in every way than in a traditional job interview and the "competition" aspect of getting the job as titleholder is made very clear. So while on the one hand it's "all about you" just remember that while winning is nice, not winning does not mean you are flawed and you don't need to over-personalize it. There's a certain element of "chance" in life and life isn't always fair. It doesn't mean we personally failed.

And so it is with getting feedback and criticism. Avoid toxically negative people—let their negativity bounce off you like you are Wonder Woman (the famous superhero) with her magic bracelets that protect her from incoming attacks. Remember we talked about Wonder Woman earlier in the book series? Let the bad bounce off but reach out for wisdom where you can find it as, remember, that Wonder Woman also had the "Lasso of Truth" in order to capture insights where you could. You can too.

"Honest criticism is hard to take, particularly from a relative, a friend an acquaintance, or a stranger."
~Franklin P. Jones

So those are ideas on how to do a Post-Pageant Review from the outside, external perspective. What about the inside? What about what was going on internally in your mind and heart? What do I mean? We've started to cover some internal aspects but read on.

"A successful person is one who can lay a firm foundation with the bricks that others throw at him or her."
~David Brinkley

Post-Pageant Review: Internal

Getting feedback from others and watching videos is worthwhile but there's another angle on how to review after the pageant. If you have the courage (and I know you do!), consider working with some of the thoughts offered here to get in touch with how your own attitudes and habits might impact how you did in the pageant. Learning from that will be powerful in improving for your next pageant and other aspects of your non-pageant life.

In It to Win?

For example, ask yourself: Did I compete to win? All we can ever do is the best we can do. But only you know if you really tried your best. Did you tell yourself that it didn't matter and talk yourself into not being your best? If so, perhaps it showed in a muted attitude, a less cheerful expression on your face, or less flattering posture. Maybe your heart wasn't in it?

It is true that we cannot be perfect all the time and do everything right 100% of the time. We have to make choices! So we may not be able to prepare in every way for every judging category. That's okay.

Self-Handicapping

But if you made choices that you know would undermine you along the way or toward the end—just before the big day—then you may have done something called "self-handicapping" which means making a choice that lets you blame something external to you (outside of you) when you fail but take extra credit if you succeed. (This is in contrast to "self-sabotage" which is when you make a choice that can only make things worse for you, making it impossible you'd succeed.)

Remember that "handicap" isn't just a term that was sometimes used in connection with "disabled" or, the better word, "differently-abled" people. It is a term from sports as well. Like you'll hear golfers say "What's your handicap?" and that has to do with how skilled the player is and how many strokes will be taken off at the end to help "even" the playing field between two players of different skill. So. As you know, terms from the world of sports work their way into other worlds...like psychology...and now pageantry. Let's look how by taking a general example first and then looking at pageantry.

> "The best years of your life are the ones in which you decide your problems are your own. You do not blame them on your mother, the ecology, or the president. You realize that you control your own destiny."
> ~Albert Ellis

Self-handicapping is when we try to even the field in our mind by trying to give ourselves an advantage around that self-imposed obstacle. Again, the advantage is that if the obstacle messes us up, we use it as an excuse. *If* we succeed in spite of the obstacle, we feel extra good about ourselves.

Let me put it another way, if we make a choice that allows or puts an obstacle in our path, we might do so because we are afraid of failing to some degree and wanted a ready external excuse handy. If we can blame something outside our self it helps protect our fragile egos! (So sometimes something that *seems* external is really based off an internal reason.) Many people do this and, of course, most of us don't realize it when we do.

Examples

Let's use taking a test as an example. Let's say "John" knows he has a test to take in school and he's gone to class half the time but did try to learn what he missed by reading the textbook pretty well. He can feel reasonably confident going in to take that test. He may not get 100% but he should do okay. Maybe he didn't study his hardest (to do the best he could). If John tends to self-handicap he might, say, stay up super late the night before so he is so tired that the chances would be slim that his brain will work right on the test. John might not even remember what he did know because he put this obstacle in his path. That way, he has an excuse for not doing well. And if, by chance, he does pass the test he can then say "Wow, I'm so good I managed to pass even though I didn't study and stayed up so late." He's set it up to try to protect how he thinks of himself regardless of the outcome.

Even if John stayed up late to study (cramming), he knew deep inside that staying up so late could undermine his performance on the test. Studying late into the night might look good on the surface but underneath the choice to stay up so late was calculated to give an outside reason to "fail" so he wouldn't have to admit that he could've or should've been preparing all along. He can tell his folks or his teacher "I'd have done okay if I just had gotten some sleep the night before." And that protects his ego and his self-esteem (but he may never learn to stop undermining himself). The ironic thing is that he did do some preparation and he may not have failed if he hadn't self-handicapped there at the end.

In the pageant world, whether you prepared well or not, let's say you change to a new pair of shoes at the very last minute when you've not practiced in them, haven't broken them in, etc. Your other pair was fine (this wasn't an emergency) but you put this "obstacle" in your path so that if you didn't walk as well or whatever you could say "Well, it was those shoes! If it weren't for them, I'd have won!" But if you *did* place or win, you might say "Well, I'm so good that even though I was struggling with a new pair of shoes, I still got 1st runner-up." Either way, you may not really be considering your true ability (or lack thereof) that impacted the quality of your performance in interview, talent, fitness, etc.

Some folks lean more toward self-handicapping than others. Maybe you'd never do that knowingly. But if what you just read feels familiar somehow, consider if you might be doing that unconsciously so you can blame that for not doing better in the pageant. If you do that, then *stop*!

You are wonderful and capable and want to give yourself the best chance you can—especially if you are in it to win! Even if you don't get to prepare just like you'd like to (again, most of us can't do *everything*), then at least don't self-handicap (and please never self-sabotage). Be willing to let things unfold as they will and then look yourself squarely in the mirror and be satisfied that you did do your personal best, knowing that you did not actually undermine yourself at the end.

"Opportunity is missed by most because it is dressed in overalls
and looks like work."
~Thomas Alva Edison

In It For Fun?

Perhaps you knew going in that you weren't competing to win and that you just wanted to try out a pageant and have some fun. Maybe make some friends, build some skills, but you weren't really in it to win. That's okay too. But be honest with yourself about whether you got the experience you intended. If not, why not? What can you adjust for next time?

And be honest with yourself about if you really just wanted to have fun or if you did secretly want to win and are just falling back on "I didn't really compete to win" to help yourself feel better. Either way is okay, just be honest with yourself. (You don't have to tell anyone else if you don't want to!) And if you really did want to win, then let that motivate you to sort out what needs to change to help you reach that goal.

Analyze But Don't Over-Analyze

Yes, whether you are in it to win or in it for fun, take a few minutes (or hours) to do post-pageant review internally and externally. Remember earlier in the book series I said not to over-analyze things while you are *at* the pageant? Well, you don't need to *over*-analyze after the pageant either but *some* "analysis" is good.

Some thoughtful reflection like this is especially important if you find you are taking it hard that you didn't win or place. If you are taking it harder than you thought, ask yourself why? Because you didn't prepare enough when you knew you should have or could have? Or are you taking it hard because you *did* prepare your best and you are truly disappointed?

Together with the external Post-Pageant Review, asking yourself good internal questions like these a few days after the pageant—after the initial emotions have ebbed—will help you sort out if you actually did prepare as well as you thought and it just didn't work out. (We can't control everything, the competition can be stiff, and a little "chance" might play a role.) Or if maybe you need to open your eyes to something you've been overlooking or get some professional guidance on how to adjust or improve.

Remember, as I emphasize from time to time, you don't have to be perfect but you do need to be perfectly *willing* to notice weaker areas with an objective eye. How can you improve what you refuse to see?

Once you have done all this, it is time to move on. Absorb it, adjust, grow, but move on. No one wins by getting stuck in the past instead of moving forward.

A Post-Pageant Review Trap

Here's a trap I'll warn you against right now! Do *not* assume that buying a more expensive dress, swimsuit, or gown will have done the trick. Unless your choice for the pageant you just finished was genuinely ill fitting, unflattering (terrible color for you?), completely out of style, or otherwise inappropriate, it probably wasn't the clothes. So don't throw money after something when it may be interview skills, grooming (good hairstyle and make-up for you, etc.), fitness, attitude, posture, facial expression, etc.

Very rarely, if ever, will any object we purchase cause a magical transformation. Be willing to look at what may need a simple tweak or an overhaul. Accept the challenge to bring whatever area of competition that is lacking up to the level of the areas that you are strong.

If you've done that—if you've looked for any glaring weaknesses or focused on strengthening a particular area of weakness—then kick it up a notch and see if you need to raise your game across the board. Do you need to improve at all levels? If everything is really pretty good then maybe it all needs to be just a bit better to bring home the crown in the most competitive pageants.

"I'm a great believer in luck and I find the harder I work, the more I have of it."
~Thomas Jefferson

If all of the levels need to come up a notch you can set goals and step-by-step improve on all levels. You can do that through working with (not just reading it once) materials like these, working with a coach or two in the areas of focus, etc.

And it may be wise to try a different pageant system for a while. Remember, as we talked about in *Book 1: Build a Strong Foundation*, there are *many* different kinds of pageants. You may benefit from trying another system to see if it is a better fit for who you are and what you want. Always read application rules, but, generally speaking, unless you are a current titleholder there usually aren't prohibitions from trying out another system.

Some contestants compete in multiple pageants a year. If your heart is set on a certain system, that's okay. There's nothing saying you can't come back to your "dream" pageant system at a later date (watch age limits!) after you've practiced your skills in a different system.

"The greatest discovery of any generation is that a human being can alter his life by altering his attitude."
~William James

In the end, yes, you may indeed need a new swimsuit or gown. You may need a new hairstyle or learn how to apply your make-up in a more professional manner. I'm not saying those things don't matter or that they don't factor in. Just don't stop looking with that surface level. In most pageants all of the contestants are lovely and well dressed so it can really come down to how well you interview, and if

you've done good work on knowing yourself (and your community, platform, etc., as appropriate). It may be nothing to do with how you look but what you communicate about who you are!

There is usually a range of ways to strengthen "weaknesses" and ways to further strengthen, or perhaps remodel, your stronger areas. If you don't have the budget or time for coaches, then use materials like these and many others available in stores or on the web. Review the section "Does Preparation Have to Cost Money?" in *Book 2: How to Prepare* for many ways to practice interview that are free or low cost. And similar resources can be found to help you with other aspects of the pageant experience.

A Final Note

Remember, pageants might look easy but often aren't—at least not for everyone or if you want to do well. They *are* fun, yes, but the fabulous pageants we see look smooth and easy because the contestants prepared and worked hard to make them that way. They made it *look* easy. They rock! And you do too. That you competed— or are considering it if you are reading this book before your first pageant—says a lot of good things about you.

If you don't do as well as you'd like, bounce back up and move on. Take your skills to the next pageant (if you wish to continue) and on into your life in everything that you do. And always be proud of your participation in pageants. You are an inspiration to others. It doesn't take a crown or a sash to be a winner!

Review

Wow, we've come a long way!

Emotions are natural and you may experience quite a variety (and some highs and lows) before, during, and after the event. Feel them, acknowledge them and what you can learn from them,

then let them go. They'll have done their job and there is no use in getting stuck in them—good or bad.

Everyone will have their own reaction after the pageant, whether they won, placed, or neither. Be respectful of yours and others experiences. Aim to be sensitive to others and kind to yourself during what may be an emotional time. The new Queen and the former Queen will be having their own emotions and thoughts too.

Remember, while we compete as individuals we are also "all in this together" so enjoy each moment for yourself and for the others. Be supportive. Next time it could be you in a different situation (winning, placing, or not) so take a second to put yourself in the other person's shoes before you say or do things that might be hurtful or misconstrued.

Sending thank you notes is always a nice touch.

Being willing to review our performance is important to having a full experience. You'll get the most out of it that way whether or not you want to compete again. Reviewing the "externals" and getting the input of others is important but so is reviewing the "internal" part of your pageant experience. Both components come into play. Working with others helps us see our blind spots. Looking deep inside ourselves might help us see if we are playing tricks on our self that might undermine our success.

Learning how to take criticism and input is important. Our own attitude goes a long way in making sure we find what's useful in even the harsh or less sensitive critiques. Still, aim to find coaches and critics that will give you the good and the bad, yes, but do so in a constructive way.

Remember that while it took me quite a few words to explain some of the techniques and approaches in this book, that doesn't mean you have to over-analyze yourself or your performance. Some healthy reflection and asking some tough questions is good. Beating yourself up or obsessing is not good.

For any area you decide to improve, you can help yourself or get others to help you (or both!). But no matter what you do or don't do, remember to spend at least as much time focusing on what you do well. You are great "as is" whether or not you won or placed. Remember that you are indeed a winner.

Exercises

This whole book was a series of exercises! Go back through it and answer any questions you can. Or at least use the details there as a guide when it does come time to handle the emotions after a pageant and review afterward.

And, as this is the last book, I encourage you to re-review the series (at least by looking at the review pages and exercises). But let's give a couple more here:

Exercise 15.1: Review or Prepare to Review

If you have competed before and didn't formally review your performance, do so now. It may have been awhile back, yes, but give it a shot and build your skill at asking good questions of yourself and others, as well as whatever you can of the other material in this book. (If the pageant was recent this will be easy for you).

If you've never competed—if you are just getting ready for your first pageant—put yourself in the shoes of the night after the pageant. Then the week after the pageant make a little plan for how you'd like to respond and review when the time comes. That plan may not work out just as you designed it but thinking through what you'd say or do can be helpful.

In any event, start noticing if you ever self-handicap. It can be hard to see in ourselves but take a look and see if you have any patterns. It is possible someone else close to you can point it out to you. (But not always! We can be pretty tricky.)

Exercise 15.2: Practice With Criticism

Some of you may be in jobs, schools, families, or other groups where criticism and feedback abound. It may be handled well, it might not be. Start building your awareness for how people say things and notice how you and others respond. Practice saying truthful things in kind ways. When you can't make it sound kinder, then at least watch the tone of your voice. (Actually, you should always do that!).

You can also practice "bookending" or "sandwiching" or the "reverse Oreo cookie" approach. That is, make sure that you say a couple good things (that'd be the bread, the bookends) and slide the thing that might be hard to hear in the middle (that'd be the sandwich filling, the book). In terms of reverse Oreo it'd be like having two creamy edges with the hard cookie in the middle! Whatever image works for you, start doing it when you can.

In terms of receiving feedback and criticism, practice dismissing the person's tone and choice of words and just listen to the content of what they say. Whether they are nice about it or not, is there any truth to it? And if you find they are not nice about it, you'll be building a callus to not letting that sort of thing bother you as much as it might usually. Sometimes we have to have "thick skin" so things don't hurt us. And, to be fair, most people don't *try* to hurt us. They just haven't practiced all these skills as much as you have.

"Promise yourself to be so strong that nothing can disturb your peace of mind. Look at the sunny side of everything and make your optimism come true. Think only of the best, work only for the best, and expect only the best. Forget the mistakes of the past and press on to the greater achievements of the future. Give so much time to the improvement of yourself that you have no time to criticize others. Live in the faith that the whole world is on your side so long as you are true to the best that is in you!"
~Christina D. Larson

Here I am taking my walk as the newly crowned Queen at the national competition.

Epilogue: Now What?
More Ways You Can Use This Book

Dr. Stephanie Raye

Wow! That was a lot of information: fifteen books brimming with advice, tips, and exercises. Your mind is probably reeling, and you're most likely wondering where you go from here.

Well, dear reader, you go on! Dive headfirst into your future. Use everything you've learned to succeed not just in pageants but in all areas of your life. After all, I chose to put "a pageant is just a beginning" on the book cover because, if you are thoughtful about the skills you learn for and in the pageant, you can use those skills beyond the pageant world.

However, I do have a few more tidbits for you before you head off into your future. In this concluding note, you'll find more about my story and some parting remarks about the value of great interviewing skills and how you can apply them to anything and everything.

Let's get started so that we can wrap this up and you can continue to apply everything you've been learning!

Then and Now

You probably know by now that I am Dr. Stephanie Raye. But I was just plain "Stephanie Raye" when I competed in pageants over 20 years ago now. The doctoral degree came later. I won pageants, yes, but since then I've had a wide range of other experiences that contribute to my expertise in interviewing and communication as it relates to personal growth and professional development.

My early work background includes the "commercial" and "visual" side of the business world. I put myself through the early years of my college education doing work that included (but was not limited to): being a print, mannequin, and runway model, appearing in commercials, being a mobile disc jockey, and representing fashion photographers to ad agencies and fashion retailers to make bookings for editorial and commercial fashion shoots.

And since 1993, among other interesting things, I've taught and conducted research at one of the largest and most well-regarded traditional state universities in the U.S.A. There I've focused more on the behind-the-scenes knowledge and concerns of organizations including families and businesses. That is, I've studied and added to the body of knowledge that helps create understanding and skill building that leads to more successful employees, leaders, and citizens. Underpinning all that, I've also spent a lot of time studying and teaching about what makes overall successful and happy *people*, from modern scientific perspectives as well as from engaging classic texts from ancient to modern times.

My work has led me to teach not only students at the university but to speak to audiences large and small on related topics. All along the way my pageant experience has always served me well.

A Pageant Success Story

During those early years, in the late 1980s—before there was a public internet—I was modeling in a large runway fashion show when someone came up and said "You're a perfect petite—you really should enter the Miss Arizona Petite pageant." It was true that, while most models were very tall, I was often hired as "the petite model" to highlight the fashions for the height that *most* women are (in the U.S. the average female height is approximately 5'4"). I was still slender and model-like, just not as tall. If I was in a photo alone, you couldn't tell how tall I was…only when I was standing next to a "standard-height" model would it occur to you that I was "petite."

The woman showed me an article from a local paper about it, and I applied to the pageant. The prize package was valued at over 50,000 dollars, and that was worth a whole lot more in 1988 than it is now!

I didn't really know what I'd signed up for as entering pageants just wasn't something we did in my family. But I figured I could learn, so while I waited for the state pageant time to arrive, I thought through what I'd need to do to succeed—what it really meant to enter, compete, and maybe win in a pageant. When the competition time finally came… I won! I became Miss Arizona Petite 1988.

Knowing that would lead me to Orlando, Florida for a week to compete in the national Miss American Petite Pageant, I did what every pageant contestant would do: got my wardrobe together, focused on proper exercise and nutrition, and so on. But I knew there had to be a way to make myself an even stronger candidate and maybe gain a competitive edge.

Interview Skills Matter

Then it hit me! I knew *all* the women at the national pageant would be beautiful and talented so to really stand out I needed to be different in how well I said things and in how well I understood what they were looking for in a Queen. I realized this was a *job interview* not just a beauty pageant.

So I thoroughly and thoughtfully prepared for the interview portions of the pageant. I had to sound like a winner. I had to show them through my words and voice that I was the best fit for the job of holding the title of Miss American Petite.

Beyond interview topical knowledge and communication skills, I also paid attention to what I was learning while I prepared, I noticed HOW I prepared and what helped the most. I already had a disciplined approach to my goals, but now I was applying that to winning a pageant.

I started to think through what other skills I was using and would need as a national titleholder. I researched what I could about "petite" related issues—their fashion needs, challenges, and opportunities—and while I naturally wanted the great prize package, I was most excited about the part that felt like a new job.

Trust me, more time goes into preparing well for the pageant *beforehand* than the time you actually spend at the pageant....and much more than you actually spend in those relatively few minutes of "competition." But it's good practice because it helps prepare you not only to do better at the pageant but to handle the titleholder's Queenly duties. And as I keep saying, it all adds up to good things for your life after the pageant.

At the national pageant, I was judged by a panel of experienced, well-respected professionals for a panel interview and for two on-stage interview questions. The seven judges included Kenn Berry who, at the time, had worked with the Miss America Pageant system for 39 years, as well as executives from a world-class talent agency (William Morris Agency), a New York City advertising agency, three of the national sponsors (two national fashion retailers and a national clothing line carried in all the best department stores), and an award-winning broadcasting anchor woman (from the Orlando area where the pageant occurred).

Throughout the pageant, I kept my eyes open and my thinking cap on. I took things seriously and still enjoyed myself. I got along well with the other contestants, as well as the pageant staff, but stayed focused on the goal. Rehearsals, appearances, photos, and so on— the time flew by. And, to my great delight, I won the title Miss American Petite 1988.

After the crown was placed on my head and I took my walk as the new Queen, camera flashes going off everywhere, the crowd started to disperse. Then we began the photos with the previous titleholder and myself, with the finalists and so on. And during all this, people would come up to say nice things and offer their congratulations.

I received many positive comments from the judges about how strong my interview was. And the director and audience who'd only seen the on-stage interview commented on the strength of my interview as well. Yes, my dress was "just right" (Kenn Berry loved my story of how I found it, selected it, and how little it cost), but it was the interview that made the difference.

I spent the next year doing what a pageant Queen does—I traveled for appearances, talked to the press, commentated at fashion shows, gave speeches, judged other competitions, appeared on television talk shows and the radio, taped commercials and more.

But a pageant is just the beginning. Something always comes next and the skills you build in the pageant can help you with it. What came next for me was choosing to continue my education. Many of you reading this book will already have completed a degree and may be considering (or have completed) an advanced education.

If you are a younger reader, however, I do hope you will consider it as well. Even if your heart is set on a career in the movies or music, you can still get an education at some point. Look up, for instance, Brooke Shields (who graduated from Princeton) and Jodie Foster (a Yale graduate). Beauty and brains are a great combination.

I'd started my education before I entered the pageant, and I decided to continue it. That included a Bachelor of Science degree in Communication (emphasizing interpersonal and intercultural communication in organizational settings) and a Masters and a Doctorate in Psychology (emphasizing social influence, organizations, family relationships/divorce, and health/wellness.)

As if understanding those areas weren't enough, I also spent two years being trained and certified as a personal and professional life coach to be absolutely sure I fully appreciated that new field and how it differed from "psychology." That and everyone was calling themselves a coach whether they'd really studied how to do it well or not, so I wanted official education in it so I knew I would offer my clients true value.

I have also studied and practiced mediation (conflict resolution) and done a lot of well-regarded professional public speaking. All that and THEN some—I've had a rich life of education and experience, and there's still so much to learn and do. I'm a "life-long learner" and many other pageant contestants are as well.

All along the way during the years since my pageant days, I've interviewed many people and have been interviewed myself many times for many different reasons (including live media/press interviews). I've always done above average—if not excellent—in interview-type situations in part because of those early days when I practiced my skills and thought so much about how to prepare for pageants.

And while I still watch and study pageants with great care, my primary "day job" is to profess at a large, well-respected major state university. In that role, I use the interview-style skills constantly for myself, in observing (and sometimes evaluating) the quality of those skills in my potential collaborators (colleagues, research assistants, etc.), and in teaching and assessing interview and interview-related skills in my students (in structured and unstructured settings).

In all I do it turns out that I work with people of all ages—in one way or another—on skills that also can help you as a pageant titleholder. Skills like this:

- how to find and use information from the world around them
- how to think from multiple perspectives
- how to more clearly communicate their thoughts/ideas in all arenas
- how to do "public speaking"
- how to know themselves better (beliefs, values)
- how to identify their skills
- how to transfer their skills to other situations
- how to narrow down "what to do" with their life and set goals

- how to present themselves better
- how to think more clearly about WHAT they need to say,
- WHEN they need to say it, and
- HOW they need to say it (without offending people)

All of the above, and then some, serves to maximize their success and effectiveness in any situation. My instruction, tips, advice, coaching—call it whatever you want—have made a real difference in many people's lives month after month, year after year.

And, trust me, I continue to know what it feels like to be in the "hot seat" as I continue to be interviewed by the press (the media) on my various areas of expertise or achievements. And I am often put "on the spot" in important meetings with high-powered people, as well as in classrooms and learning situations from the many spontaneous questions my students ask.

I must do pretty well in how I design my learning materials and answer questions because I've won recognition for my teaching, including three teaching awards so far and nominations for others.

For instance, I won "Last Lecture" in 2009. What's a "Last Lecture" award? Many universities have this honor. My university has a 14-year (so far) tradition where students select three outstanding professors from the over 2800 faculty to honor with performing a "Last Lecture" to the community. It's called "Last Lecture" because it is to be what you'd say as if it were the last time you'd ever address an audience—so nominees are typically the faculty that students find inspiring, entertaining, and educational at the same time.

And I earned recognition as one of six "Featured Faculty" in 2006 and as the recipient of the "Outstanding Faculty Award" in 2005. In the years before and after those awards, I've gotten excellent teaching evaluations by students and colleagues, year after year.

What's that all mean to you? I don't tell you that to brag—this isn't *really* about me. I tell you that so *you* can trust that the materials you just read provide excellent, reliable, and useful information! Don't worry, in case you couldn't tell, these materials aren't as hard as my college classes. They were written to be accessible to people of a wide-range of ages and educational backgrounds. ☺

Why I Wrote This for You (or your loved one)

In realizing that "interviewing" well relates to all areas of life and in noticing how a big chunk of that realization started when I was preparing for pageants, I decided to take the time to capture and share insights with others—especially pageant contestants—so they too can be the best versions of themselves when they are in an interview and in other "question & answer" situations.

When the interviewee is comfortable and confident, she'll handle herself better *and* make the interviewer feel more at ease. The interview stops being a just question and answer exchange and becomes more of a conversation where people are getting to know each other.

Also the interview can generate a "halo effect." This means that if you do well in the interview—usually the first scored event of the pageant—it can create a glow for you (like a halo) that transfers to the other areas of the pageant. The glow of your "halo" will shine on a broader area than your interview, helping you shine brighter in the other areas of competition. That can happen because you'll feel better about yourself (given how great you did interview) and…

…Without even realizing they are doing it, the judges may score you a little higher in evening gown or swimsuit as they may be expecting you do great based on your great interview! Unconsciously, the judges may be a little more forgiving of a little mistake here and there if you stand out well enough in their memory from the interview. Now if you do really poorly in other areas, a good interview may not be enough to save you. But assuming you are doing average to above average in other categories, a strong interview can really make the difference. The judges will likely have talked with *many* contestants so it can only be to your advantage if your great personality and on-target responses helps them remember you.

Transferable Skills

Being comfortable talking with people, listening well, and answering good questions (like in interviews, etc.) are key in so many areas of life. Similarly, being able to prepare for situations, researching what you need to know, getting it all together, showing up on time, handling yourself well under pressure, all with a positive attitude and smile on your face *definitely* helps in other areas of life too.

Think about it, most people prefer to live with and work with smart, adaptable, creative people. They don't have to be sugary sweet, but we usually prefer them to not be too cold or distant either. Most people also don't enjoy over-the-top "me me me" divas (except for dramatic effect or to poke fun at in the movies).

We want to be around "real" people who aim for their best but can roll with the punches. We prefer to be around someone who does their part but also admits when they need help or don't know something. (None of us are perfect!)

If we are thoughtful about what we are doing, and who we are being while we participate in a pageant, it's easy to see that "personality" is more than something we display when we are being "judged" in a category. Our personality and work ethic are in play all the time in our pageant experience and in our daily life. They contribute greatly to our pageant success.

And being disciplined, thorough, easy-to-work with, and punctual are some of the skills that are necessary to be an effective titleholder/Queen. Especially if you are participating in a well-established pageant where there are many commitments or appearances. But whether you win or not, if you learn well during your pageant it will serve you well later.

Participating in a pageant is just the beginning for many women—or an important stop along the way. Why "waste" the opportunity by focusing only (or primarily) on the beauty part? The transferable skills you learn from pageants (if you learn the skills well) will help you in every other area of your life. That's especially true after the pageant, but it can also be true during the pageant experience, if you allow yourself to be mindful and notice.

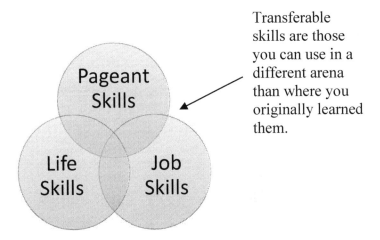

Transferable skills are those you can use in a different arena than where you originally learned them.

Just look at the range of activities that Queens have gone on to after their pageants. Plus all the ones who have gone on to Hollywood—from Raquel Welch (an all-time classic beauty) and Cloris Leachman to Jeri Ryan (for the Star Trek fans), from Oprah Winfrey (as a Miss Black Tennessee) to Diane Sawyer (America's Junior Miss). If you don't know who these beauties are, look them up. They could be you someday!

Others have worked in corporations or started their own businesses. There are surely countless examples. For instance, Miss Arkansas America 1980, Lencola Sullivan, was the first African-American woman to win the title in her state and the first African-American woman to make it to the top five at the national Miss America pageant. Among other things, Lencola went on to a career in the Netherlands organizing management workshops worldwide.

Another example or two? The ground-breaking Phyllis George (Miss America 1971) is so accomplished I could write a whole book on her alone. (So go look her up!) She has applied her skills and determination from her pageant days to many great ends. And Lu Parker (Miss USA 1994) distinguished herself by, among other things, becoming an Emmy Award winning journalist. I'm sure her pageant experience not only opened a lot of doors but the skills and discipline she learned helped her succeed in her other endeavors.

And many former contestants choose to start their own businesses—often working in areas relating to the pageant world. For instance, Cheryl Prewitt (Salem) Miss America 1980 has a successful shoe and swimwear business; Heather French (Henry) is an accomplished gown designer; and two Arizona titleholders (as you'd guess I'm a tad partial to Arizona girls!), Stacey Kole (Miss T.E.E.N Arizona 1990, Miss Arizona USA 1998) and Jessica Nicely (Miss Arizona USA 1997, Mrs. Arizona United States 2001, Mrs. Arizona International 2004), started *Savvy*, which is a successful national "beauty, style, and pop culture" magazine.

Of course there are other notable examples—I wish I could mention all the wonderful accomplishments of pageant contestants. And those are just the ones we hear about! There are no doubt many other success stores we don't hear about. (Write me and tell me your story—not just the successes but how your pageant skills helped you overcome or cope with adversity. I'd love to hear from you.)

Indeed, many of the pageants that give scholarships as prizes have many contestants that go on to finish their "four-year" degrees or beyond that for professional or graduate school degrees. While I'd recommend a college education is a good goal for most (it seems to be harder and harder to get very far without something more than a high school diploma), you certainly don't have to have a degree to be a smart person who contributes to society in all possible ways.

Many successful business people and super-stars don't (but again, that's getting rarer and rarer). Still, I'd prefer you go to school! So I hope continuing your education is part of your plan no matter your age, what pageant you are in, and whether or not you win it. The true winners follow their dreams even if they don't win.

And if you are doing pageants mainly for the fun of it, the glamour of it, or as just an activity or hobby—even if you aren't in it "to win" that's okay. The same principles apply: *have fun*, but consider the wisdom in making the time you spend in pageants extra worthwhile by learning what you can about yourself and thoughtfully improving skills along the way.

Whether you are currently a contestant or just considering entering a pageant, whether you are parent, coach, judge, director, or supportive friend, there's good information here for all. Truly, this material, while using pageants as the focus, is applicable to anyone who wants to do well in an interview situation.

My wish for you is that you understand and believe that a pageant is just one step—a fun and potentially important step. And that no matter what you want to do—small or big—you can leverage how you prepare for pageants to help you achieve your goals. (This is true even if you don't place as a runner-up or win.) That's why I call my series of materials "Pageant to PhD." Even if you don't want to be a doctor, you *are* heading somewhere! Thoughtful preparation and skill-building in pageants is a great step to help you reach your dreams.

I wish you success!

Excellence can be obtained if you:
~ care more than others think is wise
~ risk more than others think is safe
~ dream more than others think is practical
~ expect more than others think is possible

Final Review

Well, there was a lot about me in this conclusion—but the rest of the book is all for you! With this closing note, I want you to know that you have been learning from someone with pageant and professional experience and credibility. A couple take-home points from this chapter, however, include:

- Interview skills are important in all areas of life.
- Interviews can be "conversational" but are more than simple conversations.
- Pageant skills, in general, are transferable to work and personal areas of life, so we want to be thoughtful about how and what we learn (and look for the interconnections.)
- Pageants are an avenue to begin or further one's education on many fronts (whether or not you decide to pursue traditional advanced degrees).
- A great interview is important as it sets you apart from the sea of other beautiful, talented, accomplished women. A fraction of a point can make a difference between taking the crown and when everyone is physically beautiful, it is your words and personality that will help the judges select.
- A great interview is powerful in itself, but when you add the potential of the "halo effect" it's even better. In other words, a glow from a strong interview might help your scores in the other areas.

Exercise 1: Remember Your Dreams

What are your dreams? Whether you are ready to share them with anyone else or not, at least remind yourself of what they are. What do you most hope for?

Reflect on "needs" versus "wants." Where do you hope to be in 1 year? 5 years? Think about how what you will learn in participating in pageants will help you achieve your dreams.

Exercise 2: Translate Dreams in to Targets

Take one part of one dream, one step that will help you get there, and re-word it into a measurable goal. Since some people don't like "goals" (they are worried to feel bad if they "fail") just think of them as "targets" so that even if you don't hit the bull's eye you're still closer to your dream by making the effort. Here's a great way to proceed:

Make sure your target/goal is SMAART. (Pageant girls get an extra A!) We'll use a fitness goal as an example so you can see that SMAART means it is:

S–Specific	not vague "get in shape" but exactly what size dress, how much weight you can lift, how many miles you will run, etc.
M–Measurable	you'd use a measuring tape, a scale, your favorite dress, body mass index, etc. Find multiple ways to measure progress, whenever you can, so you have more input to go on and to keep yourself encouraged. For instance, if you aren't "losing weight" that can really be okay because your body may still be re-shaping itself in good ways (which you'll be able to tell with the other measures).
A–Action-oriented	make sub-goal plans for a healthy balanced diet, water drinking, and exercise
A–Ambitious	make it big enough to inspire you to reach, to grow
R–Realistic	not TOO ambitious! Choose something DO-able to help enhance your success. You can set additional goals after you get there.

T – Time based	set a specific day and date on the calendar to have achieve your goal. Set interim action plan dates to check your progress, adjust where you need to, and reward progress.

Exercise 3: Start Noticing Your Skills and Their Transferability

Sometimes we can't see the things we are good at in ourselves. They may come so naturally to us that we just don't think about it. So start noticing what you do routinely as well as things you only do once in a while. How well do you do them? Start finding the words to describe the skills you have. Start noticing how skills in one area of your life helps in other areas, directly or indirectly.

"I pray that I may never meddle, interfere, dictate, give advice that is not wanted, or assist when my services are not needed. If I can help people, I'll do it by giving them a chance to help themselves; and if I can uplift and inspire, let it be by example, inference and suggestion, rather than by injunction and dictation. That is to say, I desire to be Radiant—to Radiate Life!"
~Elbert Hubbard

Index

A

F

G

H

I

J

K

P

S

T

About the Author

Hello! I'm Dr. Stephanie Raye, though I was just plain "Stephanie Raye" when I competed in pageants over 20 years ago. Back then, I didn't really know what I'd signed up for, as entering pageants just wasn't something we did in my family. But I figured I could learn, so I thought through what I'd need to do to succeed—what it really meant to enter, compete, and win in a pageant. When the competition time came I won! I became Miss Arizona Petite 1988.

But a pageant is just the beginning. Something always comes next, and the skills you build in the pageant can help you with it.

What came next for me was choosing to continue my education. That included a Bachelor of Science degree in Communication (emphasizing interpersonal and intercultural communication in organizational settings) and a Masters and a Doctorate in Psychology (emphasizing social influence, organizations, family relationships and divorce, and health and wellness.) As if understanding those areas weren't enough, I also spent two years being trained and certified as a personal and professional life coach.

My early work background includes the "commercial" and "visual" side of the business world. I put myself through the early years of my college education doing work that included (but was not limited to): being a print, mannequin, and runway model, appearing in commercials, being a mobile disc jockey, and representing fashion photographers to ad agencies and fashion retailers to make bookings for editorial and commercial fashion shoots.

And since 1993, among other interesting things, I've taught and conducted research at one of the largest and most well-regarded traditional state universities in the U.S.A. There I've focused more on the behind-the-scenes knowledge and concerns of organizations including families and businesses. That is, I've studied and added to the body of knowledge that helps create understanding and skill building that leads to more successful employees, leaders, and citizens. Underpinning all that, I've also spent a lot of time studying and teaching about what makes overall successful and happy *people*, from modern scientific perspectives as well as from engaging classic texts from ancient to modern times.

Made in the USA
Monee, IL
05 April 2020